CRETE AND MYCENAE

I VIEW FROM NORTH OF THE PALACE OF PHAISTOS TOWARDS THE MASSIF OF MT IDA. Beneath the double peak is the Cave of Kamares where 'Kamares' ware was first found. Out of sight on the north flank of the mountain is the Idaean Cave, most famous of the ancient cave sanctuaries, where the infant Zeus grew up, hidden from his father Kronos and nursed by the goat Amaltheia (see Note page 115)

CRETE
AND MYCENAE

TEXT BY SPYRIDON MARINATOS

PHOTOGRAPHS BY MAX HIRMER

HARRY N. ABRAMS, INC., NEW YORK

LIBRARY OF CONGRESS CATALOG CARD NUMBER: 60–8399
All rights reserved. No part of the contents of this book may be reproduced
without the written permission of Harry N. Abrams, Inc., New York
Text printed in the Netherlands. Plates in color and monochrome printed in Germany.

CONTENTS

FOREWORD

THE whole story of the archaeological exploration of Crete amounts to no more than the last sixty years of excavation. The turn of the century saw the beginning of the pioneering work which brought to light the palaces of Knossos and Phaistos with many other of the island's monuments and art-treasures.

The fundamental discoveries and researches in Crete are intimately associated with the name of Sir Arthur Evans, just as those in Mycenaean Greece are with the name of Heinrich Schliemann, the explorer of Mycenae, Tiryns and Orchomenos. Intense archaeological research over more than eighty years has gradually revealed to us the extent of Mycenaean culture, down to the discovery and excavation in most recent years of another important Mycenaean centre at Pylos in the south-western Peloponnese.

Archaeologists of many countries, not least of Greece, have made known the results of their researches in numerous publications, of the greatest archaeological and scholarly value. But for the wider interested public there is no summary which presents the historical and artistic importance of the discoveries in their true proportions. The present book is designed to meet this need. The illustrations have been selected with as much regard for archaeological accuracy as for the effective presentation of the beauty of their subjects, thereby complementing and illuminating Professor Marinatos's text.

Some of the pictures are devoted to the monumental architecture and the magic of the landscape in which it is set, as well as to the frescoes of the palaces and mansions. The frescoes are illustrated in their original form, so far as it is preserved, without the misleading restorations and reconstructions of modern hands. But it is upon the enchanting products of the arts and crafts of Minoan Crete and Mycenaean Greece that the book concentrates. Outstanding among these are the treasures from the shaft graves at Mycenae: the royal gold masks, the jewellery of kings and queens, their weapons and numerous gold vessels which served them at worship or at the table, their gold signet rings, and their gems which tell us so much of their religion.

So as to present this wealth of material, these boundless riches, to the best advantage, all the photographs have been newly taken. For providing the necessary facilities I have to thank most warmly the following Greek institutions and scholars: The Archaeological Council and the Director of Antiquities in the Ministry of Education, Dr Joannes Papadimitriou; the Director of the National Museum in Athens, Dr Christos Karouzos, and the Director of the Archaeological Museum in Heraklion, Dr Nikolaos Platon, with his assistant Dr Stylianos Alexiou; and finally the Director of the Italian Archaeological School in Athens, Professor Doro Levi. In Heraklion Dr Stylios Giamalakis allowed us to photograph parts of his valuable private collection for this book, and to him special thanks are due. It is upon the helpful suggestions of Dr Franz Willemsen of the Archaeological Seminar of the University of Munich that the majority of the plans and drawings are based. I am deeply grateful to my colleague Miss Julia Asen for helping with many most difficult photographs and preparing the material for publication.

MAX HIRMER

CRETE

CRETE: THE NATURAL RESOURCES

THE history of Greek civilisation and art is as complex and full of contrasts as Greece's own chequered landscapes and rugged coastline. Man appeared in Greece about as early as in the rest of Europe. The most recent finds in Thessaly have proved that the area was inhabited in the earlier Palaeolithic periods but great floods, silting and violent geological changes brought this primitive life to a sudden end.

Crete's part in this earliest civilisation is still not clear. From the beginning it formed a small world on its own, some of its fauna, like the cave-bear and *Elephas creticus*, being peculiar to the island. We do not know exactly when it was sundered from the main mass which rose out of the primeval ocean, Tethys. In antiquity, and even today, some of the animals which are most common in Greece, such as the wolf, fox, eagle, and true owl, are absent in Crete. With the exception of the wolf these are found not only on the mainland but even in the smaller islands. Crete's wild animals comprise only the ibex—the most famous of the island's animals in art and literature—badger, wild cat and weasel. It was to this that the ancient Greeks were referring when they said that Zeus had freed the island of his birth from noxious animals, or that Heracles had cleansed the island so that it no longer had 'wild animals like bears, wolves, snakes and the like'. Admittedly this is an exaggeration because there are snakes, and among them the poisonous viper. Scorpions, whose stings are painful but not fatal, are quite common. More dangerous is a poisonous spider, called *Rogalida*, which is found especially in East Crete. The doctors of the islands say that its bite is fatal, and Pliny had already remarked on it (Diodorus IV, 17; Pliny *Natural History* VIII, 83).

The earliest true civilisations arose where man did not have to fight with the elements for his life. Thus no important civilisations were born in arctic zones or under the scorching equatorial sun. A temperate climate and rich arable land, whose yield could guarantee sustenance without too great effort, left man free to develop a civilised way of life. The ideal prerequisites seem to have been plains and valleys watered by great rivers which assured an annual harvest, and it was under these conditions that the earliest cultures arose in China, India, Mesopotamia and Egypt. Crete, which developed its civilisation—at least as early as these: it is the earliest in Europe—had no such blessings, but it possessed enough of the necessities. Its small plains, valleys and cultivable terraces, so typical of Greece, are many and fertile. The Messara Plain in the southern central part of the island is large by Greek standards: over twenty-five miles long and between three and eight miles wide. On the other hand, the parts of Crete in which civilisation grew up are poor in water. An important factor is that the cultivable areas lie at different altitudes, permitting harvests at different times. But against this, it must be admitted that the much prized rains of spring and early summer, for which men prayed even in prehistoric times, were not equally welcome everywhere. Rain in April and May, which would help the more elevated regions, could be harmful to the harvest a few miles away where the land was lower-lying. Furthermore Crete is boldly split up by three great and many lesser mountain ranges and the climatic variations have their effect. The great ranges—Leuka in the west, Ida in the centre and Dicte in the east—are all over 6000 ft. high. The summit of Ida is nearly 7000 ft. In many places their approaches are gently inclined and accessible, and the slopes were once covered with great forests of oak, cypress and fir (*Abies cephallenica*), of which there is now no trace. *Abies cephallenica* has been recognised in the carbonised remains of ancient columns in the Palace of Knossos, and the cedar-wood for the shafts of double axes was certainly hewn locally not imported. There is always snow in the deep clefts between the mountain ridges, where the new snow of each year falls on what is left from the year before. As a result some springs are well provided and there are a few rivulets which never run dry. There is not only enough water for large herds of cattle but even for the irrigation of small cultivated areas at the height of summer. High on Ida itself occupation was—and still is—possible. The small mountain-plateau, still called Nida, lies 5250 ft. above sea-level but in Minoan times it was already a centre for both cult and ordinary settlement. The famous Idaean Cave, the Cave of Kamares some two hours south of it, and others too bear witness to the flourishing communities near by. There are two springs on either side of Zeus' Cave on Ida, and to the north, deeper set, is another, yet bigger. Situated up there between heaven and earth they are known only by shepherds, from whose lips it is strange to hear that one spring is called Zominthos, a prehistoric name, otherwise unknown, which has lived on in the speech of these mountain-folk. Another of Ida's springs is called Kanethos, which is probably another prehistoric name.

A far larger fertile plain lies on the eastern mountain, Dicte, 2800 ft. above sea-level. Here too there were flourishing towns and famous caves about which legends naturally grew. The gentle slopes, even in the high places, make both grazing and cultivation possible. Deep clefts, often like tunnels from which the sky is invisible, split the mountains from north to south and offer a passage through them. Nimbros and Samaria in particular are famous for the wild beauty of their scenery.

These conditions made life possible all over Crete, from the high mountain regions, clad with snow for half the year, down to the sandy coastal plains in the south where the climate is sub-tropical and the swallows can winter. It is easy to understand how incredibly varied must be the products of an island in which a journey of only a few hours takes one from cold to heat. There is hardly another place in the Aegean today where corn and the vine, oranges, olives, currants, cherries, tomatoes, apples, bananas, nuts and melons can all be grown with the same success. Works of art and inscribed tablets tell us that there were once great herds of oxen, sheep and swine on the island, whose flora must have been more luxuriant and varied than it is now. Then there were palm trees, of which some can still be seen in the east of Crete. Perhaps there was papyrus too, at least—to judge from ancient representations—in palace gardens, and sugar cane, which can still be found here and there and is said to have been brought over by Egyptian soldiers.

II   Left: BEAKED CUP OF VEINED LIMESTONE. Height 7.2 cm. Right: JUG OF POLYCHROME STALACTITE. Height 12 cm. From the island
of Mochlos, Gulf of Mirabello, East Crete, Early Minoan II, about 2400 B.C. (see Note page 117)

All these facts show us that the island was a self-contained geographic and economic unit, with all the requisites for comfortable life, and so for the development of civilisation.

With the temperate climate, the riches of the land, and the particularly sensitive and versatile character of the Minoan people it did not take long before there emerged the happy, colourful and lively culture which was re-discovered for us at the beginning of this century. Even before the finest of the island's wares were found in their homeland they had been excavated in Egypt: 'Kamares' vases, which had found their way to the towns of the Fayum at the beginning of the second millennium B.C., more probably full of Crete's fine products than empty. The Minoans had to thank the exceptional geographical position of their island for the possibility of trade overseas: at the centre of the eastern Mediterranean 'the island lay in a most favourable position for travel to all parts of the world' (Diodorus IV, 17).

Crete's natural products were renowned throughout antiquity. Olive-oil, honey, fish, figs, and other fruit, with a mass of aromatic and medicinal herbs, are mentioned by ancient writers, many fruits themselves have been excavated in a carbonised state, and many are represented on works of art.

This produce of the land, together with manufactured goods, formed a great part of Crete's riches. They were exported over the seas which served the island as an invaluable bulwark against the sort of attack that was always threatening other early civilisations. In every period of her history Egypt was menaced, by Nubians, Lybians, Syrian nomads, Hittites or Assyro-Babylonians, and the development of her civilisation was continually being interrupted. The Sumerian civilisation of Mesopotamia was utterly destroyed by the Semitic Akkadians, and these in turn suffered severely from the attacks of Elamites and Kassites. Crete, so far as we can judge today, was never overrun by enemies until the arrival of the Achaeans. She had, moreover, at this early date attained something which the later Greeks never enjoyed: internal peace—aptly called a 'pax minoica'—in which she could cherish the gentle, idyllic arts which mirrored the calm of her life. Antiquity, and even the succeeding centuries, never forgot that Crete was once a great and blessed island. Homer expressively describes it as beautiful, fertile and thickly populated. Other writers call it 'great, fat and well-fed', the Isle of the Blessed. When the Arabs sailed from Spain against Crete at the beginning of the ninth century A.D. their leader Abu-Hafs proclaimed to his pirates that they were to sack an island in which milk and honey flowed; and many modern writers have sought to identify in Minoan Crete and her civilisation a land and people of the blessed—the Scheria of the Phaeacians, or even Plato's Atlantis.

CRETAN HISTORY AND CIVILISATION

So far as we know today man first appeared in Crete in an advanced phase of the Neolithic period, some time during the fourth millennium B.C. The Mesolithic period of the sixth and seventh millennia, which has only recently been attested on the Greek mainland, is still not represented in Crete.

It is probably true to say that the first inhabitants of Crete came from the east. Their Neolithic

III BEAKED JUG WITH FLAME-MOTTLED DECORATION. Vasiliki style. Height 33.5 cm. From Vasiliki, East Crete. Early Minoan II, about 2500–2400 B.C. (see Note page 117)

culture was characterised by black or grey burnished or 'Urfirnis' pottery and by clay figures of a
big-bellied mother goddess The number of inhabitants seems never to have particularly large. Neolithic remains are comparatively rare; they have been found in some caves, particularly the Cave of
Eileithyia at Amnisos, in a few sheltered localities, in a pair of stone-built houses of rectangular plan,
in some quantity in the deep levels beneath the Palace of Knossos and, to a lesser extent, beneath the
Palace of Phaistos. According to Sir Arthur Evans the vast levels at Knossos are as much as 20 ft. deep
(against 18 ft. for the whole of the Bronze Age), deeper than any other Neolithic level in Europe,
and he accordingly ascribed a long life to the Neolithic period in Crete. In many places on the 'tell' of
Knossos the Neolithic level is as much as 26 ft. deep, but this is a result rather of the manner of life
and building practised by the inhabitants, and cannot be taken as good evidence for an exceptionally
long Neolithic period[2]. We know that Neolithic man in Crete tilled the soil, kept cattle and caught fish.

At the turn of the fourth and the third millennia begins the sub-neolithic period, recognised by its
reddish-grey and black pottery, often with incised or burnished decoration. There is soon a greater
variety of vase-shapes; two basic forms are the so-called tea-pot and beaked jug. The first painted
vases, with mottled decoration, are associated with the 'Urfirnis' wares and are followed, towards the
end of the third millennium, by the first light-painted vases.

The Early Minoan inhabitants of Crete spread over the whole island, with the heaviest settlement
in East Crete and around the great Messara plain. It was then that the civilisation began to take on its
characteristic form. The people were established in settlements whose houses sometimes have plastered walls and floors. They were already good sailors and from their travels they brought Cycladic,
Libyan and Egyptian products back to Crete. Mochlos, in the Bay of Mirabello, became a leading and
rich centre, known to us for its gold jewellery and magnificent coloured stone vases. The inhabitants of the Messara plain seem to have been just as prosperous and well organised, as we know from
the rich offerings in their large circular tombs.

By the end of the third millennium Crete was already heavily populated. Her culture stood at the
transition between the rustic phase and that of the city and palace, between community-life and the
organised kingdom. It is notable that the west part of the island, which is just as fertile and even better
watered than the centre and east, remained almost unmoved by the cultural development. Neolithic
remains have been found, and in recent years many finds of all periods have come to light, but they
do not offer more than the imported products of the civilisation of others. The massif of Ida certainly
hindered free passage from the east, but apparently some racial difference in the population worked to
the same end[3]. It is remarkable that in the Argolid also all the Mycenaean centres were founded in the
eastern part of the plain. On the other side, and in the highlands of Arcadia, there were few if any
settlements. In the same way the areas west of Parnassus and Pindus remained backward until far into
the Hellenistic period.

The foundations of the great palaces in central Crete were laid soon after the beginning of the

IV   Above: SMALL BEAKED JUG DECORATED WITH FISH. Earliest Kamares style. Height 10.5 cm. From Vasiliki, East Crete
Middle Minoan I, about 2000 B.C.
Below, left: A SMALL JUG WITH MOTTLED DECORATION. Vasiliki style. Height 12.2 cm. From Gournia, East Crete.
Right: A TWO-HANDLED JUG. Barbotine style. Height 16.5 cm. From Hagia Triada. Middle Minoan I (see Note page 119)

16

second millennium. We cannot say whether they were founded independently of each other or through some sort of confederation led by Knossos. The recently renewed excavations at Phaistos show that the palaces there and at Knossos were foundations of the same period and magnitude. The third palace, of Mallia, some 25 miles east of Knossos, is in a different class. It lay on the coastal plain, without fortifications, like the town around it. It seems that there was no fear of attack by land or sea. Peace and order must indeed have ruled in the island for there to have been no need for fortifications, for in the rest of Greece and the Cyclades they are known from the earliest times.

The life of the 'Old' Palaces was not a long one. After two or three centuries they were all destroyed; whether simultaneously, or one after the other, we cannot say. We cannot even be certain whether the 'New' Palaces rose immediately on their ruins. More likely there was an appreciable interval, of different length in different places.

We can assume that the Old Palaces were destroyed about 1700 B.C. and the new ones built about 1600 or a little later. Both the Old and New Palaces bear traces of minor collapses and more or less extensive re-building and changes of plan. The reasons are easy to find. There were Cretan rulers with a passion for building, like those we know of in the East. Outbreaks of fire must also have been common and had devastating effect in view of the widespread use of wood in Minoan architecture. Moreover, the fabric of the great buildings must have needed renewing with the years, to say nothing of various changes in plan. But above all it was the earthquakes which occasioned continuous building activity.

The natural sciences state what the archaeologist often observes himself—that natural phenomena tend to repeat themselves. The geologists say, 'where there has once been an earthquake, there will be another.' It took a little while for archaeologists to arrive at the quite natural explanation for the destruction of the Cretan palaces, in fact until the earthquake disaster of 1926. From the records of earthquakes, incomplete though they are, it can be said with assurance that Crete, and the Knossos area in particular, suffers at least three major earthquakes in each century, of which one is catastrophic. It must have been the same in Minoan times, in the second millennium B.C.

26–27, Figs. 3–17

Crete's greatest period of building which stimulated both the architecture and other arts in the island, began soon after 1600 B.C. This is rightly called a New Era. In architecture the period is less clearly defined in the palaces, where old and new are often intimately combined, than in the mansions which rank between the palaces and ordinary houses. From the hierocratic organisation of that period and the finds from the mansions we can be certain that these minor palaces were the seats of men who held important spiritual as well as temporal offices. The mansions lie about 7 to 10 miles from each other, which may correspond to the distribution of the old administrative districts. All these important buildings, of which we know about a dozen, some of them decorated with frescoes like the palaces, have the same architectural history. They were founded about 1600 B.C. or soon after, and destroyed in 1500 B.C. or just before. Their violent and sudden destruction is made clear in every case by the excavations. In many places it was so unexpected that even valuable metal objects were not rescued in time, and everything was buried in the ruins.

The destruction about 1500 B.C. was the greatest and most thorough that the Minoan civilisation suffered. Not only the palaces with their towns, not only the great villas, but all other settlements—Gournia, Pseira, Palaikastro, Zakro—harbours like Amnisos and Nirou Chani, tombs like the Temple

V BEAKED VASE. Kamares style. Height 12.5 cm. From the Old Palace of Phaistos. Middle Minoan II (see Note page 120)

Tomb at Knossos, and even the Cave of Arkalochori, whose roof collapsed over its treasures of metal, were annihilated and abandoned. Such a comprehensive catastrophe can only be the result of something exceptional. An earthquake alone cannot account for the disaster which presaged the final end of the island's civilisation. From observations at Amnisos the conclusion has been reached that the great eruption of the volcano on Thera (Santorin) must have caused the utter devastation of Crete. Scholars in other disciplines than science are slow to pay attention to natural phenomena, but the great natural catastrophe is now generally accepted as the cause of the destruction, though still with more or less reserve by some[4].

Thera, like other volcanic islands, was once circular in plan. The volcano was inactive for many centuries, and the island was settled, no doubt by a Minoan colony, which built houses, decorated them with frescoes, made painted vases and other domestic articles. Then came the eruption. Great masses of pumice and volcanic ash were thrown up to cover the island with a layer 100 ft. thick and to discolour the sea for far around. The settlements on the island were buried beneath it. At last the force of the eruption blew up the centre and western parts of Thera, leaving the present crater, the largest of its sort. Only the eastern crescent-shaped part of the island survived.

Volcanoes can be divided into classes. A similar one was that of Krakatoa in the Dutch East Indies. Knowledge of the effect of its eruption in 1887 can help us to reconstruct the Minoan disaster. The catastrophe of 1887 turned day into night for a radius of more than 100 miles. Violent eruptions and storms destroyed buildings and the volcanic ash fell hundreds of miles away. The blast was recorded all around the world. The greatest damage was caused by a series of colossal waves, up to 50 ft. high, which struck the nearby islands of Java and Sumatra with incredible speed. Towns like Teloeg, Betoeng and Tjazingin in Sumatra were completely destroyed by them; boulders, trains and railway tracks were swept away. The steamer Maruw was thrown by the waves into a wood several miles inland beyond the town. In Tjazingin the flood caused fires by overturning lamps. More than 36,000 people lost their lives in the catastrophe.

The eruption of Thera was four times as great as that of Krakatoa: 33 square miles of land were blown up and sunk on Thera compared with 9 on Krakatoa. And the distance between Thera and the north coast of Crete is less than that between Krakatoa and the many places which were overwhelmed in neighbouring islands. Moreover, the sea is considerably deeper between Crete and Thera than around Krakatoa and the velocity of waves increases with the greater depth. The waves could have reached Crete within half an hour, and all the flourishing towns on the coast would have been overwhelmed in a few minutes.

The pottery and the style of the fresco-fragments tell us when the eruption on Thera happened: it was when the 'Floral' style in art was beginning to flourish. We cannot be more precise at present about the finds on Thera because they are in a distinctive local style and are numerically few. But Crete can tell us much, and particularly the coastal towns which would have been destroyed first by the waves. It is clear that the finds everywhere, in Amnisos, Nirou Chani, Mallia, Gournia, Pseira, and,

VI   Above, left: SMALL CUP. Height 5 cm. From the Old Palace of Phaistos. Right: 'EGG-SHELL' cup. Height 7.5 cm.
From the Old Palace of Knossos
Below: SPOUTED JAR. Height 18 cm. From the Old Palace of Knossos. Full Kamares style. Middle Minoan II
(see Note page 120)

farther away, in Palaikastro and Zakro, belong to the developed Floral style, and only a few vases of the early Marine style have been found in these places (in Amnisos none at all, but this is probably an accident). The date of the eruption should accordingly be after 1550 and before 1500, about 1525 – 20 B.C.

The explanation of the destruction of the other palaces inland, at Knossos and Phaistos, at Hagia Triada, Tylissos, Sklavokampos and many other places, remains open. Naturally the waves did not reach them. Most of the pottery found at these sites, especially the great storage-jars, are all Late Minoan IA. Some few vases are in a more developed style (Late Minoan IB) of about 1500, such as those from Tylissos and Sklavokampos. A few from Phaistos and Hagia Triada—and isolated examples elsewhere—seem even more advanced stylistically but still of the same period. The historical value of these finds can only be assessed if the exact details of their discovery are known, and these are lacking. Two explanations are admissible: either the potteries in many places were working in a more advanced style, or the destruction of the great centres was not complete, the buildings were not wholly abandoned, and life continued on a more restricted scale in some repaired parts of the structures. The latter is the more plausible, and we can assume that in many places life was not so utterly extinguished as it was on the coast. In Hagia Triada there was no break in the continuity of occupation down to Roman times.

That the great catastrophe of about 1520 B.C. laid the whole island in ruins can be demonstrated by better evidence than that of pottery, namely seal-impressions made by one and the same stone. A small find of seal-impressions on clay was made in the excavation of the villa at Sklavokampos. From this the important historical fact could be established that impressions from the same seals as those used for the Sklavokampos impressions had already been found in Zakro, Gournia and Hagia Triada[5]. This showed that the four places were in close association with each other, or with some fifth centre, before the catastrophe struck. The impressions are of the sort which would have sealed the thin cord fastening small packages or letters. There cannot therefore have been any great interval between the destructions of the various sites, always assuming that the seals were personal ones. If not contemporary they must all have fallen within very few years.

It has been observed that a series of big earthquakes usually occurs before or after each eruption on Thera, and that these are often catastrophic in the area of the volcano—the Cyclades, Sporades, Dodecanese, Asia Minor, Crete etc. We must assume that the same thing happened on the occasion of the great eruption at the end of the sixteenth century B.C.; a series of earthquakes ensued, possibly several years after the main disaster, which completed the destruction in the inland parts of Crete which the waves had not reached. All the main centres succumbed or were abandoned, and only the central power, Knossos, survived. Its palace—now the only one in Crete—remained in use, despite its partial collapse, for a hundred years or more. With reason the Praisians of East Crete, descendants of the Minoan 'Eteocretans', remembered that Crete had once been laid waste and utterly depopulated[6].

During this century the power, and with it the culture, of all mainland Greece waxed strong. Mycenae was the longest established and had become the richest centre of Early Mycenaean civilisation at about the time that the two Cretan palaces were flourishing. Pylos too may be mentioned here, and

VII SPOUTED JAR. Kamares style. Height 23.5 cm. From the Old Palace of Knossos. Middle Minoan II (see Note page 120)

traces of the same culture have been found on many of the Aegean islands. By about 1500 many Cretans were probably settling on the mainland and in the islands, but Knossos was still strong and prosperous in the hundred years from 1500 to 1400 B.C. Evans described the art of the second half of this period, particularly the pottery, as the 'Palace' style, and people are inclined today to see it as evidence of mainland influence in Crete. By this new style we understand a stiffening of the preceding naturalistic phase. It is preponderantly decorative and often amounts to a baroque translation of the previously current natural motifs. The Palace style was especially, but not exclusively, at home in Knossos, and expressed particularly in the great amphorae and storage-jars. The style is not identical with that of the mainland in the same period. It declines towards 1400 B.C., which is the beginning of the third and last phase of the Late Minoan culture. To its end, about 1100 B.C. or later, the development—or degeneration—of art in the island followed its own way, almost entirely independent of developments on the mainland.

Even less can be said about the political organisation in Crete than about the problems we have already discussed. Even the decipherment of Linear B, which has been found in Crete only in the then intact Palace of Knossos, throws no light here. The general conclusion has been that the Palace of Knossos was ultimately destroyed about 1400 B.C., after the other palaces, and never again occupied by a new regime. Where the old regime lived, if it survived at all, and how the now small communities in Crete were organised we do not know.

The script, whose partial decipherment by Michael Ventris in 1953 opened new historical horizons, followed in Crete the pattern typical of other literate cultures. A great number of early seal-stones carry devices which Evans had recognized as a pre-Hellenic script even before he had explored Crete. His theory was too bold to win much support, but Evans was able to prove with the spade the accuracy of his ideas. In fact, as well as the primitive pictographic phase which in itself demonstrated nothing, he successfully distinguished all the other stages of the evolution of writing in Crete: the two hiero-

116 glyphic phases, followed by Linear A and Linear B. The translation to Linear A fell in the first half of the second millennium. The Linear A script itself was in general use all over Crete, and there are even traces of it in Phylakopi (on the island of Melos), in Mycenae and on Cyprus. As in Egypt the older hieroglyphic script was retained for religious purposes. There are examples of it on what is either an offering table or a door-socket in stone from Mallia, and on a double axe from Arkalochori; and to them

72-73 we should perhaps add the famous disc from Phaistos.

Linear A was incised on stone or metal objects, painted on vases, engraved on gold rings, painted on walls, and—naturally its main use—inscribed on clay tablets. We can only guess about its use on perishable materials, but this must be assumed, for the ink was certainly not only used for writing on vases. Egyptian papyrus was probably employed, and there is an old tradition that the Cretans wrote on palm leaves; and finally there is the question whether skins were not also used for writing on. At all events Linear A was not only generally known, but in use for all the practical purposes of everyday life.

In complete contrast Linear B was found by Evans only in the palace, that is the New Palace of Knossos, and only on clay tablets. From the ideograms, the numerals which Evans had already deciphered and recognised as belonging to a decimal system, and from the general impression of the finds, it was soon clear that these tablets, of which there are now hundreds, were exclusively records and inventory-lists of various objects, and also of commercial transactions. At the time only few traces of

VIII BEAKED JUG. Kamares style. Height 27 cm. From the Old Palace of Phaistos. Middle Minoan II (see Note page 120)

the script had been found, painted on vases, notably on the stirrup-vases from the Palace of Cadmus at Thebes. Evans recognised in these Theban inscriptions the same combinations of letters, and therefore the same words, as were found at Knossos. He rightly treated this as a revolutionary discovery, and deduced that the same language was spoken in the two places. The language was of course—of this Evans had not a moment's doubt—the Minoan, pre-hellenic language, and this conclusion was in harmony with his own 'pancretism'.

Although there was much in favour of mainland independence which militated against Evans' pancretism, no one had seriously considered as possible that the Greek language had been spoken at the court of Knossos; yet this very fact was to be proved. Just before the outbreak of the second world war, Professor Carl Blegen went to Pylos, where he suspected the existence of a palace. In his very first trial trenches he came upon the archives of the New Palace. The first tablets, absolutely identical with those from Knossos, attracted great attention. Many thought that these tablets were loot from the sack of the Palace of Knossos; in effect this seemed the only possible answer. After the war the excavations at Pylos were resumed, and the number of tablets rose from year to year. They were soon published, and at the same time the long-unpublished tablets from Knossos appeared. Many scholars were working on the decipherment, but it fell to Michael Ventris to be the first to demonstrate that the Greek language was concealed in the clay records not only from Pylos but from Knossos. In 1953 the famous article by Ventris and Chadwick appeared, and later the book which expounded this discovery[7].

In 1952 Wace had already found the first inscribed tablets from Mycenae, which also indicated the Greek language. Short inscriptions on vessels (stirrup-vases) had already been found on other palace sites, namely Thebes, Tiryns, and isolated examples from Orchomenos and Eleusis. Linear B seems then to have been current all over Mycenaean Greece, and particularly in palaces, so far as we can see. On the other hand, in Crete it has only been found at Knossos. The historical conclusion is clear; Achaean Greeks had occupied Knossos.

The decipherment, if it is correct—and despite the problems which still exist there can be very little doubt that it is correct in all essentials—supported this conclusion. We can only touch on some of these problems here: although the Linear B documents from Knossos, Pylos and Mycenae are identical and appear contemporary, the mainland ones are to be dated after 1300 B.C. and the Knossian ones just before 1400. In explanation it is now suggested that the final destruction of Knossos might have taken place long after 1400. Reviewing the work of Evans and Mackenzie at Knossos, and their determination of the levels and chronology, it is difficult to make this assumption, but not impossible. At any rate several historical and archaeological considerations depend on the answer to this question. If the palace in whose ruins the Linear B documents were found was destroyed in 1425 (the usually accepted date) it could be said that the Achaeans had occupied Knossos soon after the great disaster caused by the eruption on Thera. The sacking of a country already overwhelmed by such a catastrophe would not seem inappropriate to their warlike and adventurous character. But we may also entertain the possibility of a peaceful change of dynasty brought about by the marriage of a

IX   THREE-HANDLED PITHOS WITH SPOUT. Kamares style. Height 69 cm. From the Old Palace of Phaistos. Middle Minoan II (see Note page 120)

Knossian queen to an Achaean prince. The Achaeans would then have got the palace scribes of Knossos to adapt their script to the Greek language. The Cretan scribes did their best but the results left something to be desired, and so the Linear B syllabary remained an inadequate medium for the Achaean tongue. The new script then spread from Knossos to the mainland, still no doubt in the hands of Minoan, Knossian clerks and only for use in the palaces. If this is not true we must explain why the syllabary was never improved and never practised by the ordinary folk in Crete and on the mainland.

The achievements of Minoan civilisation in the second millennium were carried far beyond the borders of Crete. There are already unmistakable signs of trade with neighbouring countries at the end of the Early Minoan period, particularly with Egypt and Syria. Many early seals carry representations of ships which attest the popularity of the mariner's profession. Pottery of the early Kamares style reached not only Aegina and Melos (Phylakopi, where there was probably a Minoan colony) but also as far as Egypt. And there are possible, although not certainly demonstrable, connexions with the west, Malta and Sicily. On the other hand the close relations with the east are quite clear. The range of this overseas interest must have been the same at the time of the building of the New Palaces, but in this period we are less well informed about Minoan influence abroad. Minoan and Mycenaean now become confused and it is often difficult to distinguish one from the other. Among the places where this mixing of Minoan and Mycenaean cultures took place are Cyprus, Miletus and many other eastern towns, as well as the Lipari islands in the west. Further problems are presented by the finds in the series of shaft-graves at Mycenae, the well-known ones and those recently found. Much here is local in origin, much northern, and much Minoan. But what has been called Minoan has been so disputed that only very little is left of incontrovertible Cretan provenance.

Matters are clearer in Crete itself. As we have said, the many mansions were founded at the same time as the New Palaces. They amount to small palaces with their alabaster-lined state-rooms, frescoed halls and magazines full of great storage-jars. Many of these mansions, such as that at Tylissos or the newly discovered one at Vathypetro, are about the size of a Mycenaean palace. Even the private houses in Crete appear proportionately more splendid than those of Mycenaean Greece. They had a large number of rooms and several floors; many are provided with courts, passage-ways, magazines and several kitchens, as in Palaikastro. The furnishing was always rich, particularly in clay utensils; and there were many complicated devices for cooking and heating. In Gournia, Palaikastro and Chamaizi figurines, bronze gear and all sorts of implements have been excavated on a scale which cannot be matched outside Crete. Clearly the living standards of the islanders must have been much higher than they were anywhere else.

It has now been shown that larger settlements—cities in the true sense of the word—were to be found not only around the palaces but elsewhere. They grew up without any fortifications, which were the main preoccupation of later towns. Characteristically, coastal areas were preferred. The town of Gournia was founded right on the Bay of Mirabello, and there was another flourishing town on Pseira, which was little more than a rock in the same bay. The fine villa of Nirou Chani was also built by the sea, some 10 miles east of Knossos. All this was not the caprice of magnates with a fondness for bathing, but an undertaking planned to facilitate overseas trade. The sandy beaches, protected by a rocky promontory from the north-west wind, which is the most dangerous and frequent

X   THREE-HANDLED PITHOS. Kamares style Height 45.5 cm. From the Old Palace of Phaistos. Middle Minoan II (see Note page 120)

in Crete, made an ideal anchorage for the conditions of travel at the time. There had been a market there already, by about 1600 B.C., like the agora of the mariner-Phaeacians in the *Odyssey* (VI, 265 ff.). These are signs that the soft porous rock by the water's edge had been cut to make artificial inlets which could only have been designed as wharfs. These are the oldest harbour-works in the Mediterranean, anticipating the Phoenician establishments by several hundred years.

I, Figs. 1–2

XXI, 164

The arrangement at Nirou Chani (now called Hagioi Theodoroi) does not stand alone. On the other side of the rocky promontory of Kakon Oros, only 4 miles to the west, towards Knossos, begins one of the finest and largest beaches in Crete, over a mile long. Here was the famous town of Amnisos, already mentioned in the *Odyssey* as a landing place, site of the sanctuary and cave of Eileithyia, which was renowned in antiquity, as Homer again reminds us (*Odyssey* XIX, 188–189). Callimachus thought highly of the nymphs of Amnisos, and Strabo says that Minos built the harbour town for Knossos there. All this it has been possible to rediscover: the landing place with its many establishments, including a villa decorated with frescoes, a watering place for the crews, and a sanctuary with an altar where Zeus Thenatas was worshipped in later, Roman times.

Two miles farther west, at the mouth of the Kairatos which flows past Knossos, was another harbour. Parts of its walls are still preserved below sea-level. Remains of the houses in the town have been found, and recently an interesting chamber-tomb with fine offerings, including an Egyptian alabastron with the cartouche of Thutmosis III. Three great harbours stood in the neighbourhood of Knossos along a coastal strip barely 7 miles long. This is clear indication of the scale of the overseas traffic in the mid-second millennium.

The ancient tradition, recorded by Herodotus, Thucydides and Plato among others, tells much of the fame of Minos' command of the seas. Some details seem to be historical, such as Thucydides' report that Minos recruited his crews from the pre-Hellenic population in the islands. We can only tell whether this Minos (the tradition refers to at least two) was a Minoan or an Achaean when we have answered the question of when the Achaeans occupied Knossos. From what we know today it seems that he was an Achaean. It has long been remarked that the archaeological evidence points to a Cretan command of the seas in the middle of the Late Minoan period, 1450–1400 B.C.[8]

If the assumption is right that the Cretan tablets are at least as old as 1400 B.C., then Knossos was at the time in the hands of an Achaean king. Triaconters, fast, sea-worthy and reliable ships with thirty oars on either side, were already being made. It is quite understandable that this 'Minos' could have built up his command of the seas with the help of the seamen of the islands. They had always been fine mariners but had never been led by a warlike character who was more than a mere pirate-chief, but this man they found at last in the Achaean who won control of the rich and organised power of Knossos. It is in keeping with the typically belligerent nature of the Achaeans that they should have attacked even their own folk, as the Attic stories about Nisos and Theseus tell. Idomeneus, who went to Troy, was of this dynasty. Already in Homer's time the tradition was established that the Achaeans had ruled in Knossos for at least three generations, but if we keep to the conventional dating of the Trojan War it must have been much longer.

XI   THREE-HANDLED PITHOS DECORATED WITH FISH. Kamares style. Height 50 cm. From the Old Palace of Phaistos. Middle Minoan II (see Note page 120)

The hopes that modern scientific method would give us a more accurate means of dating have not yet been realised. The measurements made by Radio-carbon 14 set many problems and are partly contradictory, although they do not seriously conflict with results gained by other means. The pre-Hellenic chronology of Crete has been excellently worked out by Evans and Mackenzie from the evidence of excavation. The latter dealt with the pottery styles, which give the archaeologist the best evidence for chronology, in an exemplary fashion, while Evans, relying more on the evidence of Egypt, brought all the material together into a single system.

Evans chose the most appropriate of the various chronological schemes used by prehistorians, that of triple divisions which correspond with the natural sequence of Youth, Maturity, Old Age. Apart from the Neolithic period he arranged the Bronze Age in Crete into three periods, named after Minos, the great legendary king of the island: Early Minoan (EM), Middle Minoan (MM) and Late Minoan (LM). His theory agreed so well with the evidence that the same system was adopted for the rest of Greece, and we now speak of Early, Middle and Late, Helladic and Cycladic cultures. Evans subdivided the three Minoan periods each into three further parts, but these are designed rather for the specialist and do not always agree so readily with the evidence.

The stylistic development of the pottery is as follows: the monochrome Neolithic wares survive into the Early Minoan period and are followed by vases decorated with dark paint on the light clay-ground. In the last phase of the Early Minoan period the opposite technique begins to appear, and remains characteristic of Middle Minoan pottery: white or yellowish paint is used for decoration over the dark-painted background of the vase. The transition to the Late Minoan period is made without a sharp break. The painting is now again dark-on-light, and the style of the decoration naturalistic. This development had already begun in the Middle Minoan period with the white-painted patterns. There is no clear stylistic boundary between the second Late Minoan period, the so-called 'Palace' style, and the preceding one, and Evans was led in his later years to propose further sub-divisions, A, B and C, although the distinction between, say, LM I C and LM II A is very fine and quite subjective.

Historical divisions made on the basis of the architectural evidence do not entirely agree with this system. The pre-Palace period is covered by the Early Minoan. The period of the Old Palaces is of the first and second phases of the Middle Minoan period, the floruit of the polychrome Kamares style.

The period of the New Palaces embraces the last Middle Minoan period (MM III) and earlier Late Minoan (LM I–LM II). The period following the great Palaces begins at Knossos with the third phase of the Late Minoan period (LM III), for the rest of Crete with LM II.

The absolute chronology, in years, is based on Evan's assessment of parallels between Crete and Egypt. His date for the start of the Early Minoan period was somewhat too high, but in general the rest of his dating is still acceptable. He set the beginning of the Bronze Age before the third millennium, but today a date about 2600 B.C. is preferred, and this serves also for the rest of Greece. Some

XII   CRATER WITH ADDED CLAY BLOSSOMS, PERHAPS IMITATING WORK IN METAL OR STONE. Kamares style. Height 45.5 cm. From the Old Palace of Phaistos. Middle Minoan II (see Note page 121)

scholars still support the high dating. We are entitled to assume that the general use of metal in Crete began about 2800 B.C. and on this basis the chronological chart opposite page 177 has been prepared[9].

MINOAN RELIGION

Minoan civilisation and art present a colourful but not readily comprehensible picture. It becomes particularly difficult when we try to understand the essence of Minoan religion in Crete, and with it that of Mycenaean Greece. Despite the many exhaustive studies the subject remains elusive. The decipherment of Linear B has made the task more complex rather than easier, for in the tablets we find predominantly Achaean deities[10].

All other known peoples before and after the main period of Cretan civilisation, including of course the Greeks, built temples for their gods. Great temples of stone were already being built in Middle Kingdom Egypt. In Mesopotamia there were large brick temples and colossal ziggurats. Babylonians and Assyrians, Hittites and even the minor kingdoms, had their temples in the earliest periods. Even the Israelites did not fail to build at least one great temple although their religion allowed no cult images. In these temples stood a large or small cult-statue of a god, while other statues and reliefs represented gods and demons. In Minoan civilisation we find no temples, no great cult-statues, and no monumental representations of a deity, apart from some extremely hypothetical examples.

Crete was not without her gods; no race ever was—except the Cyclopes. Small works of art, like rings, gems, and the figurines of the latest period, which may represent deities, show that the Cretans did not have a wholly aniconic religion, as did the Israelites and other nomad, or near-nomad peoples. Cretans believed in a god or gods. Chosen believers were honoured by their presence, but for their worship there was no need of temples or cult-statues. Archaeological evidence suggests that the Cretans felt themselves close to their deities under the open skies, in a sacred wood, on a mountain top, and especially in caves.

Evans had understood this from the beginning and explained it in his pioneering monograph on *The Tree and Pillar Cult*. Much new material has since been found but opinions have changed but little. The significance of a sacred tree has been generally accepted, but we cannot say whether we should recognise in it the god himself, a symbol of him, or a sign of the sacred character of the locality. Much has been written for and against the Pillar cult. Evans rightly observed that wherever there are pillared rooms on the ground floor of a building, there are also cult objects and often the apparatus of ritual. Something rather different was probably expressed in the representation of the Creto-Mycenaean columns which appear on gems, rings, and, among other things, the relief over the Lion Gate at Mycenae. The column is certainly a symbol. It often stands on a concave object, which is called an altar but cannot be one. Often it is flanked by two animals, and one or both of them may be tethered to it. Convincing analogies, as with the corresponding Egyptian symbol, show that this signifies Unity, the cherished aspiration of all nations in all periods[11]. There are many symbols in Creto-Mycenaean religion, among them the double axe and the so-called Horns of Consecration. These are the best known but not the best understood. We can only say of them that they represent the god himself, or —more often—indicate the sanctity of a place.

34

XIII INSIDE OF THE BOWL SHOWN IN PLATE 23. Kamares style. Diam. 54 cm. From the Old Palace of Phaistos. Middle Minoan II
(see Note page 121)

To return to the central question of the deity himself. We already find in Crete in the Neolithic period the figurines of big-bellied women of the sort found in the furthermost parts of Europe, Asia Minor and Africa, and which are generally thought to represent the Great Goddess of Nature and Fertility. The original deity in Crete, with its uniquely peaceful culture and united population, was not known in many different forms. There was no need for a war-god, there were no independent areas or peoples who had invented their own deities, there was no lively mythology of religion which demanded a plurality of gods. The island's possessions, the people's loves and fears, were for their fields and herds, for which they entreated fertility, their woods and mountains in which they hunted, the sea which they held in awe, the earthquake from the depth which they rightly dreaded. In these circumstances they naturally worshipped their deity as nature-goddess, huntress, queen of animals, sea-goddess, earth-goddess etc.

This gives rise to the important question whether Minoan religion was polytheistic or monotheistic. Most scholars, including the most respected, are inclined to assume many gods, and regard a monotheistic religion, as that of ancient Israel, the mark of a highly developed people. But apart from the fact that Crete was a unity and the scene of great cultural achievements there are other difficulties in the way attributing to Crete a very Olympus of deities. There were very few individual male deities in Crete, if indeed there were any at all, but there was a whole, distinctive series of goddesses. Moreover we get the impression, especially in the later periods, that the goddess represented is always the same, and the only change is in her attributes, which may be a bird, a flower, horns, snakes, weapons, or some unrecognisable symbols. The still very uncertain readings of some Linear A inscriptions give us names which seem to be derived from places, like Kupanatuna or Pipituna (the latter also in Linear B). The name which survived in Greek as *Dictynna* would have been something like *Dikituna*. The name which time and again appears on cult objects—among them the famous offering table from the cave at Psychro—is read as *Asasara*, which could be the same as the previously surmised *Akakala* ('Ακακαλλίς).

In Crete there seems to have been a stage in religious development which might be called 'unachieved monotheism'. The Cretans seem to have believed in one great deity. She was queen of the mountains, animals, the sea and the powers beneath the ground. She appeared under different names, but probably most often as eponym of a place or mountain, like the later names Idaea, Dindymene or Sipylene, Lindia or Paphia, which replaced the individual names of the appropriate deities. She also carried many, often very different attributes. The representations are so varied and changing in different religions and with different peoples, that we cannot distinguish with certainty the various functions of the deity which were indicated by the various symbols. Thus, was the goddess with the flowers so very different from the goddess with the doves that they could not be one? It is very difficult to see the difference and we should probably not attempt to do so.

The oldest cult-places were probably caves. They remained in use for cult purposes throughout all the periods, and even survived the Minoan civilisation until far into the Hellenistic period. The cave of Eileithyia at Amnisos was at first inhabited, and then, from the third millennium B.C. to the fifth or sixth century A.D., served uninterruptedly as a cult-place. It is one of the most venerable religious centres of antiquity for it kept the lustre of its fame through three and a half millennia, which saw two civilisations and three different religions. Caves were principally the centre for popular worship. In later traditions they became the refuges for greater goddesses, or the birth-places and nurseries of young gods. Offerings of all kinds, some most valuable, were dedicated in them. The wonderful patterns of their stalagmites and stalactites, rendered more fantastic in the deep gloom by the light of lamps, must have had a profound effect on the worshippers. The more important caves have walled entrances, rooms for accommodation, altars and chapels. Great storage-jars were found at Psychro and in the newly-discovered cult-cave of Lykastos on the holy mountain Juktas. The priests of the caves probably had herds, fields and slaves. According to the later tradition priestly colleges for centuries conducted religious instruction, sacred 'Logoi', even Mysteries, in many of the caves. The Idaean cave was the most famous, at least in Greek times, and we read that Pythagoras and Epimenides were associated with it.

As well as the caves there were unwalled sanctuaries. In them stood the sacred tree growing in an enclosure, one or more altars in the open, and often a small grove of olives, cypresses and oaks, or so ancient writers describe them. Everywhere there were great double axes on tall shafts. All this we learn from representations on works of art. Excavations tell us rather less about the plans of the shrines on mountain-peaks or in open country to which offerings were brought. These probably had no very large buildings and altars, or even chapels. The offerings were vases, clay figures of men and animals, and some cult-objects. Sanctuaries of this type are known from the beginning of the second millennium B.C. and the offerings found in them are valuable to us both for what they tell about the nature and function of the deity, and especially for the information they give about the contemporary fashion, dress and coiffure for men and women of the earlier Middle Minoan period. Such sites are Petsofa, Piskokephalo and at the peak of Mount Juktas. 15-18

So much for public worship. Private cults were served by small house-altars, the pillar-rooms already mentioned and, in the palaces, the royal shrines. Small cult-rooms are found already in the Old Palaces, and these, so far as we know, housed cult-figures and other small objects. The open steps and court served for ceremonies before a larger audience. One of the best known is the sanctuary in the Old Palace of Phaistos, formed by four small rooms at the north-east corner of the west court, and the long row of steps along its north edge. There was a sort of raised path into the court from which correspondingly higher steps led on to the main stand; we can imagine it as a carpeted approach to the royal box or to an altar. All cultures had their sacred ways, including the Greek. Such was no doubt the main road at Knossos which linked the Great with the Little Palace. It was carefully paved with well-worked stones, like the later processional way of Marduk in Babylon. The stone 'kernos' which stands at the south-west corner of the central court at Mallia tells us something about the type of cult-ceremonies. It served for ritual offerings by which thanks were given for fertility in each year. 50-51 28 56

The small palace in Gournia and the megara of Nirou Chani and Tylissos had similar shrines set apart. The theatral steps at Knossos are in the same position in the west court as at Phaistos, while the royal chapel in the west wing with its tripartite façade looked on to the Central Court. A tiny chapel, hardly more than a yard square, stood over the ruins of the south-east part of the palace until the very end of Minoan times. The figures of the goddess with the doves and other cult-objects were found there in situ. 29

Similar chapels of small single rooms are typical of the latest period and have been found at several places. The best known are those at Gazi, near Heraklion, and at Karphi in Lasithi; these contained a number of clay figures of the deity, some half life-size. The 'orans' type of these figures, with hands raised, is the most characteristic and popular one for the Minoan mother-goddess. The divine nature 128-131

XXIV, 70 has never been called into question, but earlier types, like the faience snake-goddess from Knossos, are held by some to represent mortals.

The goddess usually appears alone, or attended by animals. Less often is she shown as the mother with the divine child, a type already met in the early Cycladic idols of marble, if the figure on the head of one of them is indeed to be identified as a child. Another representation, also attested in the early period, shows two goddesses side by side. They are closely juxtaposed and often embrace each other. 218–219 As well as the two figures from Teke there is a second Cycladic group, hitherto unnoticed, in which the women embrace each other, as in the ivory group from Mycenae[12]. This type of group is also found among the Archaic Greek terracottas from Crete. They are best identified with the Cretan Μητέρες, whose cult was still alive in Sicily in the days of Diodorus. The valuable ivory group from Mycenae shows the divine child, as παραπαίζων, with the two 'mothers'. The 'two-in-one' mothers are covered by a single cloak, as later in the Eleusinian Mysteries. The holy trinity is also found in Creto-Mycenaean religion. The triads are not like the Egyptian, with father, mother and child, but in Crete the goddess is often attended by two young women ('Diaskourai') and later we find either a god between two goddesses (at Dreros and perhaps Gortyn), or a goddess between two men (on a gold plaque from 138–139 the Idaean Cave, and in the clay model of a chapel in the Giamalakis Collection).

Rites were conducted in the private chapels in quiet privacy, rather like the Japanese before their house-altars. This shows how much feeling there was for the individual deities of each house, of whose existence we hear much in Homer. There were also public ceremonies attended by crowds of both sexes. Standards on tall poles marked the festal occasion, such as we see on the miniature frescoes or the rhyton from Hagia Triada; much the same are those on the stele of Gudea. At religious festivals the women went barefoot, with bared breasts and wearing ritual skirts divided at the front[13].

Cretan art showed the divinity in various settings, some almost poetic. The goddess stands proudly at the mountain peak attended by lions which, in other scenes, she holds in check, or hunts through the hills. She sails calmly on the divine ship or rests on the waves. Again, she is seated on a bull or some other beast which swims through the seas; and we are reminded of the later story how Zeus raped Europa or Aigina and carried her to an island.

In a warm country like Crete, where the temperament and imagination of the people were easily stirred by religious and intensified by natural phenomena, men readily saw visions and dreamed dreams. Even today, in the gloom of the caves, the peasants discern the forms of men and animals among the shadows and pinnacles of rock. The incredibly clear atmosphere in spring and autumn produces mirages which set seas and fields floating in the air. Strange reflections over the Cretan valleys (the so-called Drosoulites in Sphakia) throw shadows like men on to the skies. In those days gods were more ready to show themselves to mortals; Homer knew this well. Specific rituals, prayers, dances, offerings, could conjure up the god and even dismiss him. So we must suppose that the god of the Minoans not only lived beneath the ground, in caves, in woods and on mountains, but also ascended to the heavens. We cannot be sure of this but the evidence of similar religions makes it most plausible.

XIV PALACE OF KNOSSOS. BULL'S HEAD FROM THE COLOURED PLASTER RELIEF IN THE PORTICO BY THE NORTH ENTRANCE. Early period of the New Palace. Middle Minoan III, about 1580 B.C. (see Note page 128)

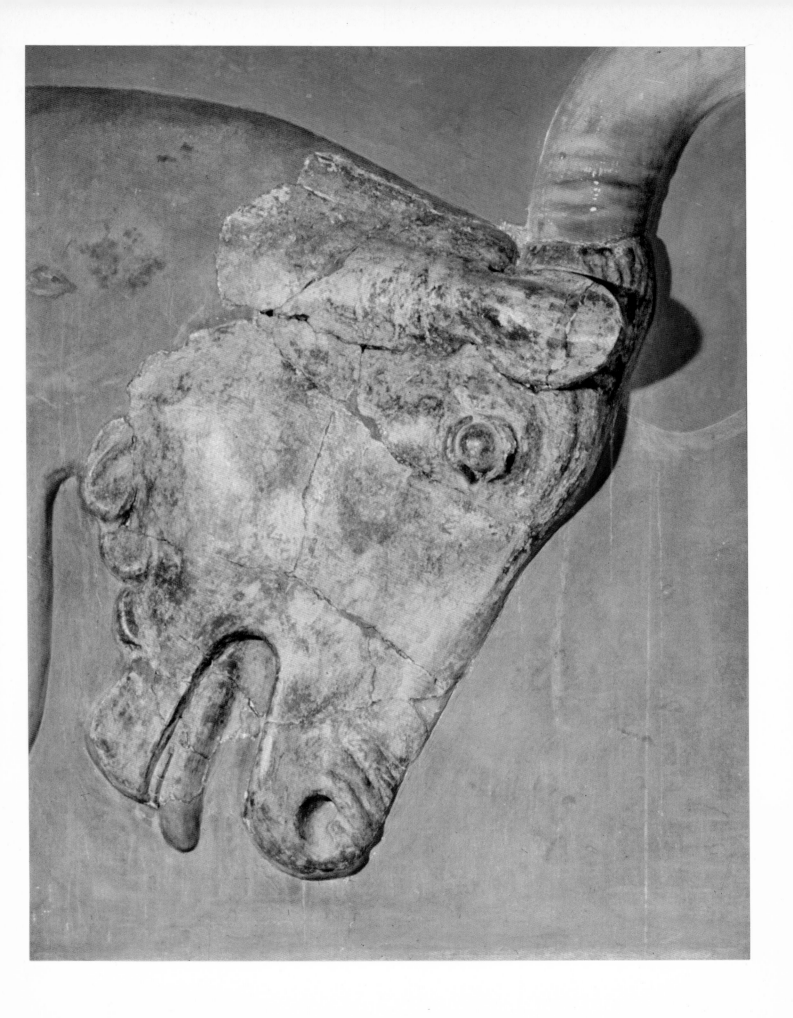

III aboveIn this context the scenes which show a young god floating in the air during some ritual enacted entirely or largely by women are particularly interesting. In most cases it is certainly a male god, and appears to be young. But we must beware of over-enthusiastic speculation about Minoan religion. Is the young god the μέγιστος κοῦρος who was summoned to make fertile the plants and animals more than a thousand years later by the Eteocretan priests in Praisos—in the Greek language but in the Minoan spirit? Is he the lover and partner of the great goddess who is embraced each year and each year dies? Is he—at least in some cases—the god who mates with a mortal queen to ensure divine blood for a mortal king?[14] The sacred marriage (ἱερὸς γάμος) between divinities, and the secret marriage between god and mortal are popular motifs in mythology and epic.

Demons also played their part in Minoan religion, particularly the donkey-headed ones which are derived from the Egyptian Ta-urt. Their concern is the watering of plant-life by the libations of holy water from heaven which they receive symbolically from the goddess. They also appear often as wild creatures with beasts, whose dead bodies they may even carry over their shoulders. We know little 119 centreabout any of the other demons; the bull-headed 'Minotaur' is the best-known. The many remarkable and disjointed monsters which are known from the Zakro sealings seem to be the inventions of one particularly imaginative artist.

The often-quoted sarcophagus from Hagia Triada is probably the most interesting single document of Minoan religion. It taxes scholarship severely, for it carries several scenes which, taken singly, may be capable of explanation, but are completely inexplicable when we try to fit them into a logical sequence.

In itself it is quite reasonable to assume that there was in Hagia Triada a tomb which had been painted in imitation of scenes of Egyptian funeral-cult and worship of the dead. In effect fragments of frescoes of this type have been found there. It is conceivable that extracts from tomb-paintings were copied on to the sarcophagus on the occasion of the destruction of the tomb itself or for some other reason. The big question is whether the scenes on the four sides, one of them divided into two parts, are possibly interrelated.

XXVII–XXXOn the long side of the Hagia Triada sarcophagus a procession brings offerings of a bull, fruit and wine to the accompaniment of a pipe. The other long side has two scenes: two women pour offerings into a vessel in a sanctuary, to the music of a cithara; the other, which is still not explained, shows three men bringing offerings of a ship (probably of ivory) and two calves (probably live creatures and not models) to the armless figure of a dead man or a god which is standing before a tomb or altar.

The short sides show two people in a chariot drawn by two creatures; on one side these are stocky, mortal horses, on the other winged griffins in full flight. A supernatural bird with powerful claws and wild eyes seems to be greeting the occupants of this chariot. Representations of strange birds appear repeatedly in Crete, and there was probably some myth about a giant winged creature such as we read of in Arabian tales.

XV PALACE OF KNOSSOS. RHYTON-CARRIER FROM THE PROCESSION FRESCO OF THE GREAT SOUTH PROPYLAEA. Later period of the New Palace. Late Minoan I, about 1500–1450 B.C. (see Note page 128)

LIFE AND CRAFTS

THE PERIOD BEFORE THE PALACES

At the outset we characterised Cretan art as colourful and individual. Modern scholars have described the artistic temperament of the Cretans sometimes as fully naturalistic, sometimes as primitive, sometimes as impressionistic, sometimes as baroque. Despite a certain primitiveness some of the Cretan achievements are incredibly bold and have almost a modern air, such as was never attained by the Egyptian artist save perhaps late in the Amarna period. Some have even found in Cretan art the sort of delicate, miniaturist, even schematic traits which we associate with the art of the Far East.

The main development of Cretan art was achieved in the third and second millennia B.C. It exhibits neither the austere discipline nor the unity of contemporary Egyptian art. The greatest single period in Crete was of the sixteenth and fifteenth centuries. The essence of its success lay in the lively use of colour and decorative sense, but there was a complete absence of feeling for monumentality, especially in sculpture. Even the great Cretan palaces, the most imposing achievements, impress by something other than their sheer size. Set on broad, often terraced sites the impression they give is more graphic than plastic, like the present-day villages on Cretan hill-sides with their colourful walls, porches and balconies.

In the Early Minoan period Cretan art was already beginning to establish its dependent character. The pottery is at first monochrome, as in the Neolithic period, but gradually the vase-shapes become more varied. High-footed cups are decorated with burnished patterns ('Pyrgos' style) and the first painted vases are made. The great innovation of the period is the appearance of bronze vessels, and these are imitated in clay by vases coated with black paint and mottled in the firing, the 'Vasiliki' style. The dark, painted surface corresponds to the 'Urfirnis' of mainland wares, with the dark brown, yellowish or red appearance produced by uneven firing in the kiln. By covering parts of the surface of the vase patterns of various shapes could be produced at will, fore-runners, as it were, of abstract art. Occasionally there is painted decoration too. Patterns were diversified; the curvilinear appears as well as the rectilinear. Towards the end of the period a new painting technique was being practised which heralds the style of the following, Middle Minoan period, the light-on-dark style, with patterns in a thick white or yellowish paint on the dark-painted ground.

Minoan appreciation for colour is seen already in the Early Minoan period in the fine vases of variegated stone which have been found particularly in East Crete. The technique of making them had been learned from the Egyptians. There are a few vases which may be direct imports from Egypt, but by and large the shapes and material are Cretan. Veined limestone, fine-grained marble and polychrome stalactitic stone from the caves were worked into vases, and the Cretan artist fully appreciated the effects to be won from an intelligent use of the natural veining. In central Crete, in the Messara plain, we find the use of stone-inlaying rather than whole polychrome stone vases.

Even at this early date the metal-worker's craft was highly developed. The bronze implements,

XVI PALACE OF KNOSSOS. SO-CALLED PARISIENNE. PRIESTESS, HER OFFICE INDICATED BY THE SACRAL KNOT AT HER BACK. Fragment from a fresco from the six-columned hall in the west wing of the Palace. Later period of the New Palace. Late Minoan I, about 1500–1450 B.C. (see Note page 128–129)

especially daggers, are moderately good and many of them may have been imported from elsewhere in the Aegean, but a special elegance and finesse inspired the gold jewellery. The necklaces and pendants in the form of animals and flowers which have been found particularly in East Crete, at Mochlos, and in the Messara plain, show how much the Cretans valued personal adornments. The only earlier pieces which can be reasonably compared are those from the Royal Graves at Ur, in particular the superb gold diadem of Queen Shubad. The contemporary gold treasures of the second city of Troy and Poliochni on Lemnos attest the wealth and prosperity of those towns, but fall far short of the Cretan jewellery in richness. Egyptologists tell us that it was the Egyptians who first realised the value of floral motifs in art, but we shall see that in this too the Cretans were second to none. In the finest period of Cretan art the flower was cherished as highly as it ever was in Egypt. We find it even at the start in the plain but gracious gold blossoms from Mochlos, gifts to the noble dead.

There is little that can be said about the early architecture. There were certainly spacious houses, with red-painted plaster on their floors, and sometimes also on the walls. We know more about the tombs, especially those in the Messara. In this, the largest plain in the island, the Early Minoan culture is seen at its richest. The small communities there lived partly off the land, and to a lesser degree from the trade with the Libyan coast, little over 250 miles away. Mochlos and the rest of East Crete were more concerned with trade with the islands and eastern countries. The Messara towns stood around the edge of the plain, and according to their size each had one or more large circular tombs, built of solid stone and generally thought to have been vaulted. The largest of them (Tomb B at Platanos) has an inner diameter of 13.10 m., about of the size of the biggest Mycenaean tholos-tombs, while its outer diameter is 18 m., the difference being due to its thick walls. The roofs were most probably wooden, not vaulted, and the walls certainly leaned inwards. In all of them there are megalithic door-jambs and lintels. All face east; an early example of fixed orientation which we will meet again in the palaces and other important buildings.

The circular tombs were communal, and continued in use for hundreds of years. Often there are subsidiary rectangular or irregular buildings attached to help accommodate all the dead. These annexes and many other rectangular graves contained poor offerings of a later period. They belong to the end of the Early Minoan period and the beginning of the Middle Minoan, at the turn of the second millennium. In them were burial pithoi, and clay sarcophagi in the form of wooden chests, often with knob-like attachments for fastening the lids to the box. The richest burials are the earliest ones, laid on the floor of the circular tombs, and the accompanying offerings are our most valuable source of information about the Early Minoan period. There is plenty of pottery, the latest being in the Kamares style. There are also figure-vases; rhyta in human form from East Crete and bulls with human figures clinging to their horns. This shows that the Cretan bull-games were first enacted on the broad plain of Messara by the young herdsmen who had to capture and tame the half-wild creatures in the well-watered pastures of southern Ida. The best of Early Minoan plastic art is seen in the greyhound carved as the handle on the lid of a stone pyxis: just the sort of creature which ranges through Cretan villages today. Other pieces of minor sculpture include many marble idols, probably imported from the Cyclades, and local imitations of them in steatite.

The most important Early Minoan artistic achievements are found in the field of seal-engraving. Many of the seals are in the form of animals, like birds and apes, or often of groups of animals. The

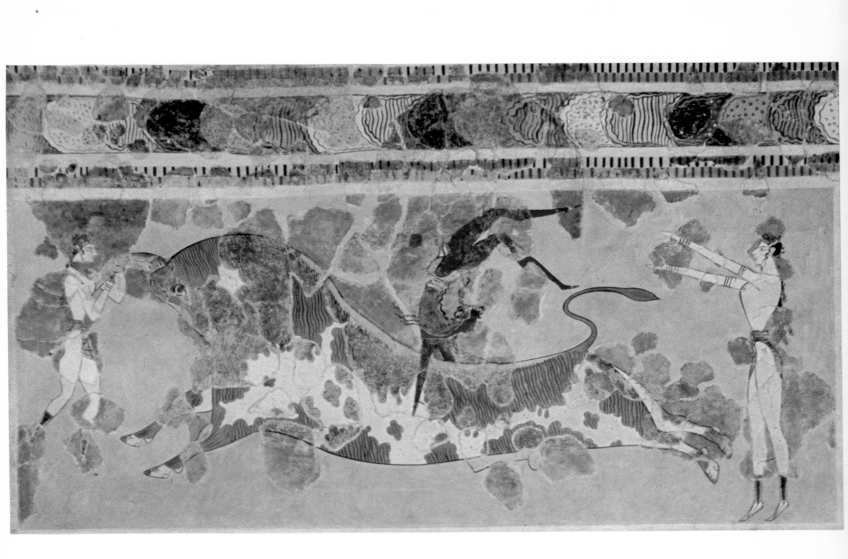

XVII   PALACE OF KNOSSOS. BULL-GAMES. FRESCO FROM A SMALL COURT IN THE EAST SHOWING THE DIFFERENT PHASES OF THE SPORT. Late Minoan 1,
shortly after 1500 B.C. (see Note page 129)

devices were cut on the flat undersides. The practice was apparently borrowed from the East and became so popular that every important Cretan came to have his personal seal. The seal-stones were probably tied around the neck, and so easily lost. As a result they appear as stray finds as often as in the tombs. Later belief had it that the stones guaranteed milk for a nursing woman so they can still be seen today suspended from the necks of Cretan mothers as they had once been long ago. Scholars and collectors still know them by their new name: *galopetrai*, milk-stones. Seals cut in a white stone are particularly prized for their milky appearance. At first they were only made of soft materials like steatite, bone, and especially ivory. Apart from the animal-forms which we have mentioned, and to which we may add seals in the shape of human and animal feet, there are head-seals and scarabs, prisms and cylinders, the last with devices at each end and not on the side. At the end of the period the softer semi-precious stones begin to come into use: rock crystal, amethyst, quartz, jasper and so forth. The patterns in the devices are an invaluable source of information about ethnological matters as well as art-history. At first they are simple and linear, especially spirals and maeanders. Animal-forms appear early as part of purely decorative schemes, and the seal may be covered with spiraliform rows of lions, or of scorpions, spiders and ants. Later, human representations became more common, showing the profession of their owner: hunter or—and this quite often—potter. The many scenes with ships show that mariners were not scarce, as we have already suspected on other grounds. One particular form of seal deserves special mention here—a round piece of bone with a suspension hole. From this was developed the later Creto-Mycenaean ring with its tiny hoop and large oval bezel[15].

Seals of the turn of the third and second millennia are particularly significant for the inscriptions which some of them carry; at first in pictographs and then in developed hieroglyphic script. Indeed Evans deduced that the groups of animals, heads, limbs, plants and implements were a form of primitive Cretan writing.

THE PERIOD OF THE OLD PALACES

It would have been difficult to envisage the transition from a peasant-culture to a kingdom if we had the evidence of only one palace. Fortunately we have at least three, and all, so far as we know, founded just after 2000 B.C. There is no evidence whatsoever for the arrival of a foreign race or dynasty at this time so the change was entirely an internal matter.

In the Messara plain the large circular tombs were still in use until about 1900 or 1800 B.C. and then the settlements which owned them seem to have been abandoned. At about the same time, however, the Palace of Phaistos was built in grand and commanding isolation. The decisive factor in the siting of the palace must have been—as at Knossos—that there was already an important settlement there, perhaps the most important in the plain. There may even have been minor palatial buildings. Ambitious and powerful leaders took over the control of the smaller communities, as they had done in Egypt a little earlier. In this country, whose political fortunes had so much in common with Crete, the local chiefs were laying the foundations of the Middle Kingdom at this very time.

A great palace was built on the levelled hill at Phaistos. At the same time were built the palaces at Mallia and, the largest of them all, at Knossos. Each of these three areas must have fallen under the leadership of one strong personality who commanded obedience. At Knossos we have the clearest picture of how things developed.

I, XVIII, 49–51

XVIII, 49–51
XX, 56–59
26–41

46

XVIII   PALACE OF PHAISTOS. WEST QUARTER AND PART OF THE WEST COURT. In the foreground ruined houses of the Greek period; in the background Mt Asterousia (see Note page 135)

The 'tell' at Knossos had seen vigorous occupation for millennia. The neolithic levels beneath the palace are the deepest in Europe, and we may yet find that Mesolithic man lived there, as he seems to have in Thessaly and even on the small islands of Skyros and Zakynthos.

In the Early Minoan period vaulted underground storerooms had been hewn out of the soft rock of the 'tell'—now called Kephala ('head')—and these bear some superficial resemblance to the 'Hypogaea' of Malta. At the beginning of the Middle Minoan period the top of the hill was occupied by close-set, solid buildings with rounded corners, one of which is still to be seen by the entrance to the Throne Room in the west wing of the New Palace. The powerful chief, who was to become the king, incorporated these buildings into a single structure. This in itself is enough to prove that the palaces were built by local chiefs and not newcomers.

Figs. 4, 11, 13 From the Old Palaces of Crete we have only the slight remains which were preserved in the New Palaces, so we can only make general remarks about their plans and construction. There are two things in common to all the palaces. First, they have two courts: a central rectangular court around which the various apartments are grouped, and a west court against the outer wall of the palace and of no particular shape. Secondly, the palaces are all oriented in the same way. As in eastern countries they were set out according to certain, probably religious canons. The long axis of the central court runs almost exactly north to south, so that the four sides of the court, and so the whole building, lie facing the four points of the compass[16]. The same orientation applies in the mansions or large villas and for whole towns, so that we can speak of deliberate palace- and town-planning in Crete.

48

XVIII The towns grew up around the palaces. At Mallia the private houses were standing until the last days of the palace and fell with it in about 1500 B.C. At Knossos and Phaistos the towns survived the palaces and lived on into Greek times, as it were in the reflected glory of the great palaces which had stood there. These are the oldest towns in Greece, if not in Europe, and Knossos at least has continued occupied to the present day.

For the appearance of these earliest towns of Europe we have the evidence of some small faience plaques which must have been inlaid on a wooden chest to give a picture of a whole town. These plaques were found deep beneath the floor of the New Palace of Knossos and are certainly Middle Minoan although we cannot be more precise than that about their date. As well as figures of men, animals and plants they represent the façades of houses of some architectural elegance. These show horizontal coursing, the pillars of windows and doors, decorative rows of circles which must represent beam-ends, and signs of isodomic construction with bricks or stone blocks. The façades are symmetrical: the door in the centre of the ground floor and two or three windows on each story. All the houses seem to have three stories and many have what appears to be a pent-house on the roof with a door and slightly sloping terrace-roof. Similar Egyptian representations suggest that this would be the summer bedroom where the Cretans, like the contemporary Egyptians, sought cool air at night. Many of the faience houses have no doors, or only narrow windows in the upper stories. These must be the backs of houses; at the fronts there were broad, airy windows which we may imagine fitted with thin skins, like parchment, which would be semi-transparent.

This spate of ambitious building for the living was, oddly enough, not accompanied by a comparable concern for the accommodation of the dead. The tombs which have hitherto been used were completely abandoned in the Middle Minoan period, a change which may reflect a change of attitude

XIX   PALACE OF HAGIA TRIADA. VIEW FROM THE CENTRAL COURT WITH THE MASSIF OF MT IDA IN THE BACKGROUND
(see Note page 135–137)

to belief in life after death. Communal graves are now almost entirely unknown and the bodies are simply buried in a pithos or clay sarcophagus. Where there are any offerings they are comparatively poor.

In this period the first public sanctuaries were built on mountain-tops and in open places. The deity appears in different forms: protectress, healer, goddess of fertility. The dedications give us a valuable picture of the sculptural achievements of the time. Animals are made in a summary fashion, and are often found set in the base of a cup which may have been used for libations of milk, wine or honey. These, and the offerings in the form of worshippers, herdsmen with their beasts, domestic animals and doves, are readily explained as gifts inviting the protection of the goddess for the donor. Some other types are more puzzling, like the weasels, which may then have been kept in the house to keep down mice. Models of parts of the human body are votives for the healing of disease or injury. Many limbs show clear signs of a particular pathological condition or deformity. Where only half of a human body is shown—usually the right half—we may suspect paralysis, and in many respects these offerings can tell the specialist much about the diseases then prevalent.

The clay figures of men and women worshippers are particularly important for us. The men are almost all alike, naked youths wearing penis-sheaths and carrying a dagger at their belts as the Cretans do today. The women are more elegant with a variety of modish dresses and coiffures. Their skirts are broad and ground-length, and their jackets leave the breasts bare, perhaps a survival of ritual nakedness. The hats, and especially the hair-styles, are strikingly artistic and modern in appearance, and the standard of the modelling of many of these figures is of a very high order.

There was notable progress in seal-engraving in the period of the Old Palaces, accompanied by a reduction in the number of shapes employed. The seal itself was generally cut from a hard, semi-precious stone, and in elegant forms which clearly imitate metal originals. The Cretans, who had no taste for monumental art, have left us masterpieces in miniature in their seals. The devices have scenes with trees, birds and other creatures, often in lively motion. Many bear complete tableaux: an ibex in a rocky landscape, a doe resting by a stream, a shepherd-boy with his grazing flock, even the fantastic pattern of stalactites in a cave. One seal-impression carries two superb portraits, no doubt of father and son. A notable cultural advance is shown by the stamp-seals with developed hieroglyphic inscriptions. Clay tablets and other objects carry these hieroglyphs simply incised but on the seals the symbols appear as fine plastic forms and the inscriptions are works of art, like the monumental hieroglyphic inscriptions in Egypt.

Pottery of the Old Palace period has survived in quantity and is the most striking achievement of the age. The products of the palace workshops soon travelled far beyond Crete. The first vases were found in Egypt, and called simply 'Aegean'. A few years later similar vases were excavated by English and Italian scholars in Crete, particularly in an almost inaccessible cave on Mount Ida which is hidden by snow until May each year. This is the famous cave of Kamares (the Cretan term for 'bridges') which takes its name from the nearest town, a difficult journey of several hours away. From the find the title 'Kamares' style was applied to this colourful ware. We have already remarked that the light-on-dark system of decoration was invented at the end of the Early Minoan period. The vases were coated all over with black paint and then decorated in yellowish-white. At the beginning of the Middle Minoan period the vase-shapes, the quality of clay, paint, colour and pattern, were improved and refined to a degree which still wins admiration. It would be hard to find better examples of the

XX   PALACE OF MALLIA, SEEN FROM THE WEST (see Note page 137)

potter's art at so early a date. One reason for it was the use of the mechanical potter's wheel, which now became known in Crete for the first time. With it, and with better refined clay, it became possible to throw a variety of shapes with extremely thin walls. The so-called 'barbotine' technique involved the application of pieces of damp clay to part or all of the vase to make a rough surface, and many potters preferred a thorny type of decoration in this technique in which we may recognise imitation of certain sea-shells.

A fine malleable clay was needed for making the thin-walled Kamares vases. Modern experiments by expert potters in Crete have shown that the clay must be refined, moistened and kneaded for months to produce the plasticity which was required, not only for the thin walls, but for the wavy rims and other imitations of metal vases, shown also in the fancy handles. The fine quality of the fabric is matched by that of the paint: dark lilac to black, and with a metallic sheen. The Kamares potters must be considered the inventors of this fine gloss which reappears centuries later on Greek pottery. Almost all the Kamares cups are thin-walled. The finest of all, the so-called 'egg-shell' ware, could perhaps only be made in the palace potteries from a combination of fine clay and the paint which strengthened the fragile fabric. These vases are all very small, generally one-handled cups.

VI above Such fine technique and elegant colouring were always to be prized, and Lucian speaks of vases like these as ἀνεμοφόρητα καὶ ὑμενόστρακα, 'light as the wind, as thin as skin' *(Lexiphanes 7).*

The rich imagination and skill of the Cretan potter excelled in this technique. The marbling of stone vases and breccias could be imitated to perfection with a palette enriched by so many shades of red and yellow. Shells, octopuses, fish and frogs, were used as decorative motifs, and even human figures, as we now know from the finds at Phaistos.

Plant-life was the richest source of inspiration for vase-decoration. The painter never represented the blooms naturalistically, but stylised them into decorative patterns; in some the model can still be easily recognised—daisies, irises, anemones, which enrich spiral designs—in others the form has been 20–21 completely translated. On a superb spouted vase from Knossos we see amid the foliage leaves which recall the later Greek anthemion, and on a fine, handleless cup of egg-shell fabric from the same site VII we can recognise the water-lily.

So far as we can tell the Kamares style of Knossos was more conservative and naturalistic. In contrast the latest finds at Phaistos show that here naturalistic forms were almost entirely abandoned. V, VIII–XIII Every element which presented the opportunity for more formal decoration was boldly and cleverly 20 below, 23–24 exploited by the painter: simple systems like regular brick-patterns, scales, wavy lines and ivy wreathes, rosettes, fire-wheels, lattice and coral-like designs, combinations of maeanders, plumes, spirals twists and blossoms—in short, an infinity of forms and combinations to excite attention. The variety in the vases and fragments which have recently been found in the deeper levels in the Palace of Phaistos is so great that one comes to expect some new pattern or shape with every new find.

It is a great pity that we have in the island no well-preserved remains of a palace of the first period. It is inconceivable that a lively and imaginative culture and art, such as is revealed by the pottery, did not also deck the palace-walls with paintings. Scraps of fresco from the Middle Minoan levels at Phaistos show that the buildings of that date were decorated with paintings, at least of simple linear patterns. We know of no important private houses of the Kamares period, except for the famous oval house at Chamaizi which is in some ways comparable with the mansions of the following period.

XXI   MANSION AT VATHYPETRO, SOUTH OF KNOSSOS. GENERAL VIEW FROM THE NORTH. Late Minoan 1, 16th century B.C.
(see Note page 137–140)

I. ARCHITECTURE

We cannot say whether the Old Palaces were destroyed all at one time, or indeed for what cause. There can certainly not have been any great interval between the disasters at the various palaces, and we can assume that they took place about 1700 B.C. or a little earlier. The Kamares pottery of this time is of the highest quality and shows no signs whatever of degeneration.

We pick up the thread of development again about 1600 or 1580 B.C. The New Palaces were under construction and the extant works of art are stylistically still Middle Minoan. We begin the Late Minoan period in about 1550 B.C. Evans rightly called the period following the turn of the seventeenth century 'a New Era'. The feverish building activity over the whole island, artistic innovations —notably monumental painting—and the general increase in prosperity in all parts of the island, are all expressions of it.

All this stands in marked contrast with the preceding century. It has generally been thought that the rebuilding was completed between 1700 and 1600 but in fact not a single building can be attributed to this period with certainty except, doubtfully, one or two parts of the Palace of Knossos. There are no great works of art from this century and even the pottery is scant and difficult to date securely in this span. It was a century marked neither by decline nor disaster, and seems rather to have been an empty transitional stage. Again we see much the same picture in Egypt. In the Nile valley this is the period of the Hyksos, the second 'Intermediate' period in which political insecurity left culture at a low ebb. It is easy to attach too much significance to the find of an alabaster lid at Knossos with the name of the Hyksos King Khyan. It probably has no historical significance although no less a scholar than Edward Meyer took it as evidence that the Hyksos had sacked Crete.

Many difficulties beset the attempt to date exactly the re-building of each palace. At all events the three New Palaces will all have been under construction after 1600, all on the same sites and in part incorporating the ruins of their predecessors; and so they were to stand until their second and final destruction. We have every reason to suppose that continuity of tradition and culture was not broken. In the earlier period Knossos and Phaistos seem to have enjoyed equal rank and importance; in fact the latest excavations might suggest that Phaistos was the senior during the Kamares period. After the re-building Knossos is clearly predominant. It looks as though the rulers of Knossos had taken the initiative in this renaissance of Cretan prosperity, as did the rulers of Thebes in Egypt at the end of the Hyksos period. Not only the local nobles, but also, it seems, the other palaces contributed to the construction of the New Palace of Knossos. This is in effect the unification of Crete under the sole rule of Knossian Minos which ancient writers recorded. The two other palaces, at Phaistos and Mallia, are imposing structures which imply some measure of independence, so it may be that the supremacy of Knossos was not achieved immediately.

XXII   WHITE LILIES IN A FLOWER-GARDEN. Fresco from the Villa at Amnisos (plate 64). Height about 1.80 m. Middle Minoan III, about 1600–1580 B.C. (see Note page 140)

KNOSSOS. The seniority of the Palace of Knossos over the others is shown not only by its size and luxury, but also by its massive store-rooms. These are far more extensive than those of the other two palaces put together. Large pits, sunk deep in the floor of the magazines and corridors, held the riches of the harvest and other treasures. We must presume that the other palaces conceded to Knossos part of their own produce.

The Palace of Knossos, including its courts, covers an area of some 24,000 sq. yds. This is greater than any Mycenaean palace, and indeed than many others. Nebuchadnezzar's palace in Babylon covered about twice this area but it included five courts and had only one story, while at Knossos there were at least three floors. The palace could have housed several hundreds if not thousands of people.

Even when ruined the building still showed clearly the plans of its large rooms and corridors with traces of the paintings of bull-games on the walls, and it was still possible to make one's way into the gloom of the lower floors in the east wing. All this had a profound effect on the Greeks who came later, and is reflected in the tradition. The extent of the palace gave an impression of a maze without an exit. They called it 'the Labyrinth'. The popular, but not strictly accurate derivation of the name is from the Lydian *labrys*, the double axe, which appears often in Knossos as a cult-symbol: 'house of the labrys', house of the double axe. From the paintings of bulls the Greeks wove the Minotaur legend. They never dared to live in the very place where trod the ghosts of King Minos and Pasiphae, Daidalos and Ikaros, Theseus and Ariadne. And so the ruins remained bare of new building, and the sacred grove of cypresses which surrounded them was dedicated to the goddess Rhea, as was fitting.

Fig. 3   DEPENDENCIES OF THE PALACE OF KNOSSOS. The 'New Era' which began in about 1580–1550 B.C. is characterised by the spread of building activity over the whole island. Knossos was the most active centre. Not only was the palace re-built and, perhaps for the first time, decorated with fresco-paintings, but the whole district of what Homer calls 'the great city of Knossos' saw new foundations of annexes to the palace, rich private houses and monumental tombs. Not many of them have so far been excavated; the area around the palace is a mass of ruins and there is work there still for generations of excavators. Most of the buildings could, or rather must have been private houses for all that they actually abut on to the palace walls; such are the buildings called the 'South House', the 'South-East House,' the 'House of the Chancel Screen,' the 'North-West Treasure House' and so on. It seems that the king lived surrounded by his subjects in a great City, as we see in other periods of European history. There is no proof that what we call the 'Royal Villa' in fact belonged to the king. Only in the 'Little Palace' do we find good reason to suspect very close association with the main palace. Some of its rooms are even larger than those of the palace, and it seems to have a predominantly religious character, with its lustral basins, pillar-rooms and regal cult apparatus. The famous bull's-head rhyton in steatite was found here. The sacred nature of the building survived its destruction, for the newcomers, in the 'Reoccupation period', built an altar exactly over the old room for ritual purification. The difference was that there were no more offerings of faience figures and elegant rhyta; the successors to the Golden Age used for their cult-figures crude, natural stone-formations which resembled human forms. The indisputably religious character of the Little Palace justifies us in calling the monumental road which linked it with the cult-place of the main palace (the so-called 'theatral area') a

XXIII   VIEW FROM THE EAST OVER THE RUINS OF GOURNIA. In the background the Gulf of Mirabello. Late Minoan 1, mid-16th century B.C.
(see Note page 141)

true Processional Way. The cult-figures and sacred symbols were brought along this finely paved road to the cult-place, where there was probably a shrine to accommodate the crowds who took part in or watched the ceremonies.

50-51　　There was a similar arrangement in each palace. The cult-area at Phaistos is in the same place at the north edge of the west court, while at Mallia it lies beside the south-west corner of the central court. The miniature frescoes at Knossos probably represent a ceremony taking place in the cult-area by the Sacred Way.

42-43, Fig. 7　　The Little Palace is the second largest building at Knossos but it is poorly preserved and the east façade is entirely missing. Today we can still see the great colonnade with the megaron to the north, but we do not know where the entrance was nor what it was like. West of the megaron was the shrine with the fetishes and stones which we have already mentioned. Farther to the west and south lay a complex of rooms. The main staircase, and another farther west, lead to the great pillar-room on the south. The sacred character of this room is shown by the cult-objects which were excavated within it, including a double axe. A yet larger pillar-room lay at the south-east corner of the building; its excavated part is about 100 yds. long and over 30 yds. broad. To the west there is another building which seems to have been just as large and significant, but this is still covered with a deep accumulation of earth and has not been excavated.

44-45, Fig. 8　　The so-called Royal Villa is reached from the north-east corner of the palace. It was built in a cutting into the hillside and faces east. The entrance is reached through a small walled court with two columns between two antae, a plan typical of the Mycenaean megara. A small niche in the back wall of the main room is cut off by a balustrade and probably held a throne or altar, ready for the possible appearance of the divinity rather than for a living king. It is interesting to note that the first floor had a doorway giving directly on to the higher ground behind the villa.

There were very many houses south of the palace, not all of which have been excavated. We may also mention the stepped portico and viaduct which provided a monumental approach to the palace from the south. By them was a singular building to which Evans gave the Turkish name 'Caravanserai', 'guest-house'. It was supplied with water for men and animals, and its main room was decorated with a painted frieze of partridges and other birds.

46-47, Figs. 9-10　　Farther to the south lies one of Evans' last finds, the famous Temple Tomb[19], which stood in one of the more populous districts of the town. It was certainly a royal burial place. A partly excavated house nearby has a balustrade and altar like those in the Royal Villa, and was called by Evans 'the Priest's House'.

PHAISTOS AND HAGIA TRIADA. The Italian excavations in Crete began at about the same time as the British, and concentrated on two most important sites in the southern part of the Messara plain. The palace which was brought to light at Phaistos matches Knossos for its monumental quality, while half an hour's walk to the west another complex of buildings was found at Hagia Triada which has been variously called a palace or a villa. The establishment there was certainly very closely associated with

XXIV　FAIENCE EARTH-GODDESS WITH SNAKES. Height 29,5 cm. From the underground treasury of the central sanctuary in the Palace of Knossos. Middle Minoan III, about 1600–1580 B.C. (see Note page 142)

Phaistos but it is no palace in the true sense of the word for its lacks several of the characteristic features of a Cretan palace. Again, the Cretan palaces are generally sited at some distance from each other. But before considering further the relationship between Hagia Triada and Phaistos we must discuss the history of Phaistos itself.

Phaistos was not completely forgotten in the later tradition, as was Mallia. It was mentioned several times by Homer and traditionally its men followed Idomeneus to Troy. A famous Greek theologian, Epimenides, once reckoned as one of the Seven Wise Men, came from Phaistos. In the Greek period it was a town of no importance, and Strabo's remark that it was founded by Minos is no more than a local glorification of its Minoan past. One of the most famous Cretan figures, Rhadamanthys, lawgiver and benefactor in many lands and noted for his fairness as Judge of the Dead, was of Phaistos, and, according to the *Genealogies* of Kinaithon, he ruled in the palace there as a king. Legend knows him only as a brother of Knossian Minos, and the story that Minos banished both his brothers, Rhadamanthys and Sarpedon, is no more than a memory of the absolute power of Knossos. Sarpedon was perhaps the lord of the third palace, Mallia[20].

XVIII, 49–51, Fig. 11

At Phaistos some trace of the Old Palace can still be detected in the plan of the west court, and before we turn to Hagia Triada there are one or two things about Phaistos which may be noted because they help to explain how the title of 'palace' might be considered for the former site. The Palace of Phaistos exhibits some singular phenomena: despite its general wealth there are no frescoes on the walls, such as there are at Hagia Triada. No royal treasure or particularly valuable finds have been made at Phaistos, while they abound at Hagia Triada. The magazines at Phaistos are small and poor, and the empty rooms and lack of signs of building in the north-east, east and perhaps south-west suggest that the New Palace was never fully completed. Only the part north of the central court and the northern part of the west wing seem to have been properly finished.

XIX, 52–55, Fig. 13

By contrast the building at Hagia Triada, only two miles away to the west, rivals all the other palaces in its luxurious appointments, so it can hardly have belonged to a private person. There is everything at Hagia Triada which we have found lacking at Phaistos. The answer seems to be that Phaistos was in fact being re-built by its rulers for some generations, but that one of the later kings preferred to live nearer the sea, at Hagia Triada. The original palace at Phaistos retained its importance as the more sacred and traditional seat, but the king was probably in residence at Hagia Triada by the time of the great catastrophe just before 1500 B.C. For this reason the royal treasures, works of art, archives (inscribed tablets and sealings), and frescoes were found at Hagia Triada.

The building there was laid out in the centre of a settlement which had already been long occupied. Its plan is not quite that of a palace, nor yet a mansion. The main complex forms a right-angle, but obeys the rule of orientation. One side runs to the east, the other almost exactly south. The highly elegant reception rooms lay at the angle, set to catch the cool north-west wind.

It had long been an important site. There was a flourishing town there in the Early Minoan period, as is shown by the two circular tombs found only 165 yds. away to the east. Around lay the cemeteries

XXV VASE DECORATED WITH LILIES. Height 27 cm. From the Palace of Knossos. Middle Minoan III, about 1600–1580 B.C. (see Note page 143)

of the later Minoan periods which have yielded important finds, such as the famous painted sarcophagus which lay in a rectangular stone-built chamber.

In the time of the Old Palace of Phaistos there was a small settlement at Hagia Triada, east of Court I, and it was probably destroyed in the same period and for the same reason. According to the excavators the 'villa' was built just after the construction of the New Palace of Phaistos. Both palace and villa were destroyed suddenly at the end of LM I, but they did not remain empty afterwards. The north part of the villa houses a great market, whose eight roomy halls and colonnade remind one of a Hellenistic or Roman agora. This gives us evidence for a renewal of prosperity, and trade was probably actively conducted there for a very long while. The memory of the cult which was still practised there in the early classical period was longer-lived than the fame of the Palace of Phaistos. In the Hellenistic and Roman periods the cult-places of Hagia Triada, as others in Crete, took on new life. Clay tiles show that there was at least a small temple there, and the impressed inscriptions on the tiles tell us that Zeus Velchanos—certainly a pre-Hellenic deity—was worshipped.

Travel between Phaistos and Hagia Triada in Minoan times must have been quick and comfortable to judge from the impressive remains of the old paved road. This approaches the villa from the south, with a branch to the east side of the main court and another farther west which must have ended at the main living quarters.

The finds in the rooms at the north show that they must have been offices, but they are well-built and the staircases to the upper floors are carefully planned. Another hall, lined with alabaster, was the office and archive-room of the ruler. Here were found seal-impressions: small, sometimes minute, pieces of clay which had once been attached to two thin strings and then stamped one or more times. They are probably from papyrus documents or palm leaves, which Pliny says were used for writing. There were stone cupboards in the room, probably for filing the correspondence. We have already mentioned the importance of the fact—recognised some years ago—that the seal-impressions found here are from the same seals as impressions from Sklavokampos (central Crete, seven miles west of Tylissos), Gournia and Zakro (East Crete). They suggest that all these sites depended on some other administrative centre, and show that they were all destroyed at the same time.

A famous fresco from one of the small apartments shows animals and plants in a 'river-scape' which is very like Egyptian representations of the same setting. This is of the best period of naturalism in Cretan art. In a thick-walled store-room behind this apartment was found the greatest bronze hoard to have been recovered from a prehistoric site: nineteen 'talents', copper ingots in the rough state in which they had been cast. These angular slabs, with concave sides, each weigh some 64 lbs. which corresponds with the Sumerian 'gun' (Akkadian *biltu*) which spread from Mesopotamia as a universal standard. As it has a fixed value it can be regarded as an early form of money[12]. From Egyptian representations we may deduce that the merchant-lord of Hagia Triada had in his emporium weighing devices and a trained staff which could do business with cash and not simply by barter.

It is notable that the finds prove that pillar-rooms, which were cult-places, came to be used for profane purposes, and, as at Hagia Triada, might be converted into magazines for storage-jars. We find the same in Megaron A at Tylissos and at Vathypetro.

MALLIA. 16 miles east of Heraklion lies the ancient, and modern, town of Chersonesos, once a centre

XXVI SPOUTED VASE FROM THE PALACE OF HAGIA TRIADA. Height 16.5 cm. Developed
naturalistic style. Late Minoan 1, about 1500 B.C. (see Note page 144)

for the worship of Britomartis. A few miles farther along the coast is a place called Stalida, which is certainly an ancient, no doubt a Dorian, name (στάλα, σταλίς, a small stela). Farther still in the same direction, 25 miles from Heraklion, the coastal strip widens into level fields, ὁμαλά in Greek (a common place-name still). From these 'omala', and their 'omalia' derives the modern name of the town of Mallia. Its deep red soil warms quickly in the late winter sun and gives an early harvest. The small farms raise the water for their fields with hundreds of primitive windmills, and all around there is an air of wealth and abundance.

The palace lies a mile beyond the town, to the east, and barely a furlong from the sea at the foot of the hills which run up to the heights of Dicte. We do not know the palace's ancient name but the locality is today called Tarmaros[22].

xx, 56-59, Fig. 13 The palace is laid out north-south like others. There is reason to think that the construction of the more important buildings in Crete was begun from the west side, where the walls of the palaces and mansions are more monumental in their masonry, and the majority of the most important rooms are in the west wings, although this is not entirely true of Knossos. If there was ever any interruption in the building it was always the east wings which were left incomplete or roughly finished. Thus it was at Phaistos, and at Vathypetro only the west wing was ever completed. At Mallia much the same happened. The west wing with its many rooms was completely fitted out and the quarter north of the central court also finished. On the east side of the court only a row of rather simple storage-rooms was built to close off the court on all sides. At the west side of the court were all the reception and cult-rooms, and no magazines.

The Palace of Mallia falls short of the other palaces in its architecture and furnishings. The most important quarter lay at the north-west corner, as at Phaistos, with the 'ἐσχάρα', porticos and lustral basin. The broad main entrance lay at the south-west corner of the central court, with a small room for the watchman, but there was no propylon. A large rectangular niche in the south façade is reminiscent of a similar one in the west façade at Vathypetro. The west court contains eight round cisterns, but there is no other provision for water in the palace.

56 below At the south-west corner of the central court there is an interesting cult object: the disc of stone with sinkings at its centre and around its edge. It has reasonably been called 'κέρνος', the ritual vase of the later Greek Mysteries, in which the first-fruits were offered to the god. The central court at Mallia is the only one in Crete with the ἐσχάρα, or low altar, at its centre. Pillars and columns alternate in the colonnades on the east and north sides. There are drains in the floors of the storage-rooms in the east wing, presumably because the pithoi were not packed close together, or were too readily broken.

The pillar-room at the end of the north wing has six columns in two rows in both its anteroom and the main hall. The arrangement of this hypostyle hall excited considerable discussion. It is most probably a religious building, but this cannot be proved. Beside this pillar-room at the north-west corner of the court there is a corridor which runs to the north quarter through another court; this shelters a second building, like a temple with anteroom and cella, but it is differently oriented. It is the only evidence for a 'reoccupation' period at Mallia, after the palace and town had been suddenly and terribly destroyed just before 1500 B.C. and then abandoned.

Recent years have seen the start of excavations in the private houses around the palace. These are simple dwellings and villas with interesting plans, apartments and lustral basins. Traces of paved

XXVII LIMESTONE SARCOPHAGUS PAINTED IN FRESCO TECHNIQUE. Length 1.375 m. From a chamber-tomb near the Palace of Hagia Triada. Early in Late Minoan III, about 1400 B.C. (see Note page 151–152)

roads leading to the houses from the palace have also been uncovered. This town, so close to the sea, must have been overwhelmed together with the palace by the sudden onslaught of the waves aroused by the eruption of Thera.

MANSIONS. Between the palaces and the ordinary private houses come the Cretan villas or mansions. These were always roomy buildings, often luxurious and decorated with frescoes. Some are as large as a Mycenaean palace. They are generally sited on their own and about seven to ten miles away from each other. They must have been the residences of important administrative officers, as the finds of sealings in them suggests. They are to be distinguished from a different type of building which has recently been recognised and which involves single houses of various plans, with big storage-rooms packed with large pithoi. No other pottery has been found at all in them, so it seems that they must be large estate houses. Their existence reflects yet again the peace and security enjoyed by the island.

Many mansions have already been found and there are certainly many more to be located. Examples have been excavated in Tylissos, Sklavokampos, Amnisos, Prasa (near Amnisos), Nirou Chani, Vathypetro. A very ruined mansion has been found at Apodoulou, south of Rethymnon, in the heavily populated area of central Crete. In it were found a small golden double axe and two important inscribed vases of steatite. In the same area another large mansion was found and excavated during the war, and there are two others in East Crete (Sitia) which have yet to be fully excavated.

63, Figs. 14–16 At Tylissos, where there was a whole town, three mansions have been excavated quite close to each other. One was richly decorated with revetments and frescoes. It had a round cistern and water supply. A Greek temple or sanctuary was later built over its ruins. All three houses yielded valuable finds, 108 including bronze statuettes of men praying, costly stone vases, great bronze cauldrons (the largest weighing over one hundredweight), and clay tablets inscribed in Linear A[23].

64 The villa at Amnisos has a portico at its north-east corner and fine frescoes in the main room of the first floor, but, unlike the other mansions, no magazines or pithoi. This house is so close to the sea that it may be thought of as a sort of royal bathing resort.

65, Fig. 18 One of the finest of the mansions, that of Nirou Chani, lies by the sea five miles to the west. Here beneath the water are remains of a harbour mole. The house had magazines filled with large storage-jars, and in its rooms lay dozens of offering tables and large double axes of thin bronze sheet. It seems that merchandise was kept in the rooms of the merchant's own house until it was shipped. Thus too are to be explained the finds of dozens or hundreds of vases in the palaces at Thebes and Pylos, in rooms which were certainly not storage-rooms. The villa at Nirou Chani has an eastward-facing court with a sort of theatral area. The façade had two columns between antae. Four doors led from the portico into a paved apartment with gypsum revetments on its walls. A corridor with frescoes led farther to the west, and on either side were rooms (one with benches), a light-well, stairs and magazines. Here was found the largest double axe so far known, nearly 4 ft. long.

XXI, 60–62 The most spacious of the mansions is still being excavated at Vathypetro, 10 miles south of Knossos, in a fine setting under the sacred Mount Juktas (ancient Iyttos). It was first laid out as a palace with west and central courts, and state-rooms built of great poros ashlars. Construction began in about 1600 B.C. the period of greatest building activity in the island, but the ambitious plan was soon abandoned, perhaps because of the soft clay soil. Only the west wing was completed and part of the first

XXVIII FRESCO FROM THE OTHER LONG SIDE OF THE SARCOPHAGUS IN PLATE XXVII. Sacrifice of a bull with offerings of fruit and wine in a sanctuary, to the music of pipes (see Note page 151–152)

floor occupied; the rest was converted into an agricultural establishment, probably the first of its sort in Europe. There was an olive-press in the west court, and a stone-built part of the south quarter housed a wine-press and weaving shop. A pottery stretched along the 100 ft. of the east-west corridor on the south side, where the workshops lay. A niche in the west façade probably served some religious purpose; behind it was an offering pit, and, farther east in the same line, a room with a three-column portico opening on to the east court. In this court were the foundations of a slight, but important build-

60 below ing: the only extant example of a sanctuary with three naves of the type otherwise known only from representations. Vathypetro did not long survive. The building collapsed a few decades after 1550. Only a very few sherds found in it are decorated in the early Marine style, and most have wave patterns or are in the Floral style. There are no signs of fire on the ruins but the great heaps of stone blocks which have been excavated suggest that they were overthrown in an earthquake[24].

TOWN PLANS. We can say but little about Minoan town-planning. The towns around the palaces at Knossos and Mallia developed over such a long time that their plans must have been quite irregular. Knossos, it seems, was made up of separate quarters often quite far apart, and the same may be true of Mallia. We know little of the town at Phaistos at the time of the New Palace, and there was only a village at Hagia Triada[25].

What is most impressive for us are the living conditions in ancient Crete, which can scarcely be matched in Europe. Even the smaller houses had several stories, with wide windows, courts, and often several kitchens. The pottery reflects gracious living, and in general the standards were probably higher than they are today in some parts of the East.

XXIII, 66–67 GOURNIA. The most completely preserved Minoan town is at Gournia. It lies near the sea by the Bay of Mirabello in East Crete, and its ancient name is not known. The heart of the settlement was on a low hill, the saddle of which was occupied by the small palace of the local governor. The remains of private houses are visible around the hillside.

The impression is given that there is hardly a square inch which was not built over on the whole line of the hill, from north to south, and especially on the east flank. The small houses often abut on to each other, and have few, sometimes very few, and very small irregular rooms. In many places there is a small open court, and almost all the houses have an upper floor which was usually reached by an outside staircase. Often the ground floor had no entrance from outside and served only as a storage-room, reached from within the house[26].

The network of streets was laid out according to a plan. There was an upper ring-road on the hill, and a lower one around the east quarter on the plain. Cross-streets link them, sometimes stepped up the slope. All the streets were carefully paved. The small palace on the southern part of the hill is poorly preserved. Its spacious court had a small row of steps with a large, smoothly-worked stone which is strangely reminiscent of the 'bath' in the palace at Tiryns.

The highest point of the hill, north of the palace, was not built on, perhaps for religious reasons. The shrine adjacent on the north belongs to the latest period of reoccupation. The town was destroyed suddenly just before 1500, and carpenter and smith left the tools of their trade on the floors of their workshops. The same flood which overwhelmed the other towns on the north coast of Crete after the eruption of Thera must have overtaken Gournia also.

XXIX A   FRESCO ON THE SIDE OF THE SARCOPHAGUS IN PLATE XXVII. To the left the presentation and pouring-out of liquid offerings to the music
of a cithara; on the right two calves and a ship are carried before the image of the dead man (see Note page 151–152)

There was no true monumental art in Crete. The nearest we come to it is in the wall-painting and related plaster reliefs which carried life-size figures and served as architectural decoration.

The earliest frescoes and plaster reliefs must have been made about 1600 B.C. to decorate the New Palaces and villas. After the somewhat abstract and stylised art of the Kamares pottery and Old Palaces the new, more naturalistic style is evolved with no appreciable transition.

A full history of the style of Cretan wall-painting cannot yet be written, but the general outlines are now clear. At first there are the simple frescoes at Amnisos, and their kin at Knossos[27]. It seems possible that the technique of fresco played its part in determining the character of Late Minoan art. It demands rapid execution which favours the sort of 'impressionism' we find in Crete. Preliminary sketches were incised in the damp plaster and the framing lines set out with cord.

The painters showed a deep appreciation of the different types of flowers but declined to represent details; this we can see well in the famous lily-fresco from Amnisos. The lily seems to have been, as it were, the national flower of Crete right to the end of this period. The interweaving of the blossoms of iris and crocus, ivy, papyrus, reeds, grasses and palms, were particularly favoured; although the palms are admittedly more familiar from vase-paintings.

Human and animal representations begin to appear soon. The finest of this type are from Hagia Triada but they have been much damaged by fire. The design is now much freer. In one rather more compact composition we can recognise a woodland setting, probably by a stream, with a woman, a hare, a pheasant and a wild cat. The similar scene in the House of the Frescoes at Knossos is more loosely composed. The rocks, crocuses, roses in a rockery, pancratium lilies, myrtle, sage, papyrus and reeds, and the blue monkeys among them were painted in bold and brilliant colours[28].

A later phase of the Palace of Knossos sees the final stage in the development of wall-painting. It resembles the decoration of the Egyptian tombs of the eighteenth dynasty. Typical of these scenes is the one rhyton-carrier preserved from the immense Procession Fresco. There were certainly differences here in the dress of the various figures and in the offerings they carried, and variety was provided by the women who were also painted in the frieze. But these life-size figures stood in two rows, one over the other, and there were in all more than five hundred of them, so that it must have been impossible to avoid some feeling of monotony.

On the miniature frescoes large areas are filled with crowds watching some cult-ceremony, all painted on a very small scale. Men are shown schematically, close-set and with only the upper part of their bodies visible. Women sit comfortably side by side in their rich dresses and indulge in lively conversation. Each figure is only some few centimetres high. Elsewhere the painter treated the same theme at almost life-size with the 'Ladies in Blue', striking models of contemporary fashion.

Unfortunately only a few substantial pieces of Minoan painting have survived but they give us a good idea of the great variety of the themes handled, and are helped by representations in other materials, which were clearly derived from the wall-paintings. Bulls and bull-games were the most popular, then processions with sacred symbols, ritual-dress, demons, mythical creatures, dances and sports. The scenes of sacred and profane life are most informative, and we may mention particularly the frescoes with the so-called 'Parisienne', the Minoan officer and his men, and the children at play. More monumental is the fragment of a bull from the west portico by the north entrance at Knossos.

XXIX B FROM ONE END OF THE SARCOPHAGUS IN PLATE XXVII. Symbolic representation of the earthly
journey with two female figures in a chariot drawn by two horses (see Note page 151–152)

The modelling and straining vigour of the creature, bellowing in agony, allow us a glimpse of the significance of the complete work.

State-rooms decorated with frescoes generally have a dado with painted imitation marbling, and above it the main decoration which may run around the whole room. It would be framed above by bands or dentated friezes. The background to the scenes may be monochrome or varied with horizontal and oblique wavy lines in two or three basic colours while ceilings are sometimes painted with over-all patterns. The floor might also have been painted, at least in the later period, as we know from remains at Hagia Triada. Similar floors decorated with dolphins and octopuses are also to be found in Tiryns, Mycenae and Pylos.

70 There was no monumental sculpture in Crete. The taller of the snake-goddesses, 34 cm. high, is about the largest of the surviving Minoan figures. There probably were larger works, and in one instance we may suspect that there was a more than life-size wooden statue of a goddess.

Works of minor sculpture had antecedents in the Middle Minoan period, unlike the wall-paintings. They are made of faience, bronze, ivory and clay, and as well as our two snake-goddesses we find mortals at prayer or bull-leaping, we find children and animals.

108 Minoan sculpture differs from the strong formalism of early Greek sculpture in its greater interest in movement. The worshippers with one hand raised are slim, elastic figures, strongly muscled, with their upper body thrown back. The figures of women are always clothed. Among them the so-called 'Bayadere' in Berlin is a masterpiece, and there is a similar statuette from Hagia Triada. These are generously modelled, slightly bowed figures with gently inclined heads. Their features are usually more summarily treated.

96–97 The small ivory figures of bull-leapers are more cunningly worked, represented at the most danger-
109 ous point in their jump. No less remarkable are the two statuettes of children, one standing, the other kneeling at play. The smooth modelling of their bodies and features can be appreciated despite their poor state of preservation.

68 To add to the list of Minoan plastic masterpieces are the mace-head from Mallia and the stone rhyta in the form of animals' heads which were inlaid with semi-precious stones and metal ornament, like
98–99 the bull's head from the Little Palace and the lioness' head from the New Palace at Knossos. The stone
114–115 vases, lamps, shells, and the rosette and triglyph reliefs attest the sure hand and skill of the sculptor.
90 The bulls from Pseira are good examples of the finest work in clay.

Large stone reliefs were not used in Crete as architectural decoration or as independent ornament, nor did they carry narrative scenes as in Egypt. The reliefs on minor works show single occasions only. Fragments of steatite vases show us buildings, porticoes, mountain-landscapes with shrines and travelling pilgrims. The three steatite vases from Hagia Triada, which are fortunately well-preserved,
100–107 carry series of scenes. They are the Chieftain's Cup, the large conical rhyton with sporting scenes, and the Harvesters' Vase.

The art of seal-engraving, long known in Crete, is related to that of the carved stone reliefs. Already in the Middle Minoan period semi-precious stones were replacing softer stones and bone for seals. The number of different shapes is now small. At the beginning of the Late Minoan period the prism is still to be found, but now carved only on one or two of its sides, and the flattened cylinder is quite rare. Most popular are the stones in the shape of a lens or almond (lentoid and amygdaloid).

72

XXX FROM THE OTHER OF THE SARCOPHAGUS IN PLATE XXVII. Symbolic representation of the heavenly journey, with two divine or deified figures in a chariot drawn by two winged griffins, and a supernatural bird overhead (see Note page 151–152)

Since each citizen may have possessed several seals the engraver was hard put to it to ensure variety. No two of the thousands of seal-stones preserved are quite alike. A theme may be repeated but the treatment of details is always different[29]. A classic theme is of a lion attacking another animal, one long popular in the east. But we must remember that the lion was unknown in Crete, and in fact we often see in its place a hunting-dog. The animals are often represented back to back, or a bull, for example, is seized by two standing or running beasts set antithetically. We can understand this in the light of the earlier Minoan tradition in seal-engraving, in which the creatures may be shown in a circle or spiral, without relation to their background.

In the repertoire of the seal-engraver we find fish and fowl, trees and buildings, fantastic creatures and sea-scapes and finally men—a shepherd, entertainer, votary, bull-jumper, hunter, even a warrior in very rare instances. A small group of stones seem to carry individual portraits. There are no mythological scenes. Their quality as works of art is of the highest, their drawing bold, their outlines delicate, and their subjects cunningly suited to the shape of the seal; and for us they are particularly important for what they tell of Minoan life[30].

One branch of this art is represented by the signet rings. Their large bezels afforded an ample field for what were sometimes quite complicated compositions. The architectural bases for some of these scenes suggest that they are copies of other, major works of art. For us these rings are one of the most important single sources for the understanding of Minoan religion. It is odd that the rings seem never to have been worn on the finger, and that, for all we can judge, they belonged only to women. Most are of gold but some may have engraved bezels of semi-precious stones, silver, bronze or iron. Iron must not be thought to have been a sign of poverty for it was extremely rare, and its high nickel content shows that it was meteoric. So the rings of meteoric iron were probably held to have great magical properties[31].

3. METALWORK

According to the tradition Crete was the birthplace of metal-working. For all that, the finds of metal objects in Crete have not been, and are not likely to be, as rich as those in Mycenaean Greece. The answer that there are no unplundered tombs in Crete is inadequate. More probably the difference lies in the different ways of life in Greece and Crete. The Mycenaean warrior collected riches not for his pleasure on earth but, like the Egyptian, to take with him to the other world. Minoan Crete had no warriors, and the riches accumulated in a life of peace were not so considerable. This Minoan lived for the present; he provided himself and his family with all comforts, with rich and artistically fashioned furnishing, but was satisfied with clay, stone and bronze as materials. He took few of his belongings with him into the other world. With a few exceptions, which belong to the Achaean period of about 1400 B.C. and afterwards, no really richly-furnished tomb has been found in Crete.

Such luxury articles as have been found are in no way inferior to their Mycenaean counterparts: gold necklaces, gold ornaments and figures; bronze bases, lamps and shallow bowls (χερνίβα), which are described in the tablets as tableware and are probably finger-bowls, often carry the bronze-worker's most elegant decoration[32]. Some articles impress by their size alone, like the colossal basins from Tylissos, of which the largest weighs over a hundredweight and measures 1.40m. across.

Weapons are not often found in Crete, and apart from the Achaean cemetery at Knossos which contains swords with gold-covered handles, the only royal weapons of the period of the New Palaces 112–113 are from Mallia. Of the period of the Old Palace is a large sword with an amethyst pommel, presumably a ceremonial piece. A more practical sword of about 1600 B.C. has a pommel which is covered with gold leaf on which an acrobat is shown in fine, low relief.

The surprising discoveries in the cave at Arkalochori in Central Crete are exceptional[33]. It still cannot 69 be proved whether this was a cult-cave, perhaps the cave of Zeus sung by Hesiod, or the depot of a bronze-smith. A hoard of metal was found also in the Idaean cave, and there was a mysterious tradition in Crete about cave-dwellers who wrought metal. At all events there lay in the cave at Arkalochori hundreds of bronze swords and daggers, large and small double axes, as well as some unfinished pieces and ingots of unworked metal. As well as this there were some twenty-five small double axes in gold, many of them with golden shafts, six others of silver, some gold leaf and a small gold object which seems to be in the form of a rock or mountain. Many of the bronze axes have chased decoration and the gold ones are engraved. One bronze axe had on it a hieroglyphic inscription, and on a silver one appear 110 above some Linear A characters.

The most interesting of the finds were the swords which had certainly been made for use and not as dedications. Here were forged the longest prehistoric swords yet found. Some half dozen are more than a yard long and the longest, of 105.5 cm. exceeds the longest of the known Mycenaean swords even with its handle. An unfinished sword tells us something of the technique; the mid-rib and careful forging ensured the strength of the over-long blade. Even today some of the swords have not lost their elasticity. The Mycenaeans also would have used such weapons manufactured in Crete.

4. POTTERY

Many fine vases have been preserved from the period of the New Palaces. Two periods can be distinguished by style: the earlier with the naturalistic Floral and Marine styles, and the later, Palace style, which began about 1500 and was at its most flourishing from 1450 to 1400. Here there is a return to the almost geometric, symmetrical compositions of the Middle Minoan period, with the difference that on the Kamares vases the linear patterns were gradually absorbed into designs made up from vegetable and animal forms. In the period of naturalism the rich repertoire of lively, natural forms had been built up, but they were to become more and more stylised and finally completely static. At the same time the linear patterns become merely subsidiary. Throughout the period the quality of potting and painted decoration is of the highest.

At about 1600 B.C. there suddenly appear beside the polychrome vases and those with broad white spirals on a dark ground, new vases with naturalistic decoration, such as lilies and reeds, which were xxv, 74, 76 probably inspired by wall-paintings. The light-on-dark decoration is still to be met but with it there is now a different, though not a new technique—decoration in dark paint on a light ground. Most important are the characteristic finds of pottery in the stone-lined pits, the so-called Temple Repositories of Knossos, which held the snake-goddesses and reliefs with suckling animals. Here there are examples xxiv, 70–71 of both styles of pottery, as well as other pieces like the bird-vase from Melos, and some connected 75 with the finds in the shaft-graves at Mycenae.

The new dark-on-light decoration developed quickly and the transition from the Middle to the Late Minoan periods was accomplished without any real break. The favourite patterns are wavy lines, spi-

80, 82–84 below
81

xxv, 76, 78–79

91–93

84 above, 85–87

87

86 right

xxxviii, 171

84 above
86 left

93

91–92

94–95

rals, discs, dot-rosettes, double axes, papyrus, and lily motifs, partly combined with naturalistic elements like olive branches and wreathes, or magnificent bucrania, as on the pithos from Pseira. At the same time the vases with predominantly naturalistic decoration were being made. It has been said that the Egyptians first exploited the decorative value of flowers, but the Cretan artists yield nothing to them in this. The wall-paintings in Amnisos, Hagia Triada and Knossos offer us a wealth of flower and plant representations which certainly served also as models for the vase-painters. Star-anemones, lilies, crocuses, irises, grasses, reeds, ivy, pea-blossom and other Cretan plants are seen on the latest of the Middle Minoan vases and the earliest of the Late Minoan. Papyrus, in its natural or stylised form, occurs often, and the plant itself must have been introduced into the island from Egypt[34].

It is still an open question whether the other manifestation of naturalism, the Marine style, in fact appears somewhat later (Late Minoan IB) than the Floral style, which is generally put in Middle Minoan III to Late Minoan IA. It is certainly less fully represented. In the sites which were later suddenly and completely destroyed in the great disaster, like Gournia, Nirou Chani, or Vathypetro, only one or two Marine style vases were found beside several of the Floral style; which is of course no reason for a later dating. The vases of the Marine style were more distinguished and more difficult to make. It was the aristocratic style in Late Minoan art[35].

The distribution of finds so far, which may of course be misleading, shows that East Crete may have been the home of the Marine style. In Central Crete we have only a few fragments of vases in the early Marine style, including some in relief. The finest examples have come to light in East Crete, particularly the well-known octopus jar from Gournia, with an octopus swimming in a seascape. In the same style is the lens-shaped vase from Palaikastro with shells between the tentacles of a swimming octopus, but it may be somewhat later than the Gournia vase. At Palaikastro as many as seventeen rhyta were found in one house, some of them decorated in the Marine style. From Zakro is a rhyton with purple-shells *(Murex trunculus)*, starfish and seaweed. The octopus-like creature, *Nautilus argonautica*, was often represented in various media, and has most recently appeared on a fine inlaid dagger from Pylos. The forerunners of the gold and silver nautili on the dagger are to be seen on the double vase from Gournia. We cannot be sure whether the famous Marseilles jug, which was found in Egypt, was made in Crete or not. Again, dolphins are favourite motifs, and there are some characteristic vases on which the painter has attempted entire seascapes in imitation of the wall-paintings.

As we have already said the representations gradually lose their naturalistic force and we enter the transitional phase before the Palace style which Evans called Late Minoan IC.

Large vases decorated in the new Palace style have only been found at Knossos. Among them is the fine relief pithos which, from its position on the landing of the main staircase of the Royal Villa, must have been purely a decorative piece. We can recognise the papyrus in its decoration, and wavy lines which may represent water. Concentric circles complete the design. Palm-like trees, papyrus and fantastic forms reminiscent of marine plants appear on other vases. In time the natural forms stiffen and are disposed more and more symmetrically over the vase. The same change can be observed in the successors to the Marine style. The once vigorous octopus is turned into a weak creature whose terrifying tentacles have become a mere pattern of opposed spirals. All the motifs are translated in the same manner. Void areas on the vase may be filled by other objects, even representations of helmets. In the final phase of their development the various patterns completely lose their organic composition.

76

The last phase of Minoan culture in Crete developed quite independently of the Greek mainland. There were no longer palaces on the island and we do not know whether there was still anywhere any form of central power. If there was, however, it must have been at Knossos. The town was still occupied, and although it no longer had the eighty or hundred thousand inhabitants computed by Evans, it was still quite large, as its cemeteries show. Excavation has proved that the living standards had dropped. The houses still have several rooms but there are no frescoes or other fine furnishing. The household utensils are mainly clay and stone vases with occasional bronze objects.

The tombs offer a richer picture than the houses. The chamber-tombs cut in the soft rock, which were first constructed in the late Middle Minoan period, are now made with unusually long 'dromoi'—ramps by which the grave-chambers were approached. In these tombs, and in the simpler pit-graves for the poor, the dead were laid in clay sarcophagi or baths, a practice almost unknown on the mainland. 126–127

The most prominent of the grave monuments is the famous stone sarcophagus from Hagia Triada XXVII–XXX which was made at the very beginning of the post-Palace period. Its painted decoration is of the first importance for the understanding of Cretan religion (see page 40) and it is the only example we have of painting from this late period.

Apart from this piece there are only a few clay sarcophagi with representations of religious significance. Some are from East Crete, and are decorated with Horns of Consecration, double axes, bulls 127 and the winged griffins. On others the decoration had no relevance to the burial and is only of artistic interest. Baths were used as coffins and naturally pithoi were also household equipment. At Vathypetro were found clay chests which closely imitate wooden models. Their use as coffins is secondary and their decoration is as that on other pottery.

Characteristic of pottery-decoration in the late period is the transformation, almost out of recognition, of natural patterns. For the first time now the figures of animals and sometimes even men appear on vases. Large birds of indeterminate species, with big beaks, spread wings and convention- 122–124 ally painted plumage, are now seen flying over dolphins, or sitting on the ground and on bushes. Here lilies and palms may be suspected rather than identified, and the big bushes with massive leaves are perhaps meant for papyrus clumps. In other pictures we find patterns derived from palms, ivy, octopuses and shells. Many vases carry designs which must have been inspired by weaving. Again, we find on vases and sarcophagi groups of a cow with calf, rather miserable horses, goats and other animals. Many vases, particularly at the end of the period, are not painted at all. Some of the clay artefacts are of unusual and as yet unexplained forms, suggesting rather sophisticated ways of life. Several are censers, and the fact that some have been found with coal in them—at Mallia with the seeds of aromatic plants as well as coal—shows that rooms might be filled with incense fumes. The list of aromatic substances recorded on the Linear B inscribed tablets also indicates the use of these things and trade in them.

The minor sculpture of the post-Palace period is true to the general tradition, although there are also a number of poor works in clay. Metalwork is in better case. The figures of the worshippers 121 are less tense; they stand upright and calm before their god. Their often elongated limbs seem to

anticipate those of mainland Greece in the Geometric period. Clay and bronze figures of animals are
134 usually roughly made but may sometimes betray some individuality. The donkey laden with water-jars, from Phaistos, is of especial interest for the history of the period's art. Its successors today, some three thousand years later, carry water-jars of identical form in just the same way.

Human representations have been found in houses, sanctuaries and sacred caves. The group of
132 dancers with a lyre-player from Palaikastro holds our attention as a record of folk religion. Figures wearing crowns and with large round eyes are probably those of worshippers belonging to the very
128-131, 135-137 latest period. Some plastic works are very nearly half life-size. The most important of these are of the Mother Goddess and these are the largest examples of Minoan sculpture which have survived. They stood, decked with various attributes, in small shrines, of which many new ones were being built in this period, no doubt to commemorate the great past—always a feature of a period of decay. They hold up both hands, like worshippers, but the exact significance of the gesture escapes us. It may here symbolise the ever-benign, ever-helpful Mother. All are the work of ordinary potters, for their bodies and heads were made on the potter's wheel and the necessary details added later. The idols from Gazi are in a better and more disciplined style than the later ones from Karphi (in Lasithi), which are sub-Minoan. The inability to characterise the faces as female shows what a decline there had been.

This type for a goddess survived the end of the Minoan civilisation and was still used by mainland Greek artists of the seventh century B.C. From Crete itself is the round chapel, made of clay, with a goddess inside; the spirit is still Minoan although the work belongs to the Greek period. The two male figures on the roof are perhaps to be considered with the goddess as a trinity whose origins may also be Minoan. A similar trinity is represented on a find from the Idaean Cave, and its significance is probably to be sought in some local tradition.

If, as has been suggested on page 26, it can be proved that the Linear B palace-archives in Knossos were still being written as late as 1300, or even 1250 B.C., then the palace itself must also have survived in use. The end of Minoan culture might then win fresh interest from the evidence of myth. It was about 1300–1250 B.C. that Minos lived, supposedly a Greek and with a grandson who fought at Troy beside the other Achaeans. Minos was certainly an Achaean. In keeping with the warlike character of his race he extended his operations to include attacks on his own people, in Megara and Athens. The Attic tradition says that the Athenian Theseus defeated him, and so is to be explained the fact that names like Talos, Androgeos, and perhaps even Minos, are preserved in their Attic forms. Minos and his grandchild Idomeneus lived in the period of Cretan decline which we have just sketched. The glories of the great Palace at Knossos lay long behind them, and they had as little inkling of them as did the Greeks of later days.

MYCENAEAN GREECE

CASTLES AND CITADELS

The first Greek peoples to enter mainland Greece arrived at the beginning of the second millennium B.C. at about the time that the Old Palaces were being built in Crete. They brought with them a few poor bronze weapons and other metal objects, a grey-to-black monochrome pottery ('Minyan') and another ware with matt-painted decoration which they were further to develop. They buried their dead in a squatting position in small cist-graves with very few offerings, if any at all. Their houses were small and they had no public buildings unless we count some fortifications. The houses of their chiefs were often horseshoe-shaped in plan with two or three rooms, sometimes with an open porch and a fairly large hearth near the centre of the main room. This plan is the forerunner of the so-called 'megaron' which was to be the characteristic feature of Mycenaean palace architecture, but was not at home in Crete. The general aspect of Mycenaean civilisation is very Minoan, however, and has led to the theory that Greece was for a long time a colony of Crete. But this cannot be so. By and large the Mycenaeans adopted Minoan culture but they also retained part of their own tradition—their monochrome pottery, many vase-shapes, megaron architecture, the hearth, tholos-tombs and the technique of fortification. They wrought the peaceful Minoan culture to their more warlike spirit. In the period of the New Palaces in Crete the mainland Greeks first came into serious contact with Cretan culture. After the material and cultural poverty of the preceding Middle Helladic period we quite suddenly find first-rate works of art, such as those which in 1876 Schliemann discovered in the Mycenae shaft-graves; real treasures of gold and silver vessels, jewellery, gilt weapons, precious stones, amber, bronze vases, rich funeral-offerings in the form of gold diadems, pectorals and masks with other golden objects. The find was something of a puzzle until Evans undertook his excavations in Crete. When the same workmanship and types were found in Knossos it was assumed that the greater part of the finds at Mycenae were Minoan. The warrior Achaeans must have destroyed the Old Palaces of Crete, sacked the island and carried back the treasure with them. But this explanation too, which still claims some following, is untenable. The Cretan palaces were destroyed by natural causes and rebuilt without fortifications. The finds at Mycenae are not purely Minoan in their workmanship and we would not look for so much gold in a Cretan palace. The answer must lie elsewhere.

The land of gold in those days was Egypt. The correspondence found in the archives at Amarna shows how concerned all the kings were for the metal. Duschratta of the Mitanni, a contemporary of Akhnaten, reported that in Egypt gold was 'like dust beneath the feet'. At the time of the Mycenae shaft-graves the Egyptians were seeking to throw off the foreign domination of the Hyksos (1730–1580 B.C.) and looked for help from overseas. We also know that the kings of the early eighteenth dynasty paid their mercenaries with gold. Even their own officers were honoured with gifts of gold. Ahmose, son of Ebne, was awarded the 'gold of bravery' for his services in battle against the Hyksos. It needs little more for us to deduce that the Achaean warriors, with their heavy weapons, tower-shields, helmets of horn, great spears and long swords, stood at the side of the Egyptians in their fight against the eastern incursions of the Hyksos. Their reward was gold with which they returned later to Greece. In the shaft-graves of Mycenae some 33 lbs. of gold were found. In later generations too Mycenae maintained her wealth of gold and some 700 years later Homer called her πολύχρυσος, 'rich in gold'. This is the memory of a wealth for which we have archaeological evidence, at least for the period down to 1550 B.C.

Connexions with Egypt are shown not only by the gold but by some practices of funeral cult which are peculiar to the generation of the men who fought in Egypt, and which became more prominent as time passed. The warriors were influenced by the Egyptian belief in the possibility of a life after death, and on their return to Mycenae they began to dig more commodious cist-graves; that contained in the largest of the shaft-graves, grave IV, measures nearly seven metres by four. For their after-life the dead were provided with all necessities: table-ware, weapons, jewellery. The dead of a generation before had at the most one small clay vase. The mummies of Middle Kingdom Egypt have gold masks or portraits of the dead man painted on the linen covering so that the spirit could leave the body but still find its way back again and recognise its home. The royal masks were of gold and the mummies were often covered with gold. The Mycenaeans followed this example and had gold masks and pectorals. Thus Schliemann found the famous gold mask of 'Agamemnon' on a body which had been wrapped up like a mummy. It seems that the Mycenaeans also learnt the art of embalming from the Egyptians because Schliemann reported that under a heavy gold mask 'the rounded features were wonderfully preserved with all their flesh' and that 'the colouring of the body was very like that of an Egyptian mummy'[36].

146–147

To guide the wandering souls in their journeys to and from the tomb stelae with carved reliefs were set up in imitation of the false doors in the Egyptian tombs. These can have nothing to do with the simple stones which are occasionally found over Middle Helladic graves.

It was as this period advanced, and at about the beginning of the sixteenth century B.C., that Minoan culture suddenly made its appearance in Mycenae. The historian Edward Meyer thought that the Egyptians had summoned Cretan help in their struggle against the Hyksos and cited Egyptian records. We cannot believe that the Cretans themselves brought armed help in view of their thoroughly un-warlike nature, but it is quite possible that sea-going Cretans carried Mycenaean warriors in their ships to Egypt, and back again. This formed the basis for friendly relations between Crete and Mycenae which may well have led to the marriages of Mycenaean chiefs with Cretan princesses. Thus too Minoan culture could have been introduced to Mycenae in a peaceful manner. The Cretan women brought with them their gold rings engraved with cult-scenes, which have been found at Mycenae; this explains why they are only found in the graves of women, as in Crete. It may be that some of the

206–207 above

XXXI   VIEW OF MYCENAE FROM THE MOUND OF THE SO-CALLED TREASURY OF ATREUS. The Palace is above the Cyclopean circuit and Mt. Hagios Elias in the background (see Note page 154–155)

women, from shaft-graves I, III and IV, were of northern race, but most were Cretan as details of their jewellery, for instance, show[37].

Mycenae has given its name to the Greek culture which arose about 1600 B.C. because the first indications of it were found there and because to the end it seems to have been the cultural centre of Greece. Nowhere else is the Early Mycenaean period, 1600–1500 B.C., so richly represented. In the years between 1550 and 1500 B.C. (Late Helladic, or Mycenaean I) traces of this culture can be detected in various other parts of Greece and on some of the islands, but from this early period we have only

157 graves. A series of chamber-tombs, and perhaps tholoi also, at Pylos show that here too was an important early Mycenaean centre. There were no palaces or fortified places and the chiefs, as at Mycenae, probably still lived in their horseshoe-shaped megara. Some traces of fortification walls at Mycenae and Tiryns can perhaps be attributed to this period. It is first in the Middle Mycenaean period— which embraces practically all the fifteenth century B.C.—that flourishing provinces appear all over Greece, apparently acknowledging the suzerainty of Mycenae. In the later Mycenaean period this was certainly true and Homer tells us of the obligation of all men to fight for Mycenae when called upon, although there were already signs of some loosening of allegiance.

148–151;
Figs. 24–25;
160–161 The culture of this Middle period can again only be appreciated from the rich finds in the royal tombs. Unfortunately most of the graves which have been found, like the royal tholoi at Mycenae and Orchomenos, had long ago been plundered. Perhaps once in a generation some archaeologist may be lucky enough to find an intact tholos-tomb, as at Vaphio in Laconia, at Midea in the Argolid, and, three years ago, at Pylos. Again, the architecture of this period is little known and even the graves are generally poorly preserved.

XXXI, 141–144
152–155 With the third Mycenaean period we begin to see the real character of Mycenaean architecture. The beginning of the period is fairly well set at the start of the fourteenth century; its end, for almost all the palaces, in the years between 1250 and 1200 B.C. But it is possible to trace the survival of Mycenaean culture on to about 1100 B.C. The most imposing and extensive remains are of walls. In their present form they belong mainly to the later thirteenth century but their basic form was established earlier. They seem the work of giants, and the ancient Greeks said they had been made by the Cyclopes. To

153 Pausanias the walls of Tiryns were no less remarkable than the pyramids of Egypt. The walls are made of colossal, roughly faced stones which were set without mortar. The blocks fit together so well that only a few small stones were required to fill crevices. The walls are usually 6 m. thick; 10 m. at places in Mycenae, and at Tiryns as much as 17.5 m. at the point where the galleries were built on the east and

152 south sides. These galleries are among the most important monumental stone structures of antiquity. Their walls are built of projecting stones in their upper part, to meet at an angle in the ceiling.

The best-known Cyclopean walls are those of Tiryns, Mycenae and Arne (Gla), beside what used to be the Copais Lake in Boeotia. On the Athenian acropolis too there are considerable remains of the so-called 'Pelargikon' wall[38]. These were held in such respect that Mnesicles left his masterpiece, the Propylaea, unfinished at the south corner so as not to damage the stretch of the Pelargikon which stood there. The longest circuit walls are at Arne, where they are nearly two miles long. Those at Mycenae are about half a mile. The walls at Arne have two small and two large gateways and they

158–159, Fig. 28 enclose a palace-like building which is laid out like that at Hagia Triada, with two wings at right angles. It is strange that the name of this important Mycenaean town is still not known. It has been call-

XXXII KORYPHASION, HOME OF NESTOR, ACCORDING TO THE ANCIENT TRADITION, FROM THE NORTH, WITH THE CAVE OF NELEUS. To the right is the Ionian Sea, on the left Bouphras and Pylos Bay. In the foreground an excavated tholos tomb which was pointed out in antiquity as the grave of Thrasymedes, son of Nestor (see Note page 161)

ed Arne, Gla, Phlegya, Glechon or Gyrton. Since there is no accompanying settlement and there are no graves it was perhaps a town of refuge for the neighbouring cities and remained nameless. The walls have the same regular jogs or setbacks, about 12 m. apart, as those of the Mycenaean city of Troy VI, or at Tiryns and Mycenae.

141–142, Fig. 18 The most famous of the fortifications are those of Mycenae itself where the two gateways—a small north door and the Lion Gate—are well preserved. The latter is a megalithic construction of four colossal blocks. The relieving triangle above the lintel holds the relief which shows the blazon of the town and the royal family. In the middle stands a column, like the Egyptian 'Unity' sign, and this sacred symbol of the might of Mycenae is flanked by two boldly modelled lions or lionesses. They lay their forefeet on two concave objects which have been called altars[39]. The Lion Gate with the bastion to its right, the north door, and a tower at the north-east corner of the circuit are built in an almost isodomic style with ashlar blocks of conglomerate, which are never found otherwise in the Cyclopean walls. The explanation for the technique is simple. The conglomerate from near Mycenae is quarried in distinct horizontal layers. Once the Achaeans had learnt to trim these colossal and natural ashlars with the saw they used this excellent building material also for some of the tholos-tombs.

Fig. 18–19, 26 The acropolis walls of Mycenae and Tiryns were probably finished by about 1300 B.C. After the mid-thirteenth century some extensions and modifications were undertaken. The extensions can easily be recognised: in Mycenae at the north corner, in Tiryns in the lower town. More significant are the alterations in the main approach to the acropolis at Athens, Mycenae and Tiryns, which seem to have been made at the same time. The approach to the citadels was hitherto from the hinterland but is now turned to face the sea and the road of trade. At Tiryns a bastion was built with a door and stairs on the seaward (west) side of the walls to spare visitors taking the road round to the east gate. There are grounds for thinking that at Mycenae the original entrance lay at the north where the doorway was still retained. On this side too lay the old entrance to the palace and propylon. The Lion Gate and stairway to the palace were constructed on the seaward side at a later date[40]. To protect the city gate which now stood at an easily accessible point a tower was built to the left of the entrance to threaten the left, unshielded side of an attacking force.

The attention which was paid to ensuring the supply of water shows that the towns had to reckon with enemy attacks. We do not know who the enemies could have been: Dorians or Turscha, Shardana or Sekelesh, races which no doubt passed through Greece and Crete before they reached Egypt. At all events the later thirteenth century saw several catastrophes and destruction by fire.

The system of water-supply at Tiryns is not yet clear. For the Mycenaean citadel at Athens there was an ingenious and bold arrangement. In a natural fault in the rock, just a few paces north-west of the later Erechtheum, a stairway was built, partly cut in the rock and partly of stone and timber, which gave a covered approach to a spring of drinking water beneath the Cyclopean wall.

The water-supply at Mycenae was more monumental and was attributed by the local tradition to the mythical founder of the town, Perseus. The secret well-house on the acropolis, for which the eastern part of the fortification was built, is an imposing affair. An underground way leads beneath

Fig. 18 the foundations of the Cyclopean wall to a tunnel where some hundred steps lead down 15 m. to water. The besieged could literally get their water from beneath the feet of their enemy.

We know as yet nothing about the palaces of the earlier period. With the possible exception of

86

XXXIII   VIEW OF THE BAY OF BOUPHRAS (VOIDOKOILA) FROM KORYPHASION. Behind lies Englianos and the so-called Palace of Nestor. In the
foreground the Aigaleon range (see Note page 161)

the somewhat older remains of the Palace of Cadmus in Thebes, all that is preserved is of the later years. In their ground-plans the Mycenaean palaces are quite unlike those of Crete. Their outlines are simple and clear, forerunners of the bold and basic forms of the classical Greek temple.

The life of the palace was concentrated in the main megaron which lay at its centre. As in Crete the buildings are orientated with the points of the compass. The megaron, a long rectangular building, always faces south, although there are some minor exceptions, as at Mycenae, dictated by local conditions. It was a characteristic which can be observed as early as the Neolithic megaron-houses in Thessaly and reflects the northerners' craving for light and warmth.

The Mycenaean megaron usually has three rooms, and opens on to a large court which may be surrounded by colonnades. For its rooms we use the terms which Homer uses, and which are certainly Mycenaean in origin. The porch lies within the façade of two columns between the two southern ends of the side walls. It is called the *aithousa*, 'place of brightness', because it was flooded with sunlight from its open south side. Behind is the anteroom of the main hall, the *prodomos*. Here visitors might be accommodated. A large door leads into the last, northernmost room, the true megaron or *domos*. In Mycenae the megaron measures nearly 12 × 13 m. It is notable that neither here nor in any of the other megara do the thresholds have any provision for bolting the doors[41].

In the middle of the megaron floor stood a low, but capacious hearth. In Tiryns it is 3.50 m. ft wide, in Mycenae 3.70 m. and in Pylos about 4.0 m. It is always edged by four columns which probably supported a roof or shelter over the hearth. In the palace at Pylos clay chimneys were found. But the fires were not laid with wood, which would have produced much smoke, for all that Homer calls Odysseus' megaron αἰθαλόεν, 'smoke-blackened'. The fresco-decorations on the walls of the megara in Mycenaean palaces have never been found to be blackened with smoke. In cold weather the king would have held court by the warmth of the hearth. That it had religious significance also is surely true, but its main function was for cooking the palace meals. The king himself sat on his throne which always stood opposite the hearth and by the right wall as one entered the megaron. The walls might be decorated with friezes of painted frescoes with battle or hunting scenes. If there were any windows they would have been set high in the walls[42].

Figs. 26–27 In Tiryns and Pylos there was a so-called 'Women's Megaron', which is a small copy of the larger one. The other rooms of the palace, the corridors, baths, and apartments, some of them with fresco-paintings, were grouped around the megaron in no particular order. There was certainly an upper story, no doubt occupied by the women who lived more apart from the men than they did in Crete.

Fig. 27 At first sight the Mycenaean palaces seem far more modest than the Cretan. The best preserved is that recently discovered at Pylos which has three separate annexes, one in the west, two in the east. It occupies an area of only some 80 × 70 m., that is little more than a quarter of the area of the Palace of Knossos. This does not necessarily reflect truly the relative sizes of the establishments. The Mycenaean palaces were built in the restricted areas on tops of hills, and the buildings for industry, trade and administration lay in the lower town. Thus at Mycenae the Palace archives, per-

XXXIV GOLD FUNERAL-MASK OF A MYCENAEAN PRINCE, THE SO-CALLED AGEMEMNON. Height 26 cm. Citadel of Mycenae, grave v. See plate 162 (see Note page 166)

fumeries etc. were found outside the citadel in the lower town. In Tiryns too the lower town held a considerable number of houses[43].

The Mycenaeans fell far behind the Minoans in the planning of their settlements and homes. At Mycenae the citadel held only the king's palace and a few other houses, probably for the royal family or high palace officials. Though they are quite roomy and decorated with frescoes they cannot compare with their counterparts in Crete. What little we have learnt from the lower towns, and from a provincial settlement at Malthi in Triphylia, shows that the standard of living was quite modest.

So far as we can see, trade, which was probably brisk, in this period was under the control of the king himself. In many parts of the Argolid the remains of roads and bridges have been found which would have served merchants as well as the war-chariots of the nobles. A construction rather like the viaduct at Knossos has been found at Mycenae and was probably a particularly large and strong bridge which secured communication with Prosymna. Near it the Heroön of Agamemnon was discovered a few years ago.

TOMBS AND BURIAL CUSTOMS

Unlike the Cretans, who lived for the present, the Mycenaeans took particular thought for their life after death. We have already remarked that this attitude appeared suddenly about 1600 B.C., probably as a result of Mycenaean relations with Egypt.

For our first information about Mycenaean graves we have to thank Schliemann who discovered 'Grave Circle A', within the citadel of Mycenae, in 1876. This was a circular area, about 27.5 m. across, bordered by a double row of upright slabs. Its entrance was in the west, and it contained six shaft-graves marked by several stelae, some of them carved. Here had been buried the great kings of Mycenae together with rich offerings. Although the position of the graves and their treasures must have been long known, they had been treated with a sort of religious respect and remained virtually unplundered.

Sixty-five years later, in 1951, the second Grave Circle (B) was discovered. This was outside the citadel, unlike the other which had been deliberately included in the circuit despite considerable difficulties. It lies 130 m. west of the Lion Gate and its diameter of 28 m. is about that of Grave Circle A. The border is of simple stones, and the entrance again was in the west. It held 24 graves but only 14 of them can really be called shaft-graves. The biggest of these measures about 3.8 × 2.8 m. Three of the graves had stelae and two of these were decorated. Many of the tombs are simple cist-graves, as were those in Grave Circle A, although this was not at first recognised. Circle B is a little older than Circle A but some of the burials there must have been contemporaneous with those in A. The first impression was that here too were royal tombs, and some of the offerings are indeed costly. Only one burial had a mask: a simple one of electrum. These two almost contemporary Grave Circles had been constructed at the end of the seventeenth and beginning of the sixteenth century B.C. on the site of an earlier cemetery. This suggests that the royal house that occupied them was newly come to power in Mycenae, and it may be that there was some form of double kingship, or at least two families in the royal household[44].

The last burials were made in the Circles before the end of the sixteenth century. Shaft-graves have been found elsewhere, and at Lerna, in the Argolid, there seems to have been some form of a circle.

At Mycenae, and generally in the whole Mycenaean world, two new forms of burial appear at the same time: royal tholos-tombs, and chamber-tombs for lesser folk.

It is generally thought that the earliest of the tholos-tombs at Mycenae was built about 1520 B.C., but it may be that some of them are as early as 1600 B.C. Both types of tomb had a dromos-approach cut level or slightly sloping in the soft rock. After a sufficient depth for safe construction had been reached the chambers were cut out of the earth and rock, and finished with a circular or rectangular plan. Some which are irregular and more like caves are for humbler burials. At the end of the dromos there was generally a fine, rectangular doorway into the chamber. A series of early chamber-tombs has been found at Pylos where the round chambers are often vaulted.

When the walls of one of the more substantial tombs are built of stone we speak of a tholos-tomb. The chamber-tombs at Pylos which are at least as old as the earliest of the tholoi can be taken to be their forerunners. Where the walls of the chamber are supported by a stone wall it was not necessary to cut it out of rock and it was enough to heap earth over it[45].

The oldest tholos-tombs have only their doorways and chambers lined with stone, and here only small flat slabs were used. The lintels are comparatively short: an improvement in technique is shown by the use of larger worked stones for the lower courses in the chamber, the door-jambs and the lintel, which is often also cut to follow the curve of the tholos wall. The earlier tholoi, like the chamber-tombs, had no door, and the entrance was walled up after each burial.

In the third and final stage of the tholos-tombs we meet the finest in materials and methods of construction. The blocks are cut to follow the curve of the wall. The entrance afforded the greatest constructional difficulties because of the immense weight of the wall over the door itself. A solution was sought in the use of colossal lintel-stones, and finally the device of a relieving triangle over the door was invented, or copied from Egypt. Now the tombs have doors which can be fastened. The threshold of the Tomb of Atreus is made of three blocks, with a removable wedge which made it possible to put the massive door-post into position and remove it again for repair if need be. Only thus could the door, some 5.40 m. high and most probably covered with bronze sheet, have been hung on its two corner pivots.

Nine tholos-tombs have been found at Mycenae, three belonging to each of the three stages. The latest, which are also the most accomplished examples of Mycenaean architecture, are known as the Tombs of Atreus, Clytemnestra and the Genii. The last is the smallest and perhaps also the latest of the series, belonging to the second half of the fourteenth century. Some would date it even later but it is doubtful whether any such building could have been undertaken in about 1300 B.C. or after. The sculptured façades of the tombs and the Lion Gate relief must at any rate be dated late for their high quality. Dating by pottery finds is only reliable where there is certainty that the levels are not disturbed.

This third stage of the tholos-tombs marks the zenith of Mycenaean architecture, and the buildings must be counted among the masterpieces of Bronze Age achievement. The most impressive tomb-chamber in all Europe is that of the so-called 'Tomb of Atreus', built of finely-worked conglomerate and incredibly well preserved. Only much later, in Hellenistic Samothrace, or later still in Rome, were such buildings attempted. The diameter of the tholos is 14.50 m. and its height 13.20 m. The inner lintel is 8 m. long, 5 m. wide and 1.20 m. thick; it weighs over one hundred tons. The interior of the tholos was decorated with bronze and perhaps golden or gilt ornaments, as we can tell from

149-151

Figs. 24-25

their fastening holes. The façade was a monumental imitation of two-story building, such as we know from a prototype in Phaistos. Its decoration comprised four half-columns and plaques of porphyry and other coloured stones, carved with close-set patterns of spirals, rosettes, triglyph friezes and other designs. Large gypsum reliefs with bull-scenes also belonged to the tomb and may be either from the façade or from the interior decoration. The position of the grave was of course always clear, from its massive dromos. This was the largest funeral-building at Mycenae, and indeed in the whole Mycenaean world.

160–161   The tomb of Orchomenos in Boeotia must have been similar, and shares with the Tomb of Atreus the peculiarity of having a separate grave-chamber at the side of the tholos. This was rectangular, and its flat ceiling is exceptionally well preserved with its relief decoration of spiral and lotus patterns. The rest of the tholos is unfortunately in a poor state of preservation.

Pausanias saw the tomb and wondered at it. He called it the 'Treasury of Minyas', mythical king of rich Orchomenos, and compared it with the walls of Tiryns and the pyramids of Egypt. He did not see the great tomb at Mycenae which we know as the Tomb or Treasury of Atreus. When Pausanias speaks of the 'Treasuries of Atreus and his sons' he means the tholoi, which came to be called 'treasuries' by reason of the rich offerings they held[46].

Figs. 19–20   Another noble architectural achievement is the so-called Tomb of Clytemnestra, which is contemporary, slightly smaller but also has a decorated façade. It stands only some 10 m. from Grave Circle B, and there may have been some connexion between the Circle and the three tholos-tombs near it. The relationship of the Circle with the Tomb of Aigisthus which is of the early period, with the Lion Tomb of the middle period, and with the Tomb of Clytemnestra of the late period, suggests some family or dynastic connexion, the Circle belonging to the founders. In that case the richer Grave Circle A with the other six tholoi, two of each of the three periods, belong to the senior line in the royal family.

The chamber-tombs at Mycenae lie in groups fairly well separated from each other. The correct deduction seems to be that the lower town at Mycenae was composed of several different settlements. This may be why so many of these earliest cities of Greece have plural names: Mycenae, Athenae, Thebae etc. Most of the chamber-tombs were used for several generations.

The last phase of Mycenaean culture is represented all over Greece, and in the islands. It is interesting to remark that wherever later myth told of the Heroic period, the accuracy of the tradition has been proved by excavation. Thus in Thebes there have been uncovered the remains of an important palace, with fresco-decorated walls and other valuable finds. At nearby Orchomenos there is the tholos-tomb of which we have spoken and fragments of frescoes which may well be from a palace. Archaeological evidence about religious survivals make it seem probable that the Mycenaean palace lies beneath the Temple of the Graces, where was also built the Byzantine cloistered church of Skripou. Farther north was Iolkos, focal point of the Argonaut story. Several tholos-tombs have already been found in this area, which promises yet more important finds. In the south the heart of Mycenaean Athens lay on the Acropolis, with the graves in the area of the later Agora; and we may mention also the tholos-tombs at Menidi and Thorikos, and the many chamber-tombs found in Attica.

XXXII, 156–157   In the western Peloponnese the tholos-tombs at Kakovatos in Elis and the palace at Pylos (Englianos) in west Messenia suggest that there are other royal tholoi and chamber-tombs to be found. In Odysseus' kingdom the rich chamber-tombs on Kephallenia have been explored. These, with many similar graves in Achaea, Salamis and elsewhere, tell us something of the last days of the Mycenaean world, the period of Homer's heroes.

The Mycenaean leaders were not only warriors but seafarers and traders. Just which of these activities is responsible for the very wide distribution of Mycenaean culture still escapes us. There were already Achaean colonies in the fourteenth century on the islands, as far away as Rhodes and Cyprus. Even earlier they had appeared in Asia Minor, as at Miletus. A colonial state called Achyawa must have flourished in this area. Trade carried Mycenaean products far and wide. Olive oil was probably an important commodity, and also pottery, carved ivory and valuable inlaid metal vases, as well as bronze weapons. Mycenaean pottery has been found in settlements and graves in Asia Minor and Syria, in Egypt, Sicily and the Lipari islands. The Sicilian graves have many characteristics which remind us immediately of the chamber-tombs at Mycenae. Indirect influence may even have been felt so far away as Iberia, Ireland and even the Orkney Islands.

ART AND LIFE

Apart from the architecture, in which we have seen considerable individuality and inventiveness, Mycenaean art can by and large be considered an extension of Minoan, with only some minor original features. In the pottery, about which we know much, it is possible to discern certain differences. The Mycenaean vases are inferior to the Minoan in the quality of their clay, paint and firing. The Minoan are thinner-walled, lustrous and stronger. The Mycenaean pithoi of elaborate style are almost all thicker-walled and gaudier than the Cretan. The shapes are about the same, though they may be popular at rather different times. Moreover, the mainland had developed some variations on the native, Middle Helladic traditions. For example, there is a group of deep cups with fairly high feet which is a characteristic Mycenaean ware. The same shape appeared in the Early Mycenaean period, but made of lighter clay; this we call 'Yellow Minyan'. In their later form the cups carry small painted motifs and are called 'Ephyrean'. From the finds made so far it would appear that the so-called *alabastron* was a common Mycenaean shape, but rare in Crete. The most characteristic of all later Mycenaean vases, the stirrup-jar, appeared in Crete about 1580 B.C. It was not introduced to the mainland before 1400, and was probably associated with the growing trade in oil. Two examples, one from Pylos, which might be dated about 1500 B.C., may be imports from Crete.

The style of painting on the Early Mycenaean vases is almost exactly like the Minoan Floral and Marine styles. At about 1500 traces of the Palace style appear in the mainland more unmistakably and quickly than they do in Crete. From this time on the differences between the shapes and decoration of the Mycenaean and Minoan vases grow more and more marked, and various local styles can be distinguished. The general development, however, is in step with that of Minoan pottery. The naturalistic style, which still retained a strong decorative bias, evolved quickly and soon developed into more purely linear patterns, so that soon after 1400 all the plant and marine motifs had been reduced to linear designs.

The vases of the very last phase again carry over-all patterns and scenes, either as a reaction against the lifeless linear styles, or under the influence of wall-painting,—or even for some nostalgic or religious reason which escapes us. Unfortunately they are so limited and stereotyped that we hardly dare look for any particular historical or mythological scenes in them. Where the animals are recognisable they are bulls, stags or goats. There are several scenes of chariots drawn by emaciated creatures which are meant for horses. Men also appear on or beside the chariots on the Mycenaean vases, but especially on the Cypriot ones which belong to the Levanto-Mycenaean world. The representations are, however, so schematic that rarely can any narrative, religious or historical significance be assigned to them. As time passed the designs degenerated. There is perhaps more movement in the mainland Greek compositions but generally speaking the style was uniform everywhere. We can speak with some reason of a Mycenaean κοινή, a common idiom in vase-decoration. There are still some exceptional scenes, like that on the Warrior Vase from Mycenae, which belongs to the so-called Illustrated style of about 1200 B.C. and later.

A characteristic artistic achievement of the mainland was the carving of stone sculpture on a scale never attempted in Crete. It has been said that the relief stelae from the shaft-graves at Mycenae represent the beginning of monumental sculpture in Europe. This is something of an exaggeration for there is a lapse of some three centuries before we see the next essay in this technique in the Lion Gate relief. The Early Mycenaean stelae are as individual as the Grave Circles themselves. Nor can we see a true continuance of the tradition in a small painted stela found in the lower town, of the latest period.

Stelae had long been known in the east and Egypt, especially for the commemoration of wars and peace-treaties, like the stelae of Eannatum, Naram-Sin, Ur-Nammu and Gudea, and, in Egypt, those over graves of the Middle Kingdom. Here they represent the door of the grave itself, or may carry one or more scenes from the life of the dead man, especially at table and with his family. We have already suggested that the idea of the stela was brought back to Greece from Egypt by the Achaeans. The scenes on the Mycenaean stelae are not death-scenes but show the martial and hunting life of the dead men. The ideals of the two peoples were quite different; the Mycenaeans wished to live again to ride their chariots in the chase or the heat of battle.

The figured scenes on the grave-stelae are primitive by comparison with the linear patterns on the metal objects from the graves themselves. The artists at work were probably the same men, but there was no tradition, no models for work in stone, and the Minoans set no example for they had never practised this art. Poros and soft limestone were employed. The designs were incised or carved in low relief, in neither case with any great skill.

We have remarked that Grave Circle B contained a few stelae of the same material and technique as those in Circle A. The two which have figured scenes represent the life of shepherds[47].

The period of artistic activity represented by the finds from the two Grave Circles begins about 1600 B.C.—perhaps a little earlier in Circle B—and ends about 1500 with the latest finds from Circle A. Even in Circle A there were some vases still matt-painted in the Middle Helladic fashion. From Circle B, however, we have large matt-painted vases which already show the influence of the Cretan Floral style. There is generally not much pottery in the rich graves, the equipment for kings or chieftains being of copper or precious metals. The typical pottery-styles of the period of the New Palaces in Crete are most skilfully imitated in many of the finds from the shaft-graves, but already a trace of the true Mycenaean spirit can be detected. For example, the ivy branches on the slim jug from Circle A (grave I) are already drawn in a Mycenaean manner.

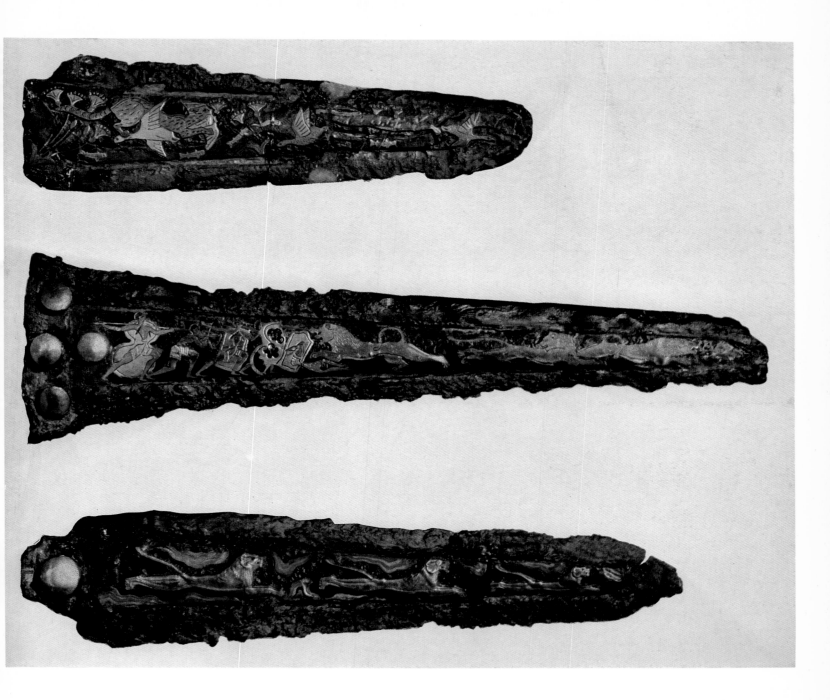

XXXV BRONZE BLADES OF THREE DAGGERS WITH INLAYS OF GOLD, SILVER AND BLACK NIELLO. About 1570–1550 B.C. Above: In a papyrus swamp.
Length 16.3 cm. Centre: Lion-hunt. Length 23.8 cm. Below: Three lions running. Length 21.4 cm. All from the Citadel of Mycenae, grave v
and two from grave IV (see Note page 167)

XXXVI   DETAILS OF THE GREAT BRONZE BLADE FROM GRAVE IV. See plate XXXV centre. Above: From the back, lion attacking gazelles.
Below: From the front, archers and warriors fighting lions (see Note page 167)

XXXVII   Above: DETAIL OF THE BRONZE BLADE FROM GRAVE V. See plate XXXV above. Papyrus swamp; leopard
among wild duck, and fish in a stream
Below: DETAIL OF THE SMALLER BRONZE BLADE FROM GRAVE IV. See plate XXXV below; one of the running lions with
clouds above (see Note page 167)

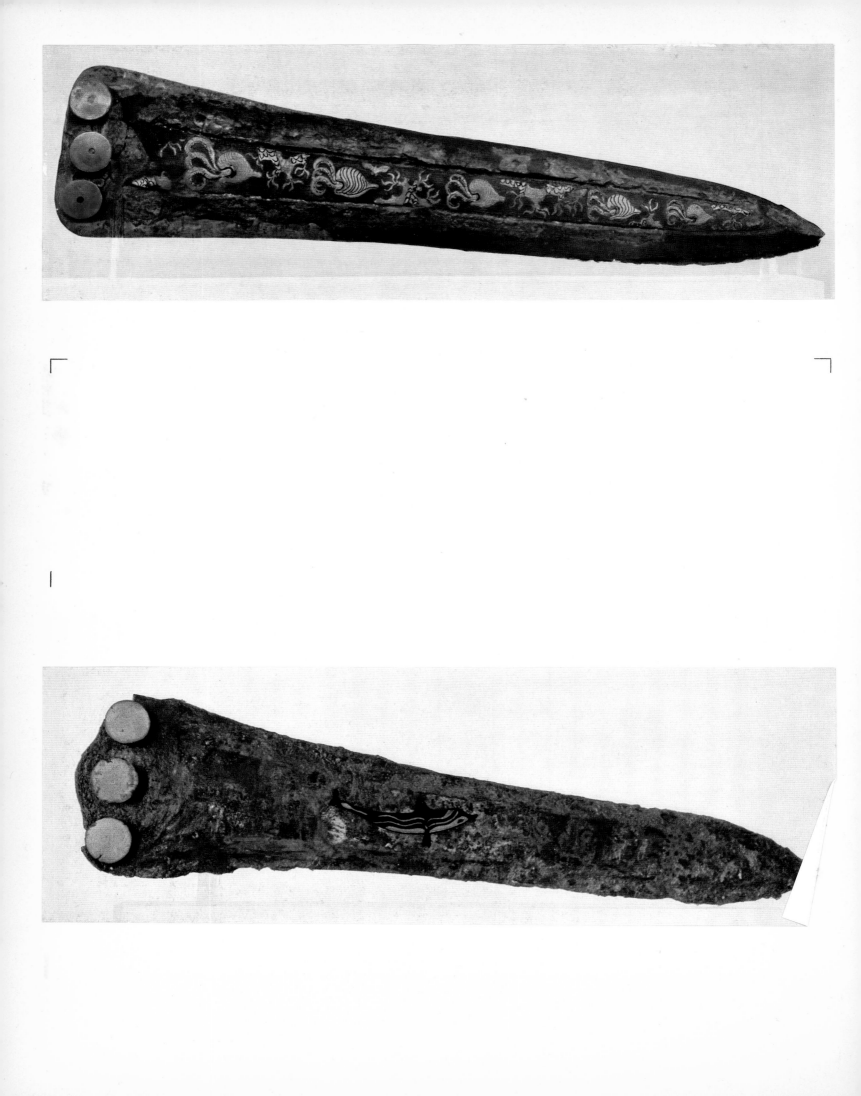

The most significant finds in Circle A were those of gold, some of them offerings, others ornaments from the corpse. The dead women wore cloaks whose hems were decorated with gold ornaments, just 200, 204 as we see them in the Cretan frescoes. Hundreds of discs of thin gold were found in the burials of both 202 men and women. The bodies of the men were wrapped in linen, like mummies, and the gold ornaments were sewn onto the shrouds. Only the most important of the dead were honoured with gold pecto- 168 rals and masks. The women wore golden diadems or half-diadems. It would seem that the decking of xxxiv, 162–166, 169 the body was carried out in the grave itself, at least in the more important burials, because scraps of gold leaf have been found in them.

Some of the other offerings in the graves are of particular interest. First, the weapons: from the protective armour, the massive tower-shields and the helmets with their crests and horns, we have only traces of the ornament because they were largely made of leather or felt. There are plentiful remnants of the helmets which were covered with boar-tusks, such as we know from many representations. Of offensive weapons we find two types of spear-heads, an older and a later variety, arrowheads, including some of obsidian, and in particular weapons for hand-to-hand fighting.

The Mycenaean nobleman carried into battle a long and a short sword, a heavy knife—which we might call the κοπίς or 'cleaver' and an axe to break through his opponent's defensive armour. We also find short javelins, sometimes all of beaten bronze, small daggers and the inlaid, ceremonial dag- gers. There may be several reasons why one dead man may have by him more than a dozen swords. He may have rejoiced in his armoury, or they may be spoils, or perhaps the number reflects some special prowess. Among the swords there are some elaborate pieces with gold covered hafts, and scabbards. The handles are terminated by a pommel of ivory, semi-precious stone or wood covered with gold. There are some differences in the swords, both as regards their hafting and their length. The shorter are about 65–75 cm. long, and the bigger ones as much as 85–95 cm. The longest blade preserved is nearly 95 cm. long and is from the so-called Grave of Agamemnon (grave v). Since the remarkable find of swords at Arkalochori in Crete there can no longer be any doubt about the source of the swords in the Mycenaean graves. Some swords which have no midrib are really elongated daggers in form, and were used for cut-and-thrust fighting, although they are not very strong. Improvements in pro- tective armour occasioned new weapons of offence. When a warrior was wearing a helmet with cheek- and neck-pieces and carrying a tower-shield the only vulnerable place was his neck beneath the chin. To reach this mark required a longer sword, and to ensure the strength of the much-length- ened blade more care was taken with the alloying and forging, and a midrib was provided. We have representations of the way the swords were handled to reach the unprotected neck. The decorated swords have blades incised with spirals, lily-patterns, griffins and horses, and beading or figure-of- eight shields on their midribs.

The smaller was called a παραξιφίς by the Greeks, that is, a second or supplementary sword. It was

XXXVIII   Above: BRONZE BLADE OF A DAGGER WITH NAUTILI. Length 25 cm.
Centre: DAGGER WITH A GOLD HANDLE DECORATED WITH SPIRALS; ON THE BLADE LEOPARDS HUNTING. Length 32 cm.
Both from a tholos tomb at Pylos. About 1500 B.C.
Below: BRONZE BLADE OF A DAGGER WITH A DOLPHIN. Length 18.5 cm. About 1450 B.C. All have inlays of gold, silver and black niello (see Note page 167–168)

about 50 cm. long and examples of it are quite common in Mycenaean tombs. It was employed in the cut-and-thrust fighting with ensued when all other weapons had been used. Against heavy armour the kopis, or battle-knife, was probably most effective, and the axe, although the latter is rare. We have examples only from grave IV in Circle A and the tholos-tomb at Vaphio. Only twice does Homer mention the use of an axe in battle but he does tell us that it was carried in the inside of the shield. The colossal shields of the Mycenaean warriors could have served as veritable armouries. We can see now why the battle-knife was cast in one piece with its handle and had a suspension ring; it was designed for dealing lusty blows, and to hang, when not in use, inside the tower-shield[48].

XXXV–XXXVII, 170 The inlaid decoration, especially on daggers, represents one of the high lights of Mycenaean art[49]. These daggers have inlays of gold, silver, or alloys of gold, silver and copper which give some variety of colour. Black niello, which is a compound of copper, lead and sulphur, was used for the background and for some details. Scratching, engraving and punching were used to pick out details to be filled with niello, so that the technique has with some reason been called 'painting' with metal. The inlaying was generally done on thin sheets of copper which were then fastened to the dagger-blades by the smith. We do not know whether these daggers are all the products of a single workshop or of more than one. It is not impossible that they were made in Crete although as yet no example of inlay-work has been found in the island.

The five famous decorated daggers from Mycenae were found in graves IV and V. There is no example of inlaying from Grave Circle B, which contained only one ceremonial sword with other 186 royal ornaments. An electrum cup, whose shape looks forward to the Ephyrean cups, has inlaid decoration of a flower-pot with lilies and sprays of dittany, an aromatic herb which was reputed to have remarkable healing properties[50].

187–194 Gold beakers and cups of various shapes and sizes were common finds, and were no doubt intended for the king's use even after death. Sometimes it is simply in the splendour of the gold and elegance of shape that their value lies, but some have hammered repoussé decoration of rosettes, running lions or 188 linear patterns, and handles with figures in the round. The so-called Cup of Nestor [51] has a bird on each of its handles, a hawk with spread wings, perhaps imitating the Egyptian hawk of Horus. The cups would have been used for libations.

A remarkable feature of the art of the shaft-graves is that there can be observed a tendency towards stylisation and stiffness even before the naturalistic style had reached its zenith. Thus it is with the 202 gold discs which had been sewn on to clothing, and the six-sided box covered with gold is also decorated in a strangely conventional style.

174 A silver conical rhyton is of exceptional historical importance. The scene on it is of a seaside town 232–233 being stormed by Mycenaean soldiers. A large bowl or *krater* has big figures of warriors carrying figure-of-eight shields and wearing strangely ornate helmets rather like those we see much later on Etruscan works.

The art of seal-engraving is related to that of relief sculpture, and is well represented by superb 206–207 rings and seals of gold, silver and semi-precious stones. As well as religious scenes the seals often

XXXIX GOLD RHYTON IN THE FORM OF A LION'S HEAD. Height 20 cm. Citadel of Mycenae, grave IV
(see Note page 168)

carry pictures of battle or the hunt. The former are usually of duels; there is only one gold ring showing four warriors. The usual schemes are for a young warrior to be fighting another who is heavily armed, or to be attacking a lion, or following the hunt in his chariot through a wild landscape. Of the

207 below

religious scenes one on a large signet ring is of unusual interest: a goddess is seated beneath a tree with a small figure wearing a full skirt standing on a base before her—a cult-idol perhaps; she receives offerings of flowers from three other goddesses or attendant nymphs. The six lion-masks at the side can be thought of as belonging two to each of the three attendants, and all four women may be considered companions of the mountain-creatures, like an Artemis and her troop.

212 above

In grave Gamma of the new Grave Circle B there was an amethyst gem with the engraved portrait of a nobleman, in the tradition of the seal-impressions of Middle Minoan I–II. His hair-style is Cretan, very like that on the portrait gem from Tylissos, and his nose is tip-tilted like those of the royal family at Knossos.

For sculpture in the round the shaft-graves offer the rhyta in the form of animal-heads. In Crete they are well-known in stone but the first examples in precious metal were from the graves at Mycenae. They have no Helladic forerunners and are another sign of the sudden intrusion of Minoan art and

175–176
xxxix

religion in Mycenae. In Grave IV there were two masterpieces of this sort, in the form of a lion's and a bull's head. The former was beaten out of a simple gold sheet, the latter from silver but the ears and horns made separately of gold, with gold inlays for the nostrils and lips, and inlaid eyes.

Semi-precious stones are represented principally by rock crystal ornaments. One of the offerings was a sort of chess-board with faïence and crystal inlays, and there were an number of pendants, beads, pin-heads, terminals and inlays of rock crystal. In many cases the underside of the piece of crystal was painted, as has been found at Knossos. There are no rock crystal vases from Circle A but grave Omi-

212 below

cron in Circle B was particularly rich in this material and has yielded one superb vase, a dish with its handle in the form of a duck's head and neck. The shape is reminiscent of the Early Helladic 'sauce-boats' but is also intimated in some stone vases from Mochlos in East Crete[52].

We cannot illustrate and describe here all the works of art which were found in the shaft-graves and will only mention some pieces of jewellery which had certainly once been worn by the living. These are a heavy bracelet and earrings, such as have been found in Crete from the Early Minoan period on, and, no doubt under Aegean influence, in New Kingdom Egypt. A necklace from grave v

205 above

may have been an insignium of honour, a sort of Order of Merit. The gold beads are in the form of pairs of hawks, perhaps again a reflection of the hawks of Horus[53].

From the end of the sixteenth century there are more and more finds from other parts of the Mycenaean world, mainly from tholoi and chamber-tombs. An exceptionally long sword of the period just

172–173

after 1500 is from a half-destroyed shaft-grave near Staphylos on the island of Peparethos (modern Skopelos)[54]. The handle is twice as thick as those on swords from Mycenae, but the blade, unfortunately, is missing. From its size this sword could never have been carried into battle but could only have been used for cult or ceremonial occasions.

There are further developments of the niello technique, especially on weapons and cups, where we

XL   FRESCO FRAGMENT WITH A WOMAN. Width about 50 cm. From the Palace of Tiryns (see Note page 176)

find what appear to be portrait-heads. There are still decorated daggers as late as 1400 B.C., but the inlaid designs are now more restricted, often of only one animal. Inlaid daggers with dolphins and

xxxviii below birds have been found at Prosymna (Argos) and more recently at Pharai (Achaea). Of about 1500 B.C. there are some daggers with more ambitious decoration on both sides of the blade. There were at least two such in the tomb at Vaphio, one with a scene of swimming youths[55]. A tholos tomb near

xxxviii, 171 Pylos, which was only partly plundered, has recently yielded two superb daggers, true masterpieces of Mycenaean art. Both have complicated inlaid scenes with nautili and leopards, and they seem to have belonged to a women. We have already come across sport-loving Mycenaean princesses and know that Queen Aahhotep and other Egyptian princesses owned decorated daggers.

208–211   The continued practice of the seal-engraver's art is shown by finds in tholoi at Pylos, Vaphio and the rather later tomb at Midea, near Argos.

     Some of the finest products of the Mycenaean artist are reliefs in gold and ivory. The former are only met in the fifteenth century but ivory reliefs remain popular to the very end of the Mycenaean period.

178–185 Best known are the gold cups from Vaphio with their fine repoussé work and balanced compositions with bulls. There is a natural interest in the life of these leaders of the herds which represented the main wealth of the nobleman. Still in Homer's Iliad we read of wealthy men described as 'rich in cattle' (πολυβούται), and in the *Odyssey* the keeper of the herd is consciously proud of his seniority over his fellow swineherds and shepherds. The bulls which wandered freely in the great herds were often half-wild and dangerous, and it needed considerable energy and courage to capture them. In a simile Homer gives us a picture of the struggling bull, tied up and dragged unwillingly along by the herds-men (*Iliad* XIII, 571). It is the work of these herdsmen which is depicted on the cups, indeed one of the scenes is very like that described by Homer. On one there is the tense and vigorous scene of the cap-ture of a bull with nets and rope, on the other a calmer scene of the bull being captured by the use of a cow as decoy. The characterisation of the hunters and hunted is superbly drawn. A rather later gold

196–197 cup from Midea, near Argos, has on it cuttlefish and dolphins; a fine piece but less lively.

     Some fragments of steatite relief vases have been found also on Mycenaean sites. They are of particular interest but there are only few of them. They were no doubt imported from Crete.

     There is considerable variety in the subjects and style of the ivory reliefs. Apart from differences of date and place of manufacture it is possible to distinguish Cypriot, Syrian and other eastern influences. Mycenae seems to have been an important centre for the art. Boxes, mirror-handles, combs and plaques for inlaying into furniture are the commonest finds. In various places ivory lyres have been found as grave-offerings, which suggests that the chieftain himself might play the instrument, as Achilles does

220–221 in the Iliad. Two striking mirror-handles are decorated with the same subject: two young seated fig-ures facing each other. On one they are shown seated on flowers, like spirits of the air, and carrying birds in their hands. The others relax, as though asleep, with their heads inclined towards each other like angels of some 'Melozzo da Forli'. A seated figure of a women, who may be a goddess, reminds us of the finest plaster reliefs from Pseira and Knossos.

218–219   The superbly worked ivory group of two women who sit beneath a single cloak—like the later

XLI   FEMALE HEAD, PERHAPS OF A SPHINX, OF LIMESTONE. Side view. Height 16.8 cm. From Mycenae
(see Note page 176)

mystai—and watch over a child playing before them is of particular interest for the light it throws on Mycenaean religion. Various explanations have been proposed but there can be no doubt that we have here the Μητέρες to whom the divine child has been entrusted. It is usual to find only two of these 'mothers'—to keep the Cretan name recorded by Diodorus—represented. The same figures appear in pairs much later in Greek terracotta groups. One of the many traditions calls them ἄρκτοι 'bears', who were translated by a grateful Zeus into the constellations of the Great and Little Bear. Another series is of ivory plaques in the form of warriors' heads wearing helmets mounted with boars' tusks and often also bearing cheek-pieces. The best of these is from Mycenae, and there is another good example from Spata in East Attica. From the latter site there are also plaques with sphinxes, a lion attacking a bull, and other scenes, in a conventional but vigorous style.

From the reliefs and works in the round made of stone, bronze and other metals we may pick out the small gold figures, of frogs, owl, grasshoppers, and particularly figures of men like that from Kampos in Laconia, and the life-size plaster head, perhaps of a sphinx, from Mycenae. Finest of the plastic works is the relief of the Lion Gate itself.

Works in faience and glass may be passed over, but the frescoes must be mentioned. The technique came from Crete fully developed but the scenes on the Mycenaean frescoes are seldom like the Cretan ones of bull-games, cult-scenes and women. No doubt the king himself dictated the themes to the artist and we find battle or the preparation for battle, the siege and storming of a city, the hunt and chariots.

We cannot date all the surviving frescoes but none seem to be as early as the Early Mycenaean period. Many of the finest belong to the older palaces, but these, including that at Thebes which is the first in date, must be of about 1400 or 1450 B.C. Amongst the earliest must be the fragments from Mycenae which include the 'Women on the Balcony'. The largest of the friezes with women from Thebes cannot be earlier than 140–1400 B.C.[56]. The frescoes from Tiryns show two different periods and styles; the older and better are probably of about 1400 B.C. like those from Mycenae. The few scraps from Orchomenos, and those found recently at Pylos, must be much later, perhaps about 1300 B.C.

It is interesting to note that the old themes were kept even after any accidents or repairs in the palaces. For instance, the re-painting of the frescoes in the palace at Tiryns were executed in a different style but with the same subjects. In the hunting scenes warriors fight a boar, and the women also join the hunt, in chariots and without escort. Even from the fragments it is possible to distinguish the refined features of the noblemen from the coarser faces of their servants. The life-size procession of women from Thebes is probably from some religious scene. The frieze in the megaron at Mycenae must have been over 40 m. long. From it we have preserved warriors and horses preparing for battle, and chariotry attacking a great structure whose defendants are toppling from its roof. The frescoes from the palace at Pylos have been seriously damaged by fire. There some of the scenes were peaceful, like that with a lyre-player; others are of battle, one with a mortal duel. Traces of frescoes were also found in the smaller buildings.

Late examples of fresco are the pieces from a house at Mycenae with three demonic figures who seem to carry on their shoulders trophies of the chase—a popular or folk theme rather than a religious one—

XLII FEMALE HEAD, PERHAPS OF A SPHINX, OF LIMESTONE. Front view. See plate XLI. From Mycenae
(see Note page 176)

and the painted stela with warriors like those on the Mycenae 'Warrior Vase'. This small and rather poor stela which had been painted for re-use marks for us the final stage of what was once a glorious city. There were to be no more palaces, no more painted walls, no bard could again sing of Mycenae as 'rich in gold'.

232–233

This, too, is the end of our story of the civilisation and art of Mycenae. Its noblest legacy, more precious than the treasures we have described, is the reflection of its greatness which shines through Homer's poems.

XLIII Above: FRESCO FRAGMENT. WOMEN ON A BALCONY WATCHING A PLAY. Width 13.5 cm.
Below: FRESCO FRAGMENT. THREE CRETO-MYCENAEAN TA-URT DEMONS. Both from Mycenae
(see Note page 176)

[1] See Netolitzky, in *Bericht* VI. *Internationalen Kongress*, Berlin 1940, p. 155.

[2] Evans, *Palace of Minos* I, pp. 34–35, sets the start of the Neolithic period at Knossos at least as early as 8000 B.C. Such an early date can only be possible if the lowest levels are 'pre-pottery' Mesolithic.

[3] An Illyrian element has been detected by some in West Crete, but such theories are hard to assess. See A. Ficks, *Vorgriechische Ortsnamen*, and *Hattiden und Danubier in Griechenland*.

[4] First proposed in *Antiquity* 13, 1939, p. 425 ff. 'The Volcanic Destruction of Minoan Crete'.

[5] *Ephemeris* 1939–1941 (publ. 1948) pp. 91–92.

[6] Herodotus VII, 171. According to the Cretan tradition the island was twice laid waste. The Eteocretans survived at Praisos into the Greek period and preserved traces of the Minoan language and, it seems, Linear A script (see *Minoica: Festschrift J. Sundwall* 1958, p. 226 ff.), as well as the early religion and some other traditions. The account of the annihilation of the population must be correct although the reasons given for it are aetiological myths. See also the account cited in note 4.

[7] Ventris and Chadwick, 'Evidence for Greek Dialect in the Mycenaean Archives' in *Journal of Hellenic Studies* LXXIII, 1953, p. 84 ff.; *Documents in Mycenaean Greek*, 1956.

[8] Marinatos, 'La Marine Créto-mycénienne', *Bulletin de correspondance Hellénique* LVI, 1933, pp. 170–235; especially p. 181 for this problem, p. 193 for the shipyards at Hagioi Theodoroi, p. 191 ff. for the sizes and p. 212 ff. for the types of Aegean ships.

[9] Latest on dating, Schachermeyer, *Die ältesten Kulturen Griechenlands*, p. 28 ff. and the table on p. 32 attributing the various systems to different scholars.

[10] The main source for Minoan and Mycenaean religion is Nilsson, *Minoan-Mycenaean Religion*, 2nd edition, 1950. Of the very many other books and monographs on the subject the following may be mentioned: Picard, *Les religions préhelléniques*, 1948; Matz, 'Göttererscheinung und Kultbild im minoischen Kreta', *Abhandl. der Akademie der Wissenschaften*, 7, 1958, pp. 358–448.

[11] Further on this see "Ἕνωσις" in Πρακτικὰ Ἀκαδημίας Ἀθηνῶν 31, 1956, p. 400 ff.

[12] Pryce, *British Museum Catalogue of Sculpture* I, I. 13 no. A 34 (from Amorgos).

[13] See *Gnomon* 29, 1957, pp. 536–537.

[14] On this possiblity see Διογενεῖς Βασιλῆες, in *Studies Presented to D. M. Robinson* II, p. 126 ff.

[15] The basic work on this period is still Matz, *Die frühkretischen Siegel*, 1928; and see his, *Kreta–Mykene–Troja*, 1956, and Schachermeyr, op. cit.

[16] On orientation in Minoan architecture see Marinatos, in *Proc. Internat. Congress of Prehistoric and Protohistoric Sciences*, Oxford 1934, p. 197 ff.

[17] One painting from Knossos, the 'Blue Boy picking crocuses', was attributed by Evans to the Old Palace, but it is certainly of the later period, and the figure is now generally recognised as a monkey. It is, however, wearing an armlet, belt and amulet (the cord is visible on the chest) which is rather surprising.

[18] Famous for its oval plan which is very rare in Greece. Here it seems to have been determined by the shape of the hill on which it was built, but it has provoked many arguments about the origins of palace architecture in Mediterranean lands. The stout outer wall has only one entrance. Inside the rooms lie around a central court from which they are lit.

[19] Diodorus Siculus IV, 79 ff., says that after the death of Minos in Sicily the Cretans built for him a double grave, in which the king's bones were laid in a hidden room while the upper part formed a temple to Aphrodite. This reminds us of Evans' discovery at Knossos of the Temple Tomb with a hidden rock-cut tomb-chamber and a built part also above ground. According to Diodorus the tomb in Sicily was still standing when Acragas was founded. It was destroyed in the time of the tyrant Theron and the king's bones were returned to Crete at the beginning of the fifth century.
The whole aspect of the Temple Tomb is most Egyptian and reminds one of the so-called 'Hemispeois' of the early New Kingdom. The Temple Tomb was erected at this time (Middle Minoan III); it was soon destroyed, and re-built. The last royal burial was in Late Minoan II. The many later robbings have left only scraps of the treasures which were once there. The Ring of Minos, which is supposed to have been found there, is certainly a forgery. The Temple Tomb was no doubt not the only royal tomb at Knossos. In Mycenae and Pylos each king seems to have built his own tomb. There are in fact two tholos-tombs near Knossos, and the Isopata Tomb, on the road to the Harbour Town, must have been royal. At Knossos, and the other palaces, further finds of royal tombs are to be expected.

[20] 'Les légendes royales de la Crète Minoenne', *Revue archéologique* 1949 (Mélanges Ch. Picard).

[21] The official character of the copper ingots found in many parts of the Mediterranean is shown by the symbols stamped on them. Their origin is not known; some say Cyprus. We should note that the ruler of Hagia Triada had his own treasury. At Knossos was found a porphyry weight with an octopus in relief on it. It weighs a talent and could have been used for checking the weight of ingots.

[22] Some miles to the east are the ruins of ancient Milatos. Sarpedon, the third brother, was an admirer of Miletos, son of Apollo and Akakallis, and followed him to Asia Minor when he was banished by Minos. Miletos founded the city named after him, and Sarpedon, with his fellow-exiles, the city of Termilai in Lycia. This tale, and the association of the modern name Tarmaros (also known in west Crete) with Termilai, suggests that the third palace in Crete was the seat of Minos' 'third' brother.

[23] Six miles to the west, in the foot-hills of Ida, is the mansion of Sklavokampos, with remains of smaller houses on higher ground. The mansion, which had two stories, presents some unusual features. Its plan was almost square with a central court, a *compluvium displuviatum*. On the cooler north side were the best rooms, and at the north-west corner there were verandahs on both floors to catch the cool breezes. We have already mentioned the find of seal-impressions here.
The room beneath the stairs (the *sottoscala*) was used as a toilet, as it is still in many country houses. The slab in the floor had a round hole in it, 21 cm. across, and a drain beneath. There was a clay lid, hardened by the conflagration. For details and reconstruction of this mansion see *Deltion* 1939–1941 (publ. 1948) p. 67 ff.

[24] Preliminary reports in Πρακτικὰ Ἀρχ. Ἐτ. 1949, 1950, 1952 (main report) and later volumes.

[25] Three miles from Mallia traces of what seems to be a house have been found with an important hoard of bronzes *Bulletin de correspondance Hellénique* 53, 1929, p. 365 ff.). At Lykastos, south-

west of Mt Juktas, are remains of a palatial building with a town around. The ruined nature of the city is unfortunate for it plays an important part in the stories about the kings of Crete, and it sent soldiers with Idomeneus to Troy. We know more about private houses from East Crete, especially Palaikastro, and there was a small settlement on the island of Pseira. We find here the same scheme of houses and streets (usually paved) of various sizes.

[26] Where space is restricted in towns the houses lie one on top of the other, as we can see today in the Veneto-Turkish fortress-town of Chania. A householder may be obliged to allow his neighbour passage through his home if the neighbour's house is higher and has no other entrance. This right of way would be hereditary. The situation in Gournia must have been much like this.

[27] Evans, *Palace of Minos* I, p. 536ff., figs. 389, 390 and especially colour pl. 6. The Amnisos frescoes, of which there are extensive fragments, certainly belong to the earliest stage of wall-painting which is barely represented at Knossos.

[28] Plants and apes, not native to Crete, might have been painted from memory by an artist who had travelled widely, but more likely the creatures and papyrus had been introduced to the island. More remarkable are the fountains which throw their blue waters high over rocks. There are water-cascades at Knossos and fountains are possible in view of the wide use of clay pipes. For the House of the Frescoes and Fountains see Evans, *Palace of Minos* II, p. 444ff. (with two colour plates) and III, p. 254 (colour plate of the fountain).

[29] Evans, *Palace of Minos* IV, p. 484ff. A fully detailed and illustrated account.

[30] These rules of composition can be observed time and again, and must reflect the true Minoan feeling for decoration. See Matz, *Frühkretische Siegel*, and many later works. Torsion, spirals, double S's and the like are used to translate natural forms into drawing.

[31] Iron was considered to have magic properties in earliest Egypt. Its name Bia indicates its meteoric origin, especially with the suffix 'ni-pet' (from heaven). Wainwright, 'The Coming of Iron', in *Antiquity*, March 1936, pp. 5–24. The Greek word σίδηρος, if it can be associated with *sidus*, *sideris*, may have the same significance as the Egyptian.

[32] Marinatos, 'Le Chernibon etc.' in *Bulletin de correspondance Hellénique* 53, 1929, p. 365, pl. 23. For bronze vases from private houses in Knossos, see Evans, *Palace of Minos* II, pp. 623–647, with several illustrations.

[33] There are only preliminary reports as the finds are not yet all cleaned: *Archäologischer Anzeiger* 1934, p. 250, fig. 3; 1935, p. 247, figs. 4–6; Evans, *Palace of Minos* IV, suppl. pl. 68.

[34] Plant motifs were adapted in innumerable ways, some of which are still hard to explain, e.g. the 'ogival canopy'. There is an important chapter on this in Evans, *Palace of Minos* II, p. 468ff., and on details of the motifs see Furumark, *Mycenaean Pottery*.

[35] The Marine style also appears seldom in wall-painting. There are some examples from the House of the Frescoes in Knossos.

[36] An oil-painting was made of the remains of this companion of the 'Agamemnon'. Schliemann, *Mykenai*, pp. 340–341, fig. 454, and on p. 385 he says that in several cases there was much of the flesh still preserved.

[37] This was suggested in an unpublished lecture by the author in 1951. On the Hyksos and Mycenae see Persson, *New Tombs at Dendra*, 1942; Schachermeyr, *Archiv Orientální* 17, 1949.

[38] Sometimes called Pelasgian, a term conveying the same meaning as 'Cyclopean'.

[39] On the Amnisos frescoes these objects are in part filled with upright zigzag lines, the Egyptian symbol for 'Sea' or 'Land of the Sea'. Thus the blazon of Mycenae might be read as the Union of the two Sea-powers. When the Lion Gate was built the 'second' power might as well have been Crete as the

Ahhijawa in Asia Minor. See Marinatos, in *Πρακτικὰ Ἀκαδημίας* 31, 1956, p. 400.

[40] For the same reason the north entrance to the Acropolis at Athens was given up and the Pelargikon Enneapylon (not necessarily nine gates) was built facing Phalerum and Piraeus. The Cyclopean tower found recently beneath the Nike bastion corresponds so closely with the tower beside the Lion Gate at Mycenae that both fortifications might have been designed by the same man.

[41] It is not satisfactory to suppose that the doorway to the megaron was hung with curtains. Rather were there doors, and no doubt windows, hinged from above; what Homer calls ὀρσοθύρη. The word means a door which is moved upwards, as does the variant εἰρεθύρη preserved in Hesychius. The lexicographers have only given the word the meaning suggested by the single passage in the Odyssey.

[42] This detail leads us to the vexed problems about the lighting and roofing of the megaron. In almost all the palaces the megaron stands between corridors or apartments on two floors, and it is doubtful whether there could have been windows high in the megaron walls. It has generally been assumed that the four columns around the hearth supported a clerestory roof whose open sides served both as chimney and windows. The Pylos excavations have shown that there was a fairly broad chimney over the centre of the hearth but go no further to answer the problem. The four columns by the hearth were too thin to be either very high or able to support any real weight. At the most they might have supported a flimsy roof or clerestory through which the main room could be lit; an arrangement met elsewhere, as in the hypostyle halls of Egyptian temples and the later basilicas with three naves. The megaron would thus not have been well lit but it might have been enough. Homer calls the megara σκιόεντα, 'shady'. A flat roof would have been technically impossible over a room 11 or 12 metres wide and without inner supports. If then the roof was pitched it must have been covered with straw or rushes for no tiles have been found. In Crete flat roofs were common. On the ground floors each small room had pillars, and in the floor above thick columns supported the roof-beams.

[43] Here and in Thebes there is a good chance of finding other inscriptions since inscribed stirrup-vases have been found already at both sites.

[44] A preliminary report in Mylonas, *Ancient Mycenae*, p. 128ff. Cf. Marinatos, *Geras Keramopoullou*, 1953, p. 54ff.

[45] When the earth or stones were too loose the dromos had to be lined with walls, as happens also in the later tombs.

[46] There is the famous story of Trophonios and Agamedes, princes of Orchomenos, and the architects who built the Treasury of Hyrieus at Aulis. They left a stone loose so that they could secretly remove the treasure placed in it by their patron. Thus, already in the seventh century the tholoi were regarded as treasuries.

[47] On one stela one of the lions attacking the bull is being slain with a knife or club, the deed of the man buried here or indeed of any herdsman. On another rather broader stela the bull is attacked by lions in the manner we see on the Vaphio gem. This representation can be traced back ultimately to the plaster relief by the north entrance to the Palace of Knossos. The rear legs of the lion are still visible beneath the belly of the bull on the new stela from Mycenae. The first stela had been re-used as a base and the hole cut in its centre has obliterated much of its decoration. The rest is well preserved. The second stela is badly worn and is still being repaired. See Marinatos, in *Geras Keramopoullou*, pp. 72–73, fig. 2 (restoration), and pls. 8–9 (discovery and present condition). The stela belonged to grave Gamma and is carved in relief while the other, over grave Alpha, is simply incised. It is badly worn at the right and incomplete but at least one warrior with a spear can be

distinguished. On the ·stelae see also Mylonas, *Ancient Mycenae*, p. 131, fig. 41 (stela of B I), and p. 135 ff., fig. 45 (stela of B III).

[48] The 'halberd' from shaft-grave VI is a great rarity, and if it is indeed this weapon it must be an import from the north. For a discussion of swords see. Evans, *The Shaft-Graves and Bee-Hive Tombs of Mycenae* (1929), p. 32 ff., and Karo, *Schachtgräber von Mykenai*, p. 200 ff. The short sword (or long dagger) was used for hand-to-hand fighting. The battle-axe is mentioned once in the *Iliad* (XIII, 611 ff.) in the hands of the Trojan Pisander against Menelaus. We read that in the fight around the ships all weapons were employed (XV, 711). We know of several small whetstones, pierced at one end for suspension, both from the shaft-graves and other tombs. That these were a warrior's standard equipment we know from the whetstone and dagger which were attached to the silver girdle worn by the body of Meskalam-Dug; see Woolley, *Ur und die Sintflut*, 1930, p. 48. Some other unusual stone objects from grave VI, the grave with the halberd, seem to be of northern origin and may have been a type of whetstone. They are of sandstone and each has a shallow groove (Karo, *Schachtgräber*, p. 63, fig. 79). Northern museums contain many such objects which are variously called amulets, arrow-straighteners, or shaft-polishers. Another example has been found in an Early Mycenaean chamber-tomb at Pylos.

[49] There are only a few other cups in this technique, and there are some examples of simple inlay-work in Egypt. In these cut-out patterns of gold and silver are hammered into prepared sink-ings, and there are many Mycenaean works which show this simpler technique.

[50] Cretans today grow them in flower-pots, and boil them to produce a physic against stomach-disorders. Perhaps the Mycenaean electrum cups were made to hold this potion to solace heroes exhausted by carousal.

[51] Nestor took with him to Troy a cup, an heirloom in his family, which had on its handles golden doves. When full it was so heavy that only that redoubtable hero could lift it. Homer does not, however, say that it was drunk from. He calls it a *depas*, a general word for a cup or bowl. See Marinatos, in *Neue Beiträge zur Klassischen Altertumswissenschaft: Festschrift für B. Schweitzer* pp. 11–18.

[52] Rock crystal cups are met in Crete at Knossos and Palaikastro. The stone had long ago been explained as 'pure water, not frozen by cold but petrified through the strength of divine fire' (Diodorus). Thus it was that in these cups, *krystalla*, which were valued at least as highly as gold, only cold drinks were offered. See Marinatos, in *Ephemeris* 1931, pp. 158–160.

[53] See Marinatos, *op. cit.* in note 51, pp. 16–17.

[54] There is a tradition that Staphylos was the Cretan who colonised the island in the time of Rhadamanthys.

[55] See Marinatos, in *Essays in Aegean Archaeology presented to Sir Arthur Evans*, p. 63 ff.; Evans, *Palace of Minos* III, pp. 126 ff.; Karo, *Schachtgräber von Mykenai*, pp. 313–314.

[56] See Reusch, *Die zeichnerische Rekonstruktion des Frauenfries im böotischen Theben*, 1956; and the review in *Gnomon* 29, 1957, pp. 533–537.

CRETE

1   Cave of Eileithyia at Amnisos.
The cave was inhabited in the Neolithic period and afterwards served as a cult-place until long into the Christian period

THE PERIOD BEFORE THE GREAT PALACES

NEOLITHIC (5000–3100 B.C.), SUB-NEOLITHIC (3100–2800 B.C.)

AND EARLY MINOAN (2800–2000 B.C.)

2   Above – Clay figure. Height 9.3 cm. Below – Cup with incised decoration. Diam. 20.5 cm. Both from Knossos. Neolithic

3 Two circular tombs at Hagia Triada, Messara. Early Minoan. First half of the third millennium B.C.

4   Two high-footed cups of black clay with burnished decoration. Pyrgos style. Height of each 22 cm.
From the cave-grave at Pyrgos near Nirou Chani, Central Crete. Early Minoan I, about 2800–2600 B.C.

5 Above – Beaked jugs with matt-painted decoration. Hagios Onouphrios style. Heights 18.5 and 19 cm. From the cave-grave
at Kyparissi, Central Crete. Early Minoan I, about 2700–2500 B.C. Below – Clay pan with incised decoration,
imported from the Cyclades. Diam. 12.2 cm. Early Minoan II–III. Giamalakis Collection

6 Lid of a pyxis in green steatite, the handle in the form of a recumbent greyhound. Diam. 12 cm.
From the island of Mochlos, Gulf of Mirabello, East Crete. Early Minoan II, about 2400 B.C.

7   Schist pyxis. Diam. 17 cm. From the cave-grave at Maronia, East Crete. Early Minoan II, about 2500 B.C.

8   Above – So-called 'tea-pot' with fire-mottled decoration. Vasiliki style. Height 14.5 cm.
From Vasiliki, East Crete. Early Minoan II, about 2500 B.C.   Below – Jug with white-painted decoration.
Height 19 cm. From the island of Mochlos, Gulf of Mirabello, East Crete. Early Minoan III, about 2200 B.C.

9 Clay cult-vase in the form of three doves. Height 12 cm. Provenance unknown. Early Minoan III. Giamalakis Collection

10   Above – Clay rhyton in the form of a bust. Height 17.5 cm.   Below – Clay ship. Length 20 cm.
Both from the island of Mochlos, Gulf of Mirabello, East Crete. Early Minoan III

11 Cycladic idols. Left – Heights: above, 5 cm; below, 8.3 cm. From a find at Teke, north of Knossos. Right – Height 23.5 cm. From the circular tomb at Koumasa. Early Minoan II, about 2400–2200 B.C.

12   Ivory seal in the form of an ape.
Height 3.2 cm. The base of the seal is shown
below. Probably from Lasithi.
Early Minoan III. Giamalakis Collection

13   Gold jewellery. Above, left – Leafy spray and blossoms. About one and a half times life-size. From the island of Mochlos, Gulf of Mirabello, East Crete. Early Minoan II. Above, right – Frog with granulation, and bead with spirals. Both three and a half times life-size. From the circular tomb at Koumasa, and from Kalathiana, Messara. Early Minoan II–III. Below – Pendant in the form of two hornets holding a granulated honeycomb. Width 4.7 cm. From the cemetery at Mallia. Early Minoan III, about 2000 B.C.

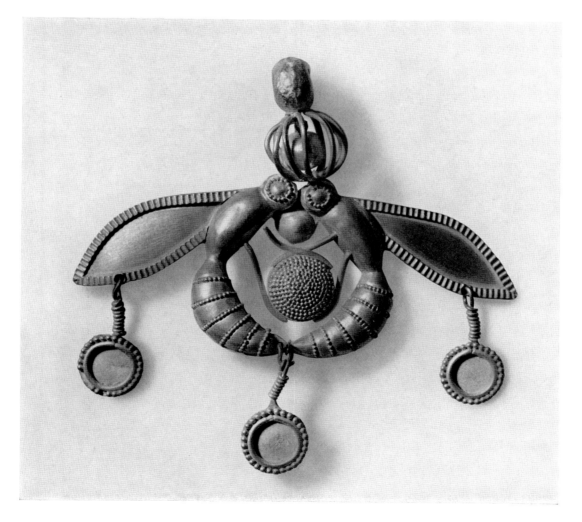

THE PERIOD
OF THE
OLD PALACES

MIDDLE MINOAN I AND II

(2000–1700 B.C.)

14   Above – Clay figure of an animal. Height 19.5 cm. Below – Clay rhyton in the form of a bull with acrobats. Length 16 cm.
Both from a circular tomb at Porti, Messara. Middle Minoan I.

15   Clay figures. Height of the largest figure 23 cm.
From the hill-sanctuary at Petsofa and oval house at Chamaizi in Sitia, East Crete. Middle Minoan I

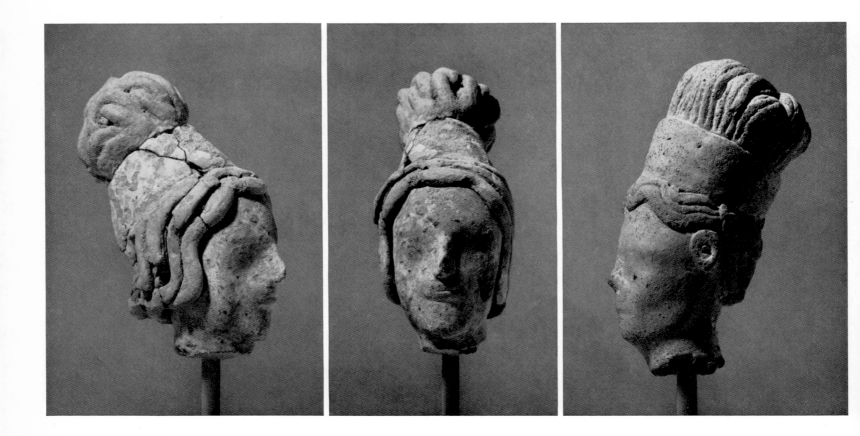

16 Heads from clay figures of women. Height, left and middle 12 cm., right 13 cm. From Piskokephalo in Sitia, East Crete. Middle Minoan II

17   Clay figure of a praying woman. Height 26.4 cm. From Piskokephalo in Sitia, East Crete. Middle Minoan II

18   Above – Clay bowl with shepherd and flock. Diam. 19.5 cm.   Below – Clay bowl with a flying bird. Diam. 11.3 cm.
Both from Palaikastro, East Crete. Middle Minoan I

19　Above – Bell-shaped cult-object of faience with horns. Height 8 cm. From a votive pit at the ancient harbour of Knossos.
Middle Minoan I. Middle and below – Painted clay cattle. Kamares style. Height of each 21 cm.
From the Old Palace of Phaistos. Middle Minoan II

20   Above – Spouted vase with painted daisies. Kamares style. Height 12 cm. From the cave near Kamares on Mt. Ida. Below – Cup. Kamares style. Height 16.2 cm. From the Old Palace of Phaistos. Both Middle Minoan II

21   Beaked jug. Kamares style. Height 27 cm. From the Old Palace of Phaistos. Middle Minoan II

22 Vase with a strainer and feeding-spout. Kamares style. Height 13.8 cm.
From the Old Palace of Phaistos. Middle Minoan II

23   Footed bowl. Kamares style. Diam. 54 cm. From the Old Palace of Phaistos. Middle Minoan II

24   Pithos. Kamares style. Height 1.10 m. From the Old Palace of Phaistos. Middle Minoan II

25   Above – Portrait of a child on a clay seal-impression. From the Old Palace of Knossos. Middle Minoan II, about 1800 B.C.
Below – Larnax. Length 74 cm. From a circular grave at Vorou, Central Crete. Middle Minoan I–II

PALACES, MANSIONS AND VILLAS

26   The main part of the Palace of Knossos from the hill, Hagios Elias, to the east

27   Above – General view of the landscape and Palace of Knossos from the hill, Hagios Elias, to the east.
Below – Palace of Knossos from the hill Gypsades to the south

28 Palace of Knossos.
The Sacred Way at the north edge of the Palace and the steps of the theatre for cult-performances, seen from the east

29   Palace of Knossos. The steps of the theatre for cult-performances, seen from the Sacred Way

30   Palace of Knossos. North entrance. To the left the Hall of Pillars, to the right the partly restored portico with the bull-relief

31   Palace of Knossos. North entrance, seen from the Central Court within

32 Palace of Knossos. View from the top the main staircase in the east wing across the Central Court to the Throne Room and
Vestibule in the west wing. To the left the verandah of the west wing, to the right the portico by the north entrance

33 Palace of Knossos. Throne Room

34   Palace of Knossos. View from the west-south-west of the pillared well of the main staircase in the east wing (left), of the
Queen's Rooms on the main floor, and one storey below

35   Palace of Knossos. Main staircase in the east wing. Pillared hall

36 Palace of Knossos. Upper section of the main staircase in the east wing

37   Palace of Knossos. Lower section and light-well of the main staircase in the east wing

38   Palace of Knossos. Above – The Queen's Megaron with pillared hall and light-well.
Below – Fragment of a fresco with a dancer from a pillar in the Queen's Megaron

39　Palace of Knossos, east wing. Vestibule to the Hall of the Double Axes, from outside and inside

40   Palace of Knossos. View from the north west: central state-room with three columns and three pillars,
on the main floor of the west wing; before it the upper Propylon, below to the left the south-east gallery

41 Palace of Knossos. Part of the west magazine with large pithoi in situ

42   Knossos, so-called Little Palace. Shrine. To the left the impressions of fluted wooden columns;
to the right, horns of consecration and natural stone figures (fetishes)

43   Knossos, so-called Little Palace. View from the south east

44 Knossos, so-called Royal Villa. Above – Inner hall with a view of the ante-room and light-well.
Below – Inner hall with a view of the balustrade and niche for the throne. On the right the entrance to the so-called Pillar Crypt

45　Knossos, so-called Royal Villa. Above – Stairs in the south-west quarter.
Below – So-called Pillar Crypt seen from the corridor to the inner hall

46   Knossos, Temple Tomb. View from the Entrance hall over the forecourt towards the inner hall and the Pillar Crypt

47 Knossos, Temple Tomb. View from the hill to the west; the upper pillared hall with the Pillar Crypt below; in the background the forecourt and entrance hall

48   Phaistos. Houses west of the Palace, mainly Middle Minoan I

49   Palace of Phaistos. View from the south across the Central Court. In the background the massif of Mt. Ida

50   Palace of Phaistos. Above – The Palace from the north-west. Below – West court with the sanctuary of the Old Palace, theatre-area for cult-performances (left) and the Grand Staircase of the New Palace (right); before it the Processional Way

51   Palace of Phaistos. Above – On the left the Great Propylon with the Grand Staircase before it; on the right the west façade of the New Palace with that of the Old Palace before it. Middle – North wall of the west court; before it the seats of the theatre for cult-performances. Below – West court and façade of the New Palace; before it the wall of the Old Palace

52 Palace of Hagia Triada. View from the north-east over the main part of the Palace

53   Palace of Hagia Triada. View from the south-east over the main part of the Palace

54   Palace of Hagia Triada. View from the north-north-east over the so-called Market and magazines

55   Palace of Hagia Triada. Above – View from the south-west across the Palace.
Below – View from the servants' quarters to the portico of the so-called Market and magazines

56 Palace of Mallia. Above – North entrance.
Below – South-west corner of the Central Court with the great stone 'kernos' for fertility-cult offerings

57   Palace of Mallia. Above – The central part from the west.
Below – View of the north end of the Central Court with the north portico and adjacent Pillar Room

58   Palace of Mallia. Above – South part of the Central Court with theatre-area for cult-performances
Below – Central part of the west wing; in the foreground the Central Court with the altar (eschara)

59 Palace of Mallia. Above – North-west part of the Central Court with the north portico and adjacent Pillar Room.
Below – View of the Central Court with the altar (eschara). To the right the east portico with alternate pillars and columns

60   Mansion at Vathypetro, south of Knossos. Late Minoan I, 16th century B.C. Above – View of the north side.
Below – East court with the foundations of the sanctuary

61   Mansion at Vathypetro. Above – On the left the east–west corridor, seen from the east.
On the right a view from the north-west of the Propylon (right), inner court (centre) and the rooms for weaving and wine-pressing.
Below – The west façade with a cult-niche

62 Mansion at Vathypetro. Above – Wine-press. Below – Oil-press. Both in situ

63   Tylissos, Central Crete. Two of the mansions. Late Minoan I. Above – House B. Below – House C

64   Amnisos, Harbour Town of Knossos. Ruins of a villa. Late in Middle Minoan III. Above – From the south-east.
Below – From the west–north-west

65   Nirou Chani, Villa of a High Priest. Late Minoan I. Above – From the east. Below – From the west

80   Pithos decorated with spirals. Height 98 cm. From the island of Pseira, Gulf of Mirabello, East Crete.
Late Minoan I, about 1550–1520 B.C.

65   Nirou Chani, Villa of a High Priest. Late Minoan I. Above – From the east. Below – From the west

66 Ruins of the town of Gournia, Gulf of Mirabello, East Crete. Late Minoan I. Above – General view from the east.
Below – Road in the north part of the town

67 Ruins of the town of Gournia, Gulf of Mirabello, East Crete. Above – View of the west part of the town from the south; on the right the Palace with court and theatre. Below – Part of the circuit road in the west part of the town

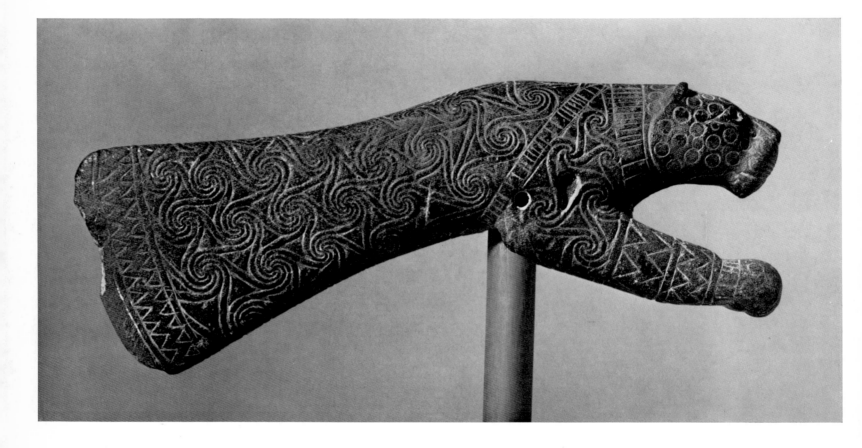

68   Mace-head in the form of a leopard and battle-axe. Grey schist. Length 14.8 cm. From the Old Palace of Mallia.
Middle Minoan III, about 1650–1600 B.C.

69   Gold covering of the pommel of a bronze sword, with the representation of an acrobat. Diam. 7 cm.
From the Old Palace of Mallia. Middle Minoan III, about 1600 B.C.

70   Faience Earth-goddess with snakes. Height 34.2 cm.
From the underground treasury of the central sanctuary in the Palace of Knossos. Middle Minoan III, about 1600 B.C.

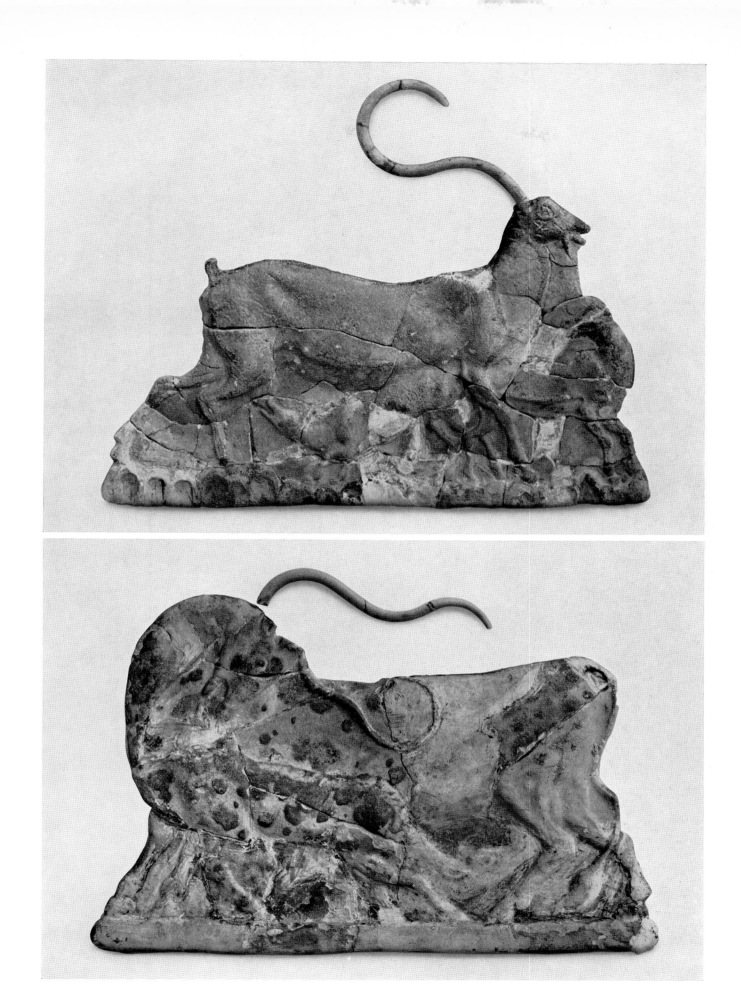

71   Faience reliefs with animals suckling. Above – Wild goat with two kids. Below – Cow with a calf. The bases of each are
19 cm. wide. From the underground treasury of the central sanctuary in the Palace of Knossos. Middle Minoan III, about 1600 B.C.

72   The Disc of Phaistos, side B, of fired clay. Diam. 16 cm.
The text, perhaps of religious import, is of stamped hieroglyphs arranged in a spiral. Middle Minoan III, after 1600 B.C.

73   The Disc of Phaistos, side A. See caption to plate 72

74 Two-handled bellied jar decorated with palm-trees
Height 57 cm. Last phase of the Kamares style. From the Old Palace of Knossos. Middle Minoan II–III

75 Jug decorated with birds, imported from Melos. Height 58 cm. From the treasury of the Palace sanctuary at Knossos.
Middle Minoan III, about 1600 B.C.

76 Two-handled vase, decorated with white star-anemones on a dark ground. Height 22 cm. From Zakro, East Crete. Middle Minoan III, about 1560–1550 B.C.

THE LATE PERIOD OF THE NEW PALACES

LATE MINOAN I AND II (1550–1400 B.C.)

POTTERY

77   Beaked jug. Height 31.5 cm. From the Palace of Knossos. Late Minoan I, about 1550 B.C.

78   Mugs and cups from the New Palace of Knossos. Heights, above, 6.8 and 6.4 cm., middle, 12.3, below, 7.5 and 6.5 cm.
Late Minoan I, about 1550–1520 B.C.

79 Beaked jug with decoration of grasses. Height 29 cm. From the New Palace of Phaistos. Late Minoan I, about 1550–1520 B.C.

80 Pithos decorated with spirals. Height 98 cm. From the island of Pseira, Gulf of Mirabello, East Crete.
Late Minoan I, about 1550–1520 B.C.

81 Cult-vase with double axes and bulls' heads as the main decoration, and stylised ivy leaves and spirals below.
Height 77 cm. From the island of Pseira, Gulf of Mirabello, East Crete. Late Minoan I, about 1550 B.C.

82 Left – Jug decorated with the double axe and sacral knots. Height 28.5 cm. From the Palace of Hagia Triada. Late Minoan I.
Right – Jug decorated with stylised papyrus. Height 24.5 cm. From Palaikastro, East Crete. Late Minoan I

83 Above – Jug. Height 24.5 cm. From Palaikastro, East Crete. Late Minoan I, about 1500 B.C. Below – Beaked jug (height 26.8 cm.) and cup (height without handle 14.5 cm.) with the sacred symbols of double axe and sacral knots. From the New Palace of Phaistos. Late Minoan I, about 1500 B.C.

84   Above – Double jug decorated with nautili. Height 26 cm. From Gournia, East Crete. Late Minoan I, about 1500 B.C.
Below – Handled jar (height 14.5 cm.) and vase in the form of a basket decorated with double axes (height 20 cm.).
Both from the island of Pseira, Gulf of Mirabello. Late Minoan I, shortly after 1500 B.C.

85   Rhyton decorated with nautili. Height 20.2 cm. From the New Palace of Phaistos. Late Minoan I, about 1500 B.C.

86   Two Rhytons. Left – with dolphins. Height 32 cm. From the island of Pseira, Gulf of Mirabello.
Right – with starfish and sea-shells. Height 33 cm. From Zakro, East Crete. Both Late Minoan I, about 1500 B.C.

87　Lentoid Flask decorated with octopuses. Height 28 cm. From Palaikastro, East Crete. Late Minoan I, about 1500 B.C.

88   Double vase with a votary; a cult-vessel. Height 16 cm. Late Minoan I–II, about 1450 B.C. Giamalakis Collection

89   Clay rhyton with a goat's head. Height 29 cm. From Palaikastro, East Crete. Late Minoan I, about 1500 B.C.

90   Two clay rhytons in the form of bulls. Lengths 25.5 and 26 cm. The lower one is covered with the net pattern as of a royal bull.
From the island of Pseira, Gulf of Mirabello. Late Minoan I, about 1500 B.C.

91　Three-handled jar with papyrus decorations. Palace Style. Height 70 cm. From the Palace of Knossos.
Late Minoan II, about 1425 B.C.

92   Three-handled jar with papyrus decoration. Palace Style. Height 78 cm. From Knossos. Late Minoan II, about 1430 B.C.

93 Pithos with a papyrus plant in low relief. Height 97 cm. From the Royal Villa at Knossos. Late Minoan II, about 1425 B.C.

94 Three-handled jar decorated with helmets which have cheek-pieces and horse-tail crests. Height 47.5 cm.
From a grave near the mouth of the Kairatos, in the harbour area of Knossos. Late Minoan II, about 1425–1400 B.C.

95 Narrow-necked jug, probably a cult-vase, with painted and relief decoration. Height 49.5 cm.
From a grave near the mouth of the Kairatos, in the harbour area of Knossos. Late Minoan II, about 1400 B.C.

THE LATE PERIOD OF THE NEW PALACES

LATE MINOAN I AND II (1550–1400 B.C.)

WORK IN STONE, IVORY, BRONZE AND GOLD

96   Ivory head of a bull-jumper, from a group representing the bull-games. See plate 97. About five times life-size.
From the Palace of Knossos. Early in Late Minoan I, about 1550 B.C.

97   Ivory bull-jumper executing the 'salto mortale', from a group representing the bull-games; once embellished with gold.
Ninetenths life-size. From the Palace of Knossos. Early in Late Minoan I, about 1550 B.C.

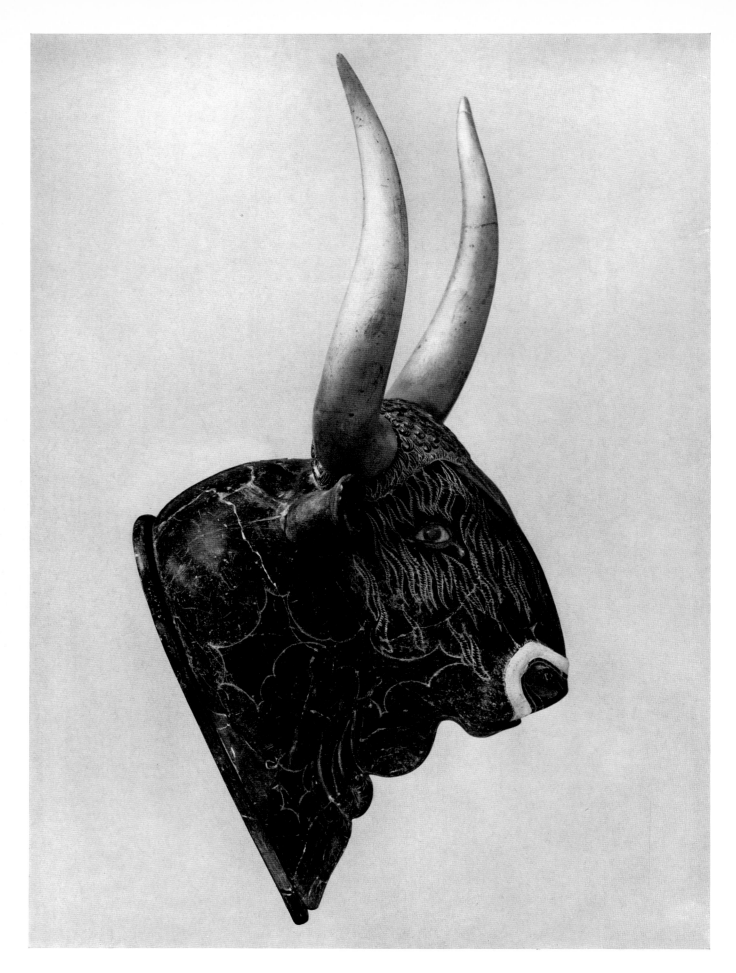

98   Black steatite rhyton in the form of a bull's head. The nostrils are of tridacna shell, eyes of rock crystal and horns of gilt wood.
Length of the head without horns 20.6 cm. From the Little Palace at Knossos. Late Minoan I, about 1550–1500 B.C.

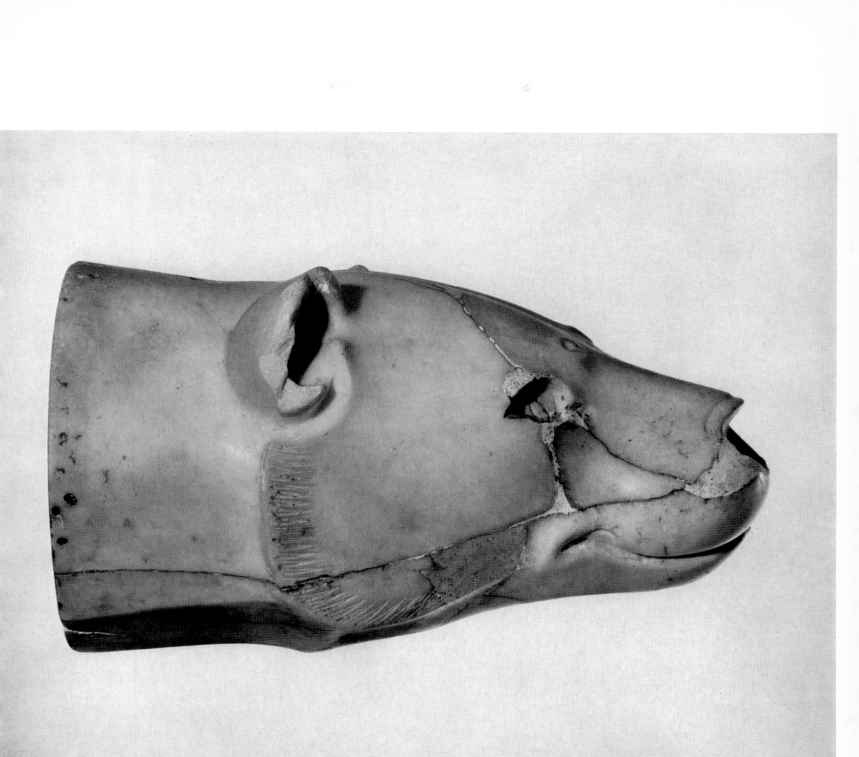

99   Rhyton of white, marmoreal limestone in the form of a lioness' head. The nose and eyes were once of red jasper and rock crystal.
Diameter at the back 16.6 cm. From the Palace of Knossos. Late Minoan I, about 1550–1500 B.C.

100　The so-called Chieftain's Cup, of black steatite, with children at play, imitating a prince, officer and three soldiers. Upper diameter 9.9 cm. From the Palace of Hagia Triada. Late Minoan I, about 1550–1500 B.C.

101   Back of the so-called Chieftain's Cup. See plate 100. From the Palace of Hagia Triada.
Late Minoan I, about 1550–1500 B.C.

102   From the so-called Chieftain's Cup: officer and prince. From the Palace of Hagia Triada. Late Minoan I, about 1550–1500 B.C.

103　The so-called Harvesters' Vase. A black steatite rhyton in the shape of an ostrich egg
with the representation of a thanksgiving procession after the harvest, probably the olive-harvest. Greatest diameter 11.5 cm;
the lower half is missing. From the Palace of Hagia Triada. Late Minoan I, about 1550–1500 B.C.

104   From the so-called Harvesters' Vase; the procession. From the Palace of Hagia Triada. Late Minoan I, about 1550–1500 B.C.

105   From the so-called Harvesters' Vase. Continuation of the procession.
From the Palace of Hagia Triada. Late Minoan I, about 1550–1500 B.C.

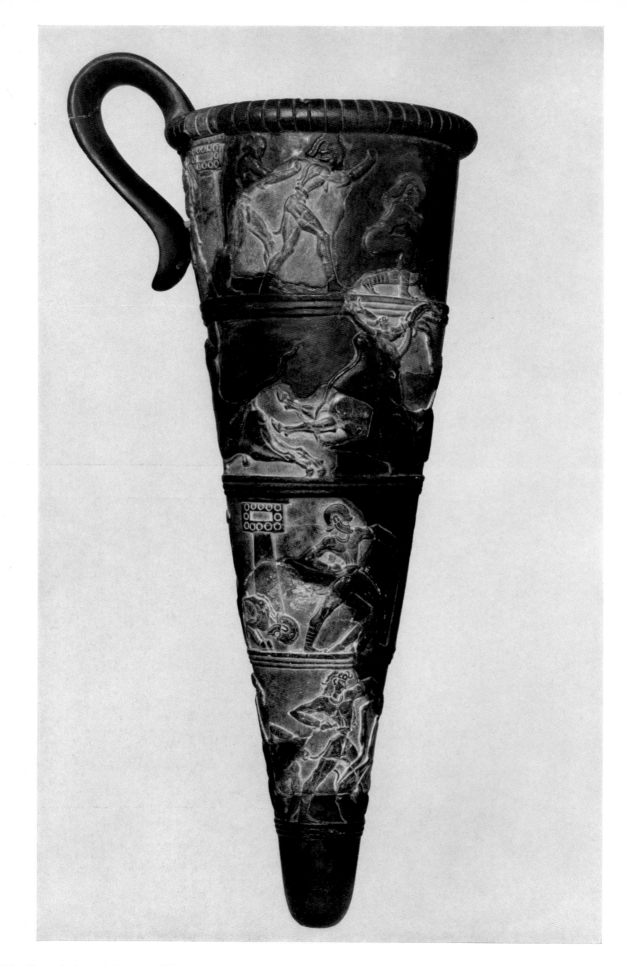

106   Funnel-shaped rhyton of black steatite with scenes of training for sports: wrestling, bull-jumping and boxing,
by both helmeted men and youths. Height without handle 46.5 cm.
From the Palace of Hagia Triada. Late Minoan I, about 1550–1500 B.C.

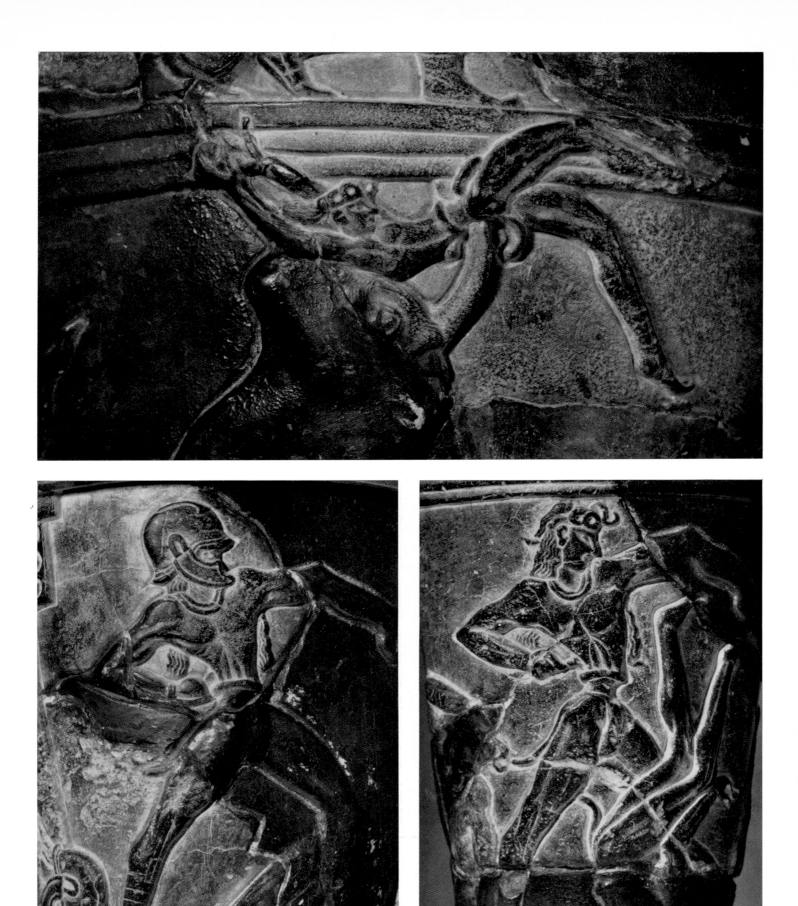

107   Details of the funnel-shaped rhyton on plate 106. Above – From the bull-games. Below – From the boxing.
From the Palace of Hagia Triada. Late Minoan I, about 1550–1500 B.C.

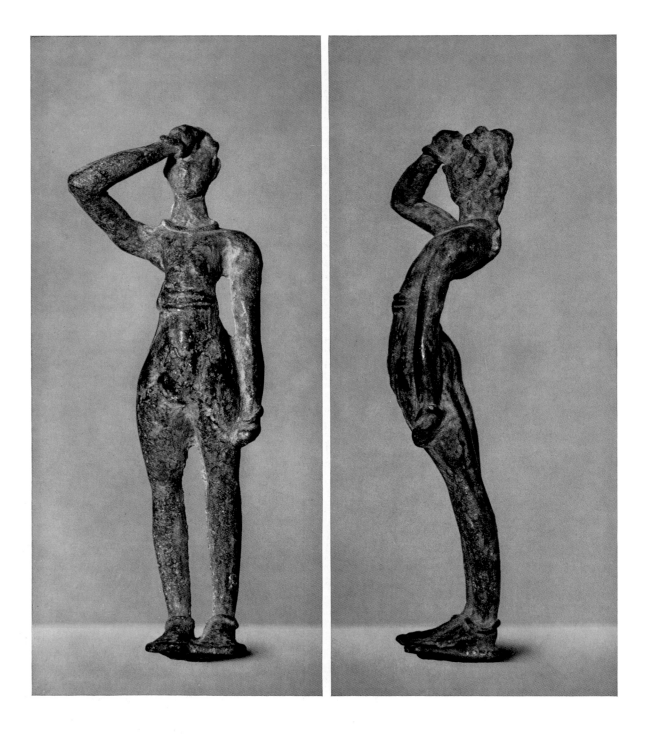

108   Bronze statuette of a man praying. Height 15.2 cm. From Tylissos. Late Minoan I, about 1550 B.C.

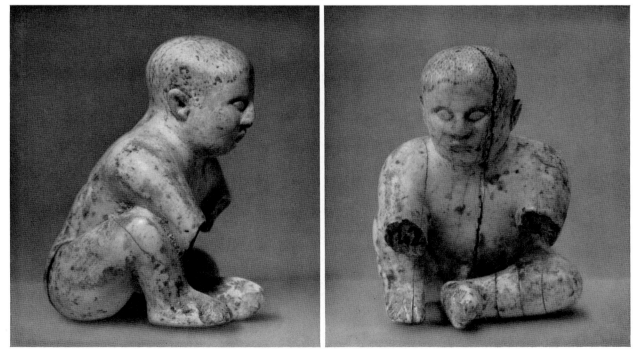

109   Above – Ivory plaque with a supernatural bird. Height 7 cm. Below – Ivory child, perhaps playing with knucklebones.
Height 4 cm. Both from Palaikastro, East Crete. Late Minoan I

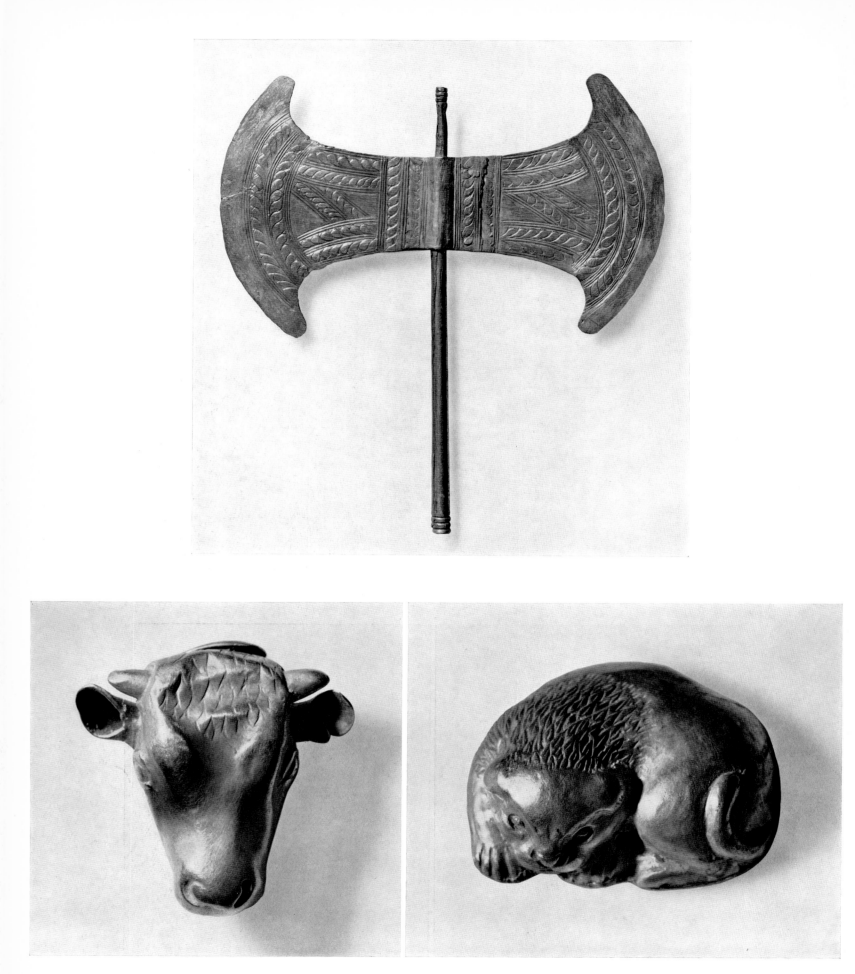

110   Above – Gold double axe. Width 8.6 cm. From the cave at Arkalochori, East Crete.
Late Minoan I. Below – Gold pendants; on the left a bull's head (height 2.5 cm.), on the right a lion (width 2.7 cm.).
From a grave near the Palace of Hagia Triada. Late Minoan I

111   Above – Gold signet rings. Views of the devices enlarged four times. From various graves in Crete. Late Minoan I–II.
Below – Clay seal impressions, probably from rings, enlarged three times. Late Minoan I, about 1550–1530 B.C.

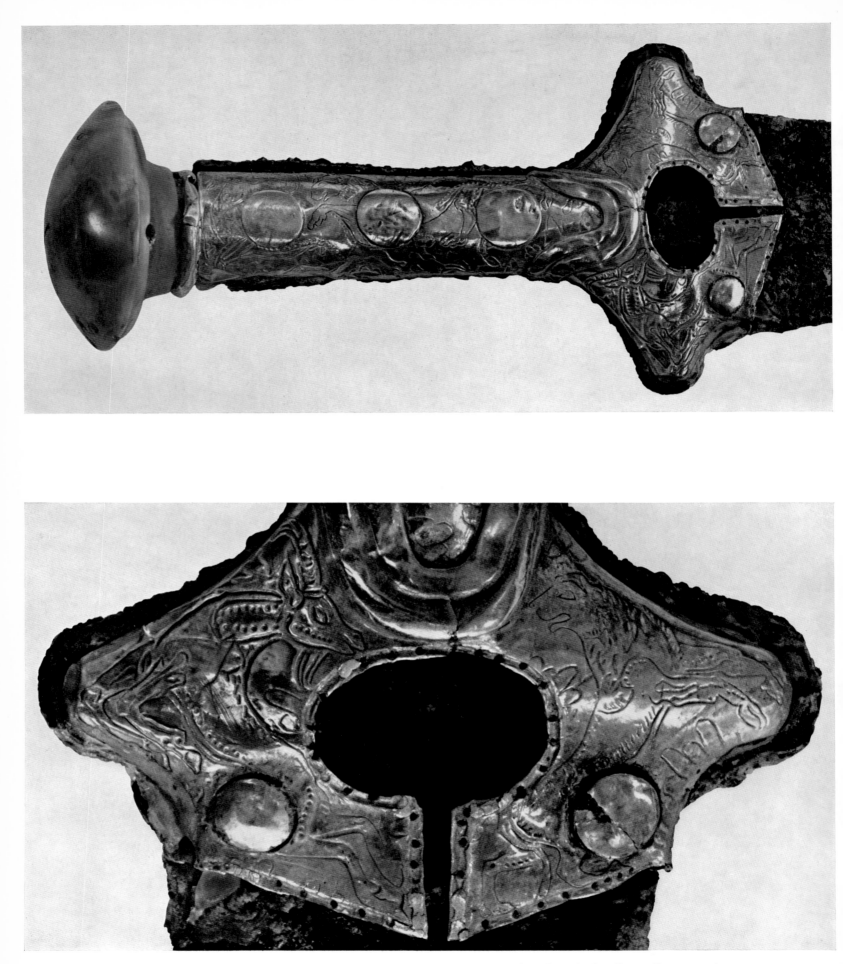

112   Gold handle of a bronze sword. Diameter of the agate knob 4.4 cm. Chased on the handle are lions pursuing goats.
Above – The complete handle. Below – The lower part. From grave 36 in the Zapher Papoura cemetery at Knossos. Late Minoan II

113 Above – Centre part of the gold handle from Zapher Papoura. See plate 112. Below – Bronze helmet with cheek-pieces. Overall height 38.6 cm. From a grave near Knossos. Late Minoan II

114 Above – Limestone frieze from the north-west gateway of the New Palace of Knossos. Height 19 cm. Late Minoan I–II.
Below, left – Upper part of a lamp with papyrus decoration. From the New Palace of Knossos.
Below, right – Part of a lamp with ivy decoration. From the South-East House at Knossos. Both Middle Minoan III – Late Minoan I

115   Above – Lamp in dark limestone. Diam. 12 cm. From the Palace of Hagia Triada. Late Minoan I–II.
Below – Alabaster triton shell. Length 30 cm. From the cemetery at Kalyvia near Phaistos. Late Minoan II

116 Above – Writing-tablets of clay. On the right with Linear A script, from Hagia Triada, Late Minoan I.
On the left with Linear B script, from Knossos. Late Minoan II. Life-size. Below – On the left, fragments of a steatite vase
with a Linear A inscription. From Apodoulou, South Crete. About 1550 B.C. On the right, fragment of a vase,
with Linear B inscription. From the New Palace of Knossos. After 1400 B.C. Probably a Mycenaean import

117 Seal-stones from various sites in Crete. Late Minoan I–III. Views of the originals and plaster impressions.
Enlarged three and a third times

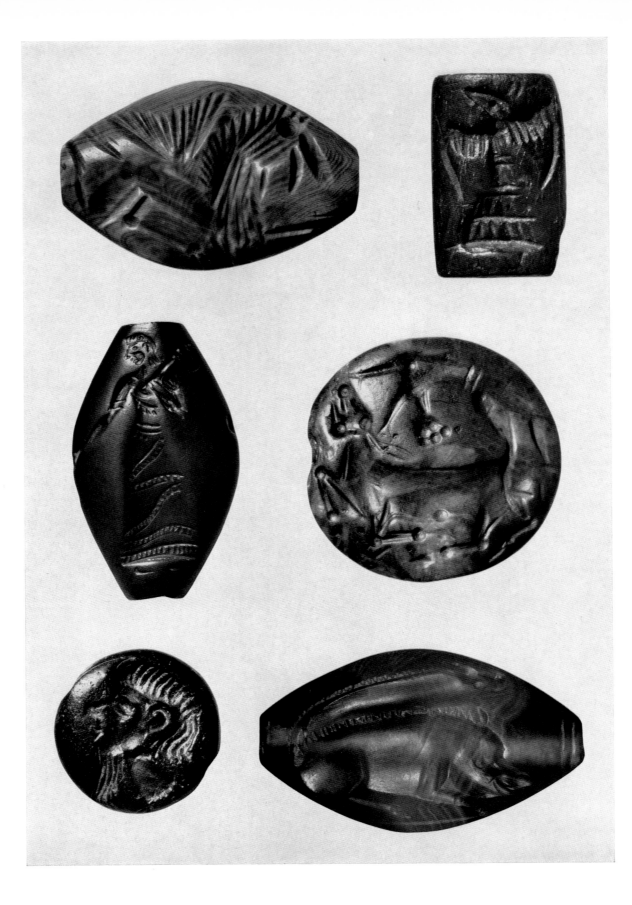

118   Seal-stones from various sites in Crete. Late Minoan I–III. Views of the original stones, three times life size

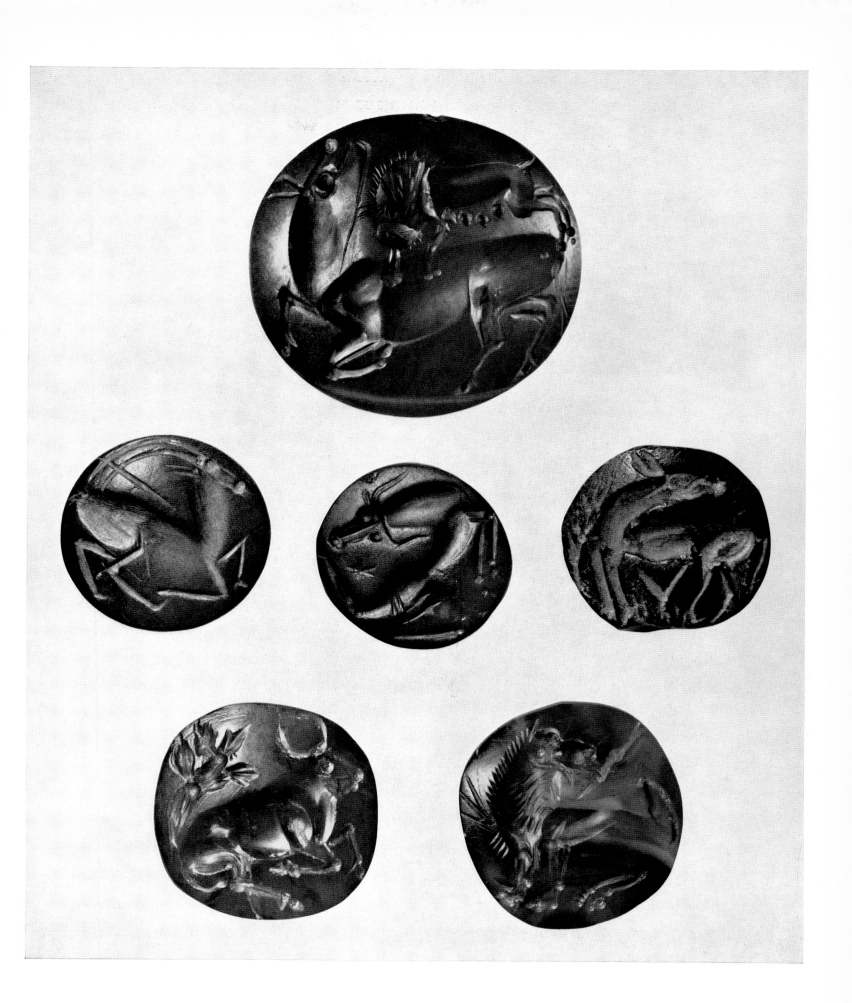

119   Seal-stones from various sites in Crete. Late Minoan I–III.
Views of the original stones, three times life size

THE PERIOD AFTER THE GREAT PALACES

LATE MINOAN III (1400–1100 B.C.) AND SUB-MINOAN (1100 to after 1000 B.C.)

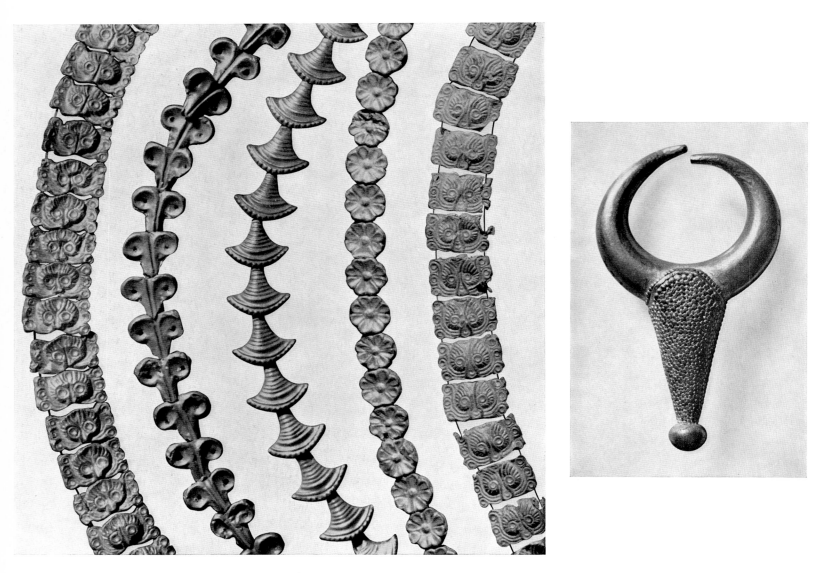

120   Left – Gold necklaces. From the Zapher Papoura graves near Knossos and the cemetery at Kalyvia near Phaistos.
Enlarged about two times. Right – Gold earring. From the cemetery at Mavro Spelio near Knossos.
Enlarged two and a half times. Both Late Minoan III, shortly after 1400 B.C.

121 Bronze statuette of a youth. Height 29 cm. From Griviglia near Rethymnon. Late Minoan III, probably about 1200 B.C.

122 Clay alabastron with water-birds. Height 23 cm. From the cemetery at Kalyvia near Phaistos. Late Minoan III, about 1300 B.C.

123   Clay alabastron with water-birds and fish. Height 28.5 cm. From the cemetery at Kalyvia near Phaistos.
Late Minoan III, about 1300 B.C.

124   Jewel box decorated with birds. Above, its lid. Height 10.3 cm. From a chamber-tomb at Pachyammos, Gulf of Mirabello, East Crete. Late Minoan III

125   Mixing-bowl. Height 24.5 cm. From a late chamber-tomb at Amnisos. Late Minoan III

126   Above – Bath-sarcophagus with an octopus and stylised papyrus. Upper length 121 cm. From Pachyammos.
Below – Chest-sarcophagus with lid; decorated with stylised papyrus, water-birds and fish.
From Vasilika Anogeia, Central Crete. Both Late Minoan III, about 1400–1350 B.C.

127 Above – Chest-sarcophagus with gabled lid. Upper length 123 cm. Horns of consecration, double axe and winged griffin.
From Palaikastro, East Crete. Late Minoan III, about 1400 B.C.
Below – Bath-sarcophagus with cattle. Upper length 117 cm. From Gournia. Late Minoan III

128   Female idol in clay with horns of consecration and birds on her head. Height 52 cm.
From Gazi, west of Heraklion. Late Minoan III

129 Female idol in clay. See plate 128. From Gazi, west of Heraklion. Late Minoan III

130   Idol in clay of the so-called Moon-goddess, probably goddess of fertility and healing. Height 77.5 cm.
From Gazi, west of Heraklion. Late Minoan III

131 Idol in clay of the so-called Moon-goddess, probably goddess of fertility and healing. See plate 130. From Gazi, west of Heraklion. Late Minoan III

132   Above – Three women in a chain dance, with a lyre-player. Height 13.1 cm. From Palaikastro, East Crete. Late Minoan III.
Below – Goddesses and votary. Height of the central figure 21 cm. From the Shrine of the Double Axes in Knossos. Late Minoan III

133   Above – Clay head. Height 8.5 cm. From the cave of Hermes Kranaios, Patsos, near Rethymnon. Late Minoan III.
Below – Rhyton in the form of a head. Height without the handle 15 cm. From the Palace of Phaistos.
Late Minoan III or a little earlier

134   Above – Clay donkey laden with jars. Height 17 cm.
Below – Clay bull. Height 37 cm. Both from the Palace of Phaistos. Late Minoan III

135   Female idol in clay. Height 63 cm. From Karphi, Mt. Dikte. Sub-Minoan, about 1100–1000 B.C.

136   Female idol in clay with movable legs, on her head the horns of consecration.
Height 67 cm. From Karphi, Mt. Dikte. Sub-Minoan, about 1100–1000 B.C.

137   Female idol in clay. See plate 136. From Karphi, Mt. Dikte. Sub-Minoan, about 1100–1000 B.C.

138 Clay model of a small shrine with the goddess within; the door shut. Height 22 cm. From Archanes, Central Crete.
Sub-Minoan, about 1100–1000 B.C. Giamalakis Collection

139 Clay model of a small shrine. See plate 138. The door is open and the goddess visible. Height 22 cm. From Archanes, Central Crete. Sub-Minoan, about. 1100–1000 B.C. Giamalakis Collection

140   Mt. Iyttos (modern Iuktas), mythical burial-place of Zeus

MYCENAEAN GREECE

141 Mycenae, Lion Gate of the Citadel

142 Mycenae. Above – Approach to the Lion Gate with part of the tower-like fortifications. Below – Upper Citadel and Palace

143   Mycenae. View from the Palace to the south-west over the Lower Town and the Argive plain

144   Mycenae. View from the east over the Megaron and the ante-room of the Palace;
in the Megaron the four column bases and hearth (restored) can be seen

145   Mycenae. The Shaft Grave Circle within the walls

146   Grave stela, originally over grave V of the Citadel of Mycenae. Hunting scene

147 Grave stela, originally over grave V of the Citadel of Mycenae. Setting out for the hunt

148 Mycenae. So-called Treasury of Atreus from the east. The entrance (dromos) and the mound covering the vaulted grave

149 Mycenae. Architectural pieces from the door to the Treasury of Atreus. Above – Parts of the plinth and spiral decoration above it. Below – Part of one of the half-columns at the side. In the British Museum, London

150   Mycenae. So-called Treasury of Atreus. Interior, with the entrance on the right, the grave-chamber on the left

151 Mycenae. So-called Treasury of Atreus. View into the roof

152 Citadel of Tiryns. View of the so-called Great Casemate on the south

153   Citadel of Tiryns. Above – View of the citadel from the east. Below – Ramp and east gate of the citadel

154 Citadel of Tiryns. Palace. Below – View from the propylon over the Great Court with the round altar.
Above – View from the Great Court over the main Megaron and the so-called Princes' Megara

155   Citadel of Tiryns. View from the north-east corner of the Palace area over the Princes' Megara to the main Megaron.
In the background the bay and mountains of the Argolid

156 The area of Pylos. Above – The bays of Bouphras (Voidokoila) and Pylos, from Koryphasion.
Below – The so-called Palace of Nestor at Englianos. In the background the Aigaleon range

157 Above – Pylos. Tholos tomb near the so-called Palace of Nestor at Englianos (the vault restored).
Below – Palaipylos (Volimidia, near Chora). One of the chamber-tombs in the Early Mycenaean cemetery

158   Acropolis of Arne (Gla). Above – View from the highest point of the Palace to the east. Below – Part of the north wall and gate

159   Acropolis of Arne (Gla). Above – North-west corner of the wall; on the left the supporting wall of the Palace, in the background Lake Copais, now drained. Below – North gate

160 Orchomenos. So-called Treasury of Minyas. View of the ruined tholos tomb. On the left the entrance to the grave-chamber

161   Orchomenos. So-called Treasury of Minyas. The ceiling of the grave-chamber in the tholos tomb

164   Gold funeral-mask of a Mycenaean prince. Height 20.5 cm. Citadel of Mycenae, grave IV

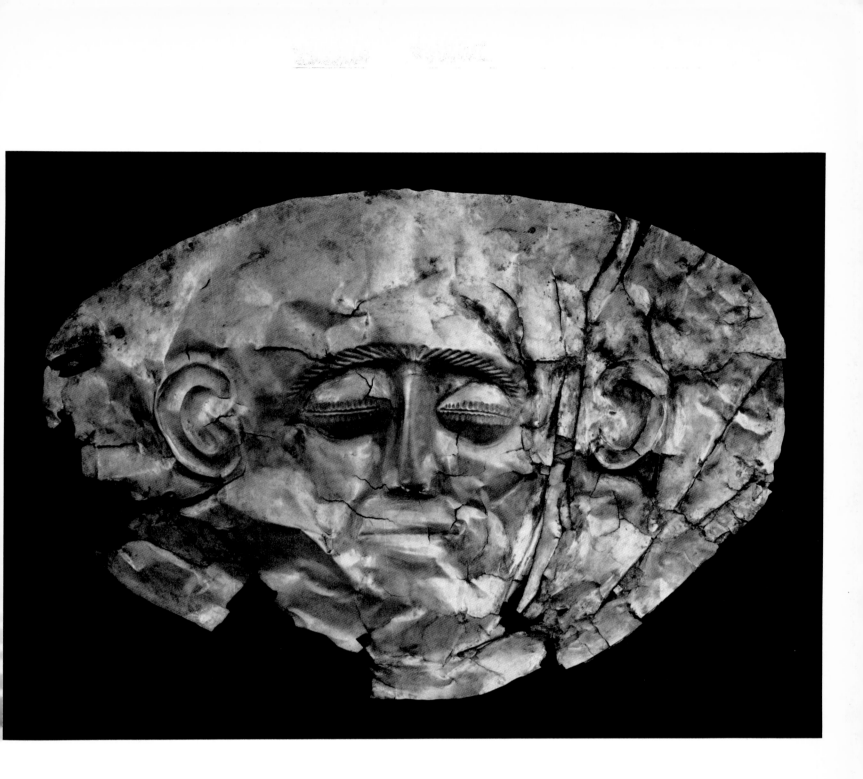

165   Gold funeral-mask of a Mycenaean prince. Height 21.5 cm. Citadel of Mycenae, grave IV

166   Gold funeral-mask of a Mycenaean prince. Height 30.3 cm. Citadel of Mycenae, grave IV

167   Electrum funeral-mask of a Mycenaean prince.
Height 22 cm. From grave Gamma in the newly-found Grave Circle B, Mycenae

174   Upper part of a silver funnel-shaped rhyton. Mycenaean soldiers storm a town. Overall height of the rhyton 22.9 cm.,
upper diameter 11.2 cm. Citadel of Mycenae, grave IV

175   Silver and gold rhyton in the form of bull's head. Height without the horns 15.5 cm. Citadel of Mycenae, grave IV

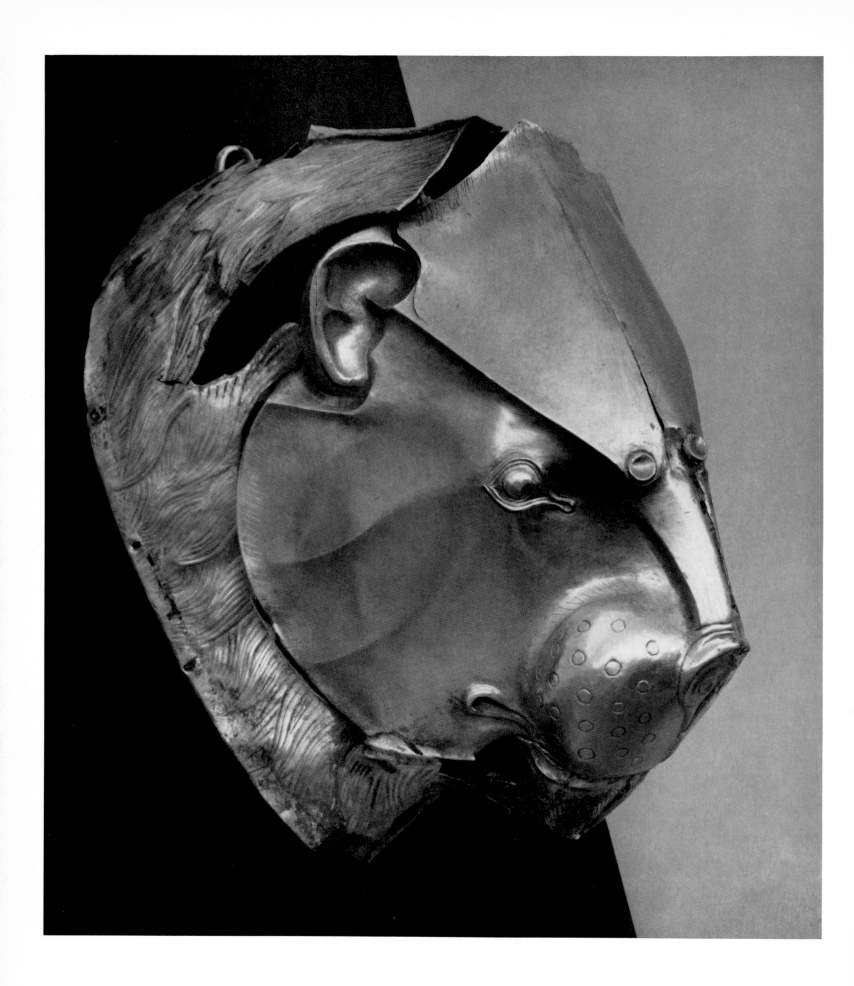

176   Gold rhyton in the form of a lion's head. Height 20 cm. Citadel of Mycenae, grave IV

177 Base silver rhyton in the form of a stag. Height to the mouth 16.2 cm. Citadel of Mycenae, grave IV

178   Gold cup I with the capture of a bull. From the tholos tomb at Vaphio in Laconia. About 1500 B.C.
Upper diameter 10.8 cm. Above – Bull attacks hunter and huntress. Below – Other side, bull in flight

179   Gold cup I with the capture of a bull. From the tholos tomb at Vaphio in Laconia. About 1500 B.C. Bull in a net

180   From gold cup I from Vaphio; bull attacking hunter and huntress. See plate 178 above

181   From gold cup I from Vaphio; bull in a net. See plate 179

182   Gold cup II. Bull captured by a decoy-cow. From the tholos tomb at Vaphio in Laconia. About 1500 B.C.
Upper diameter 10.8 cm. Above – Bull caught by its rear foot. Below – Hunter, and to his left the decoy-cow and a second bull

183   Gold cup II from the tholos tomb at Vaphio in Laconia. About 1500 B.C. Above – Decoy-cow and bull.
Below – Cautious approach of a third bull

184　From gold cup II from Vaphio; the hunter tethering the bull by its leg. See plate 182 below

185   From gold cup II from Vaphio; decoy-cow and bull. See plate 182 below and 183 above

186   Electrum cup with gold and niello, decorated with a bowl of flowers. Height 15.5 cm. Citadel of Mycenae, grave IV

187   Gold cup with rosettes in relief. Height without handle 15 cm. Citadel of Mycenae, grave IV

188   So-called Nestor-cup. On each handle a hawk with spread wings. Height without handles 14.5 cm.
Citadel of Mycenae, grave IV

189 Gold cup with dog's heads on the handles. Height about 15 cm. From a find near the Grave Circle A of the Citadel of Mycenae

190   Above – Gold cup. Height 9 cm. Below – Gold cup. Height without handle 12.6 cm. Both from the Citadel of Mycenae, grave IV

189   Gold cup with dog's heads on the handles. Height about 15 cm. From a find near the Grave Circle A of the Citadel of Mycenae

190   Above – Gold cup. Height 9 cm. Below – Gold cup. Height without handle 12.6 cm. Both from the Citadel of Mycenae, grave IV

191   Above – Gold rouge-vessel with handles. Height without the top handle 12.2 cm. Below – Gold cup. Height 7 cm.
Both from the Citadel of Mycenae, grave IV

192   Above – Gold cup decorated with running lions. Height without handle 12.8 cm.
Below – Gold kantharos. Height without handles 9.2 cm. Citadel of Mycenae, graves V and IV

193   Above – Gold cup. Height without handle 6.2 cm. Below – Tall gold cup. Height without handle 12 cm.
Citadel of Mycenae, graves IV and V

194 Above – Gold cup with spirals. Height without handle 11 cm. Below – Gold cup with plants. Height without handle 8.8 cm. Citadel of Mycenae, graves V and IV

195 Silver jug with spirals and stripes. Height 34.5 cm. Citadel of Mycenae, grave V

196 Above – Silver cup with inlaid male heads. Compare plate 204. Diam. 16.2 cm. From a chamber-tomb at Mycenae.
Below – Gold cup with sea-creatures. Diam. 17.3 cm. From Midea in the Argolid

197   Gold cup seen from beneath. See plate 196

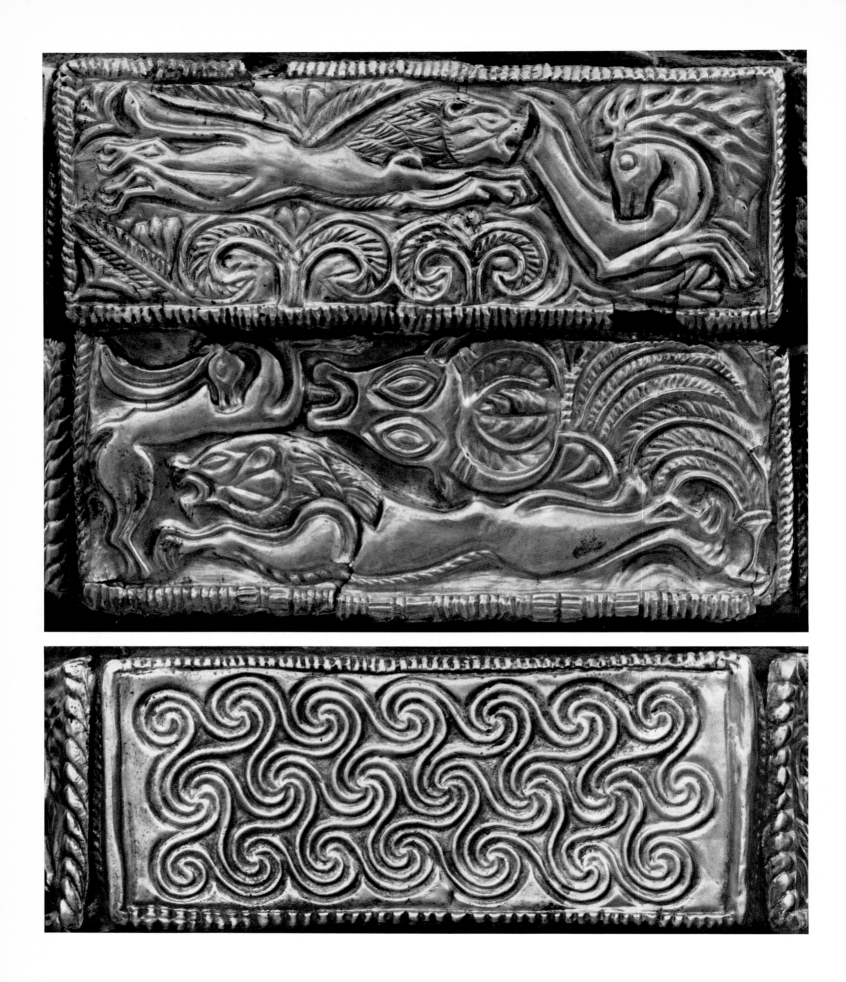

198   Gold plaques from the box in plate 199. Twice life-size

199   Below – Six-sided wooden box with gold plaques. About life-size. Citadel of Mycenae, grave V. Above – Gold recumbent lion probably from the handle of a cup. About three times life-size. From a finding near the Grave Circle A of the Citadel of Mycenae

200   Left – Silver pin with gold decoration: a goddess with arms outstretched towards stylised branches.
Height of the decorated attachment 6.7 cm., of the pin 21.5 cm. Citadel of Mycenae, grave III.
Right – Gold ornaments in the form of stylised nautili. Somewhat more than life-size. From Mycenae

201 Above – Gold armlet for a man. Diam. 9.3 cm. Below – Gold earrings. Diam. 7.5 cm. Citadel of Mycenae, graves IV and III

202   Repoussé gold discs, probably dress ornaments. About life-size. Citadel of Mycenae, grave III

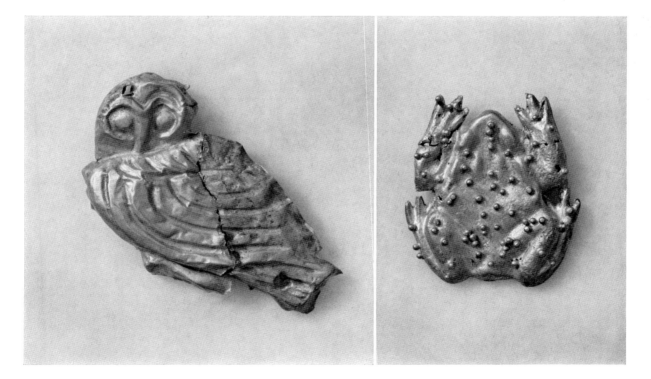

203   Above – Gold jewellery. One and a third times life size. From Prosymna in the Argolid. Below – Gold owl and frog.
Three and a third times life-size. From Kakovatos, Triphylia

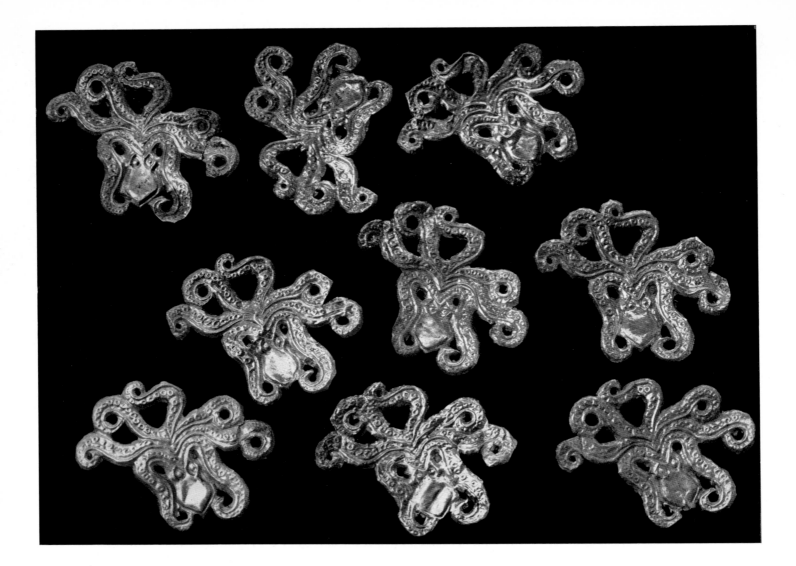

204   Above – Gold ornaments in the form of octopuses. Two-thirds life size. Citadel of Mycenae, grave IV. Below – Heads of gold and black niello, probably from the decoration of a cup like that on plate 196 above. About one and a third times life-size. From Pylos

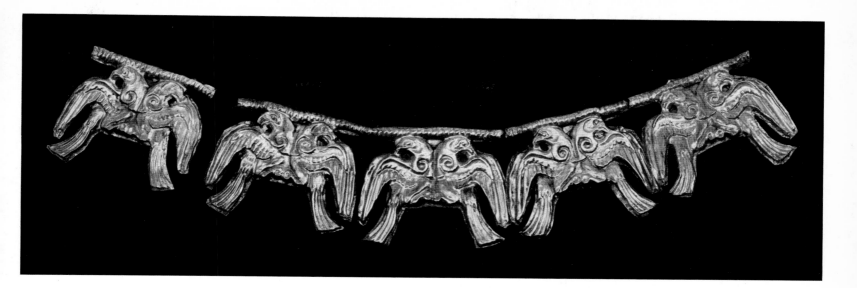

205   Above – Gold necklace; pairs of eagles. Nine-tenths life-size. Centre – Gold ornaments; altar with horns of consecration and doves.
Nine-tenths life-size. Below – Gold ornaments; female figures. Citadel of Mycenae, graves V and IV and III

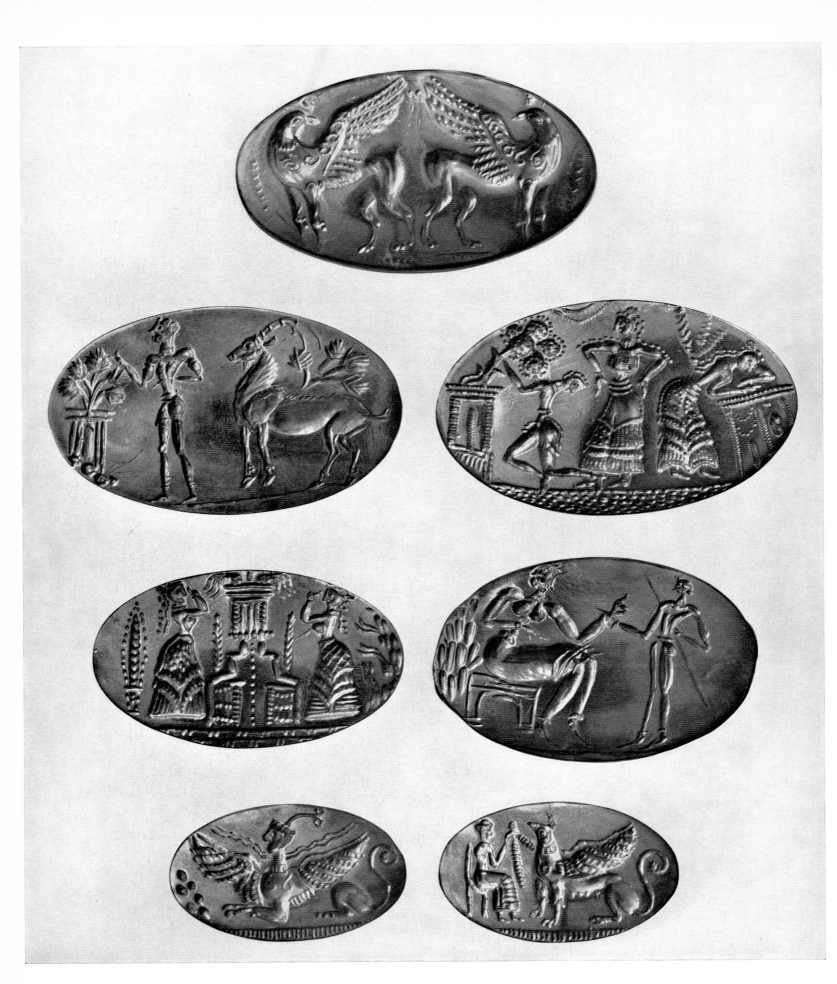

206 Gold signet rings from Mycenae. View of the devices on the originals. Three and a quarter times life-size

207   Gold signet rings. Above – From Tiryns. Three times life-size.
Below – From Mycenae. Four times life-size. Both from the originals

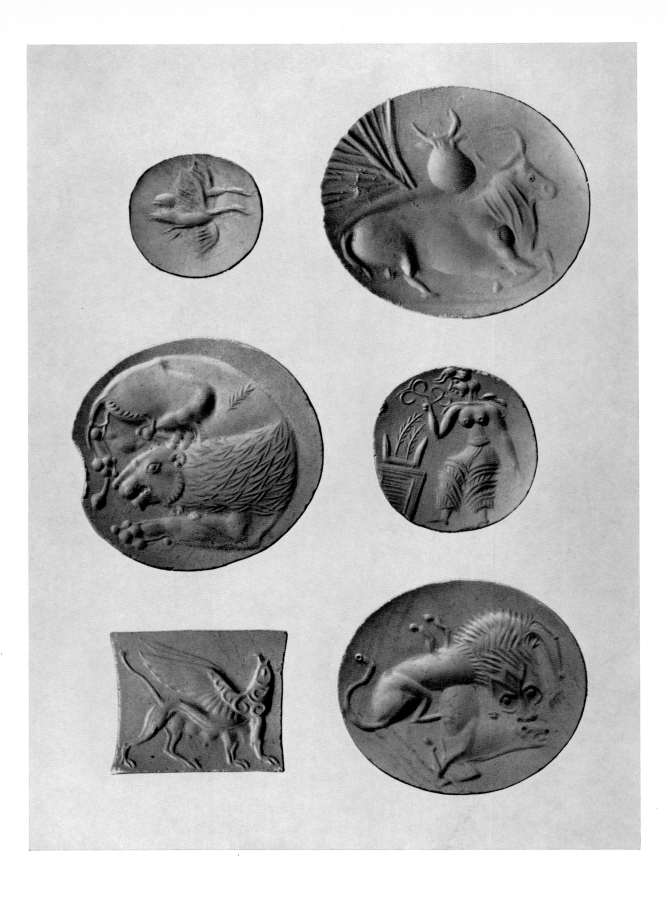

208 Seal stones; amethyst, carnelian, sardonyx. From Pylos. From plaster impressions, two and a half times life-size

209   Gold seals. From Pylos. Views of the originals, three and a half times life-size

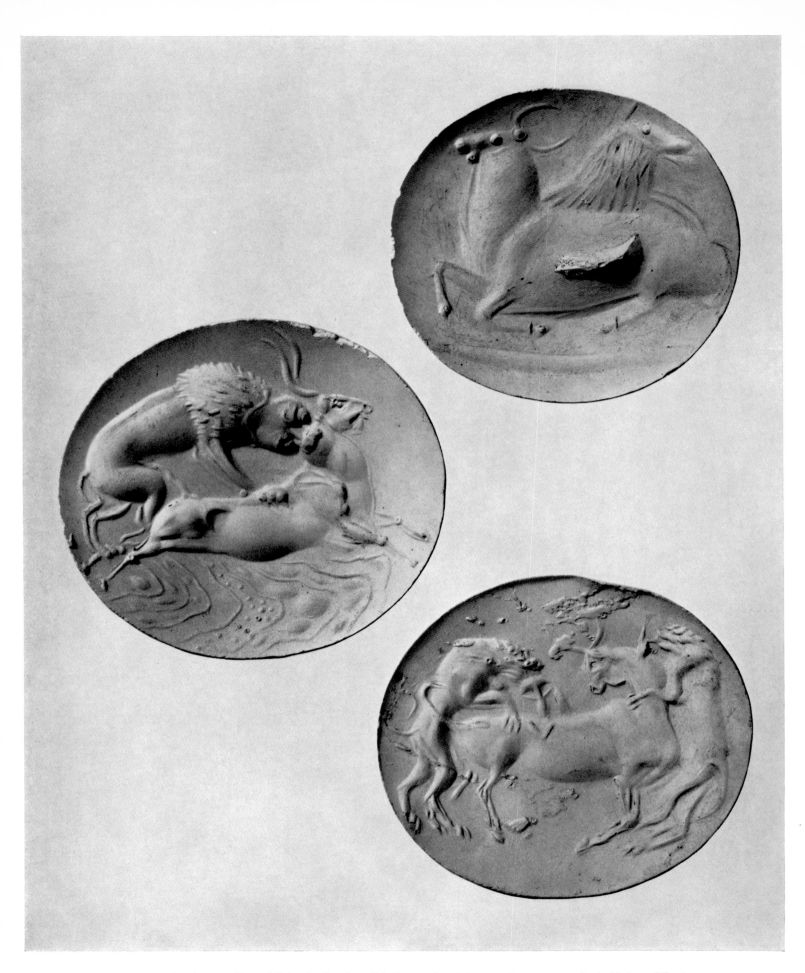

210   Seals of agate. From Midea in the Argolid. From plaster impressions, two and a half times life-size

211 Seals of various semi-precious stones. From Vaphio in Laconia. About 1500 B.C.
From plaster impressions, two and a half times life-size

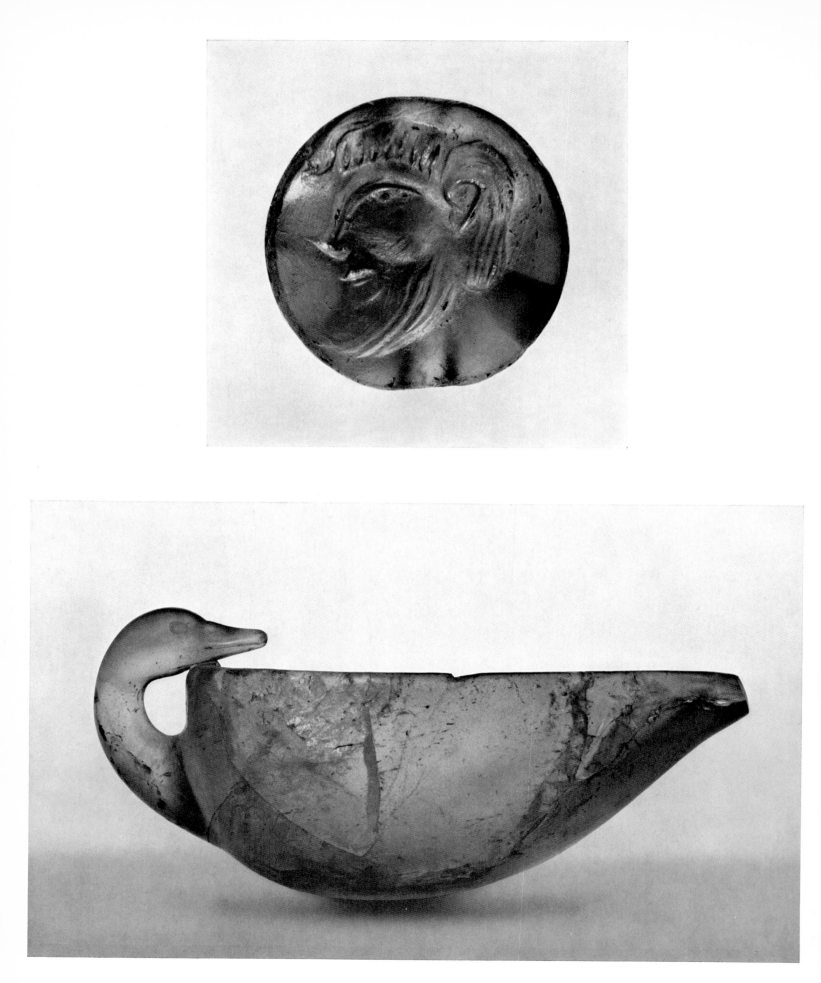

212　Above – Seal-stone of amethyst; from the original, eight times life-size.　Below – Rock-crystal dish in the form of a duck.
Length 13.2 cm. Both from the newly-found Grave Circle B, Mycenae, graves Gamma and Omicron

213   Alabaster vase. Height with handle 24.3 cm. Citadel of Mycenae, grave IV

214   Ivory head of a warrior wearing a boras'-tusk helmet.   About three times life-size. From Mycenae

215　Ivory head of a warrior wearing a boars'-tusk helmet. About three times life-size. From Spata, East Attica

216 Ivory relief plaques. Above – Winged sphinx. Below – Bull attacked by a lion. About three and a half times life-size.
From Spata, East Attica

217 Ivory figure of a goddess seated on a rock. About twice life-size. From Mycenae

218   Ivory group of the divine child watched over by two nurses. From behind.
Twice life-size. From Mycenae. 15th c. B.C.

219 Ivory group of the divine child watched over by two nurses. From the front.
Twice life-size. From Mycenae. 15th c. B.C.

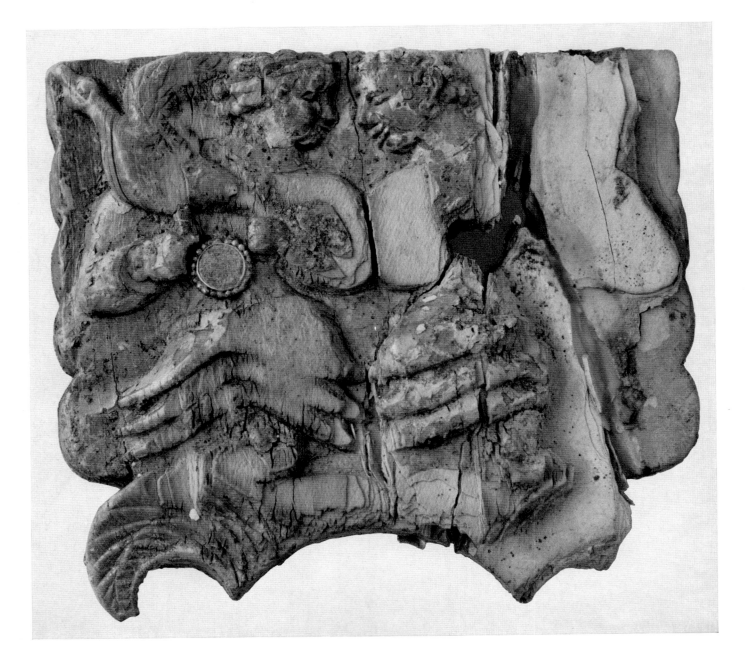

220   Fragment of the ivory handle of a mirror. Two women with a dove seated on palm branches. About four times life-size.
From the so-called Tomb of Clytemnestra, Mycenae

219   Ivory group of the divine child watched over by two nurses. From the front.
Twice life-size. From Mycenae. 15th c. B.C.

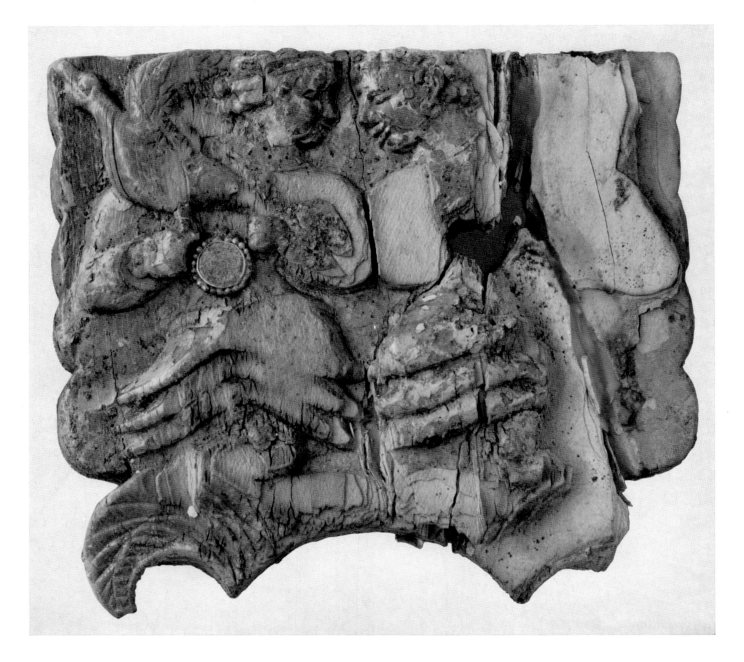

220　Fragment of the ivory handle of a mirror. Two women with a dove seated on palm branches. About four times life-size. From the so-called Tomb of Clytemnestra, Mycenae

221 Ivory handle of a bronze mirror. Two women seated on a palm tree. About twice life-size.
From the so-called Tomb of Clytemnestra, Mycenae

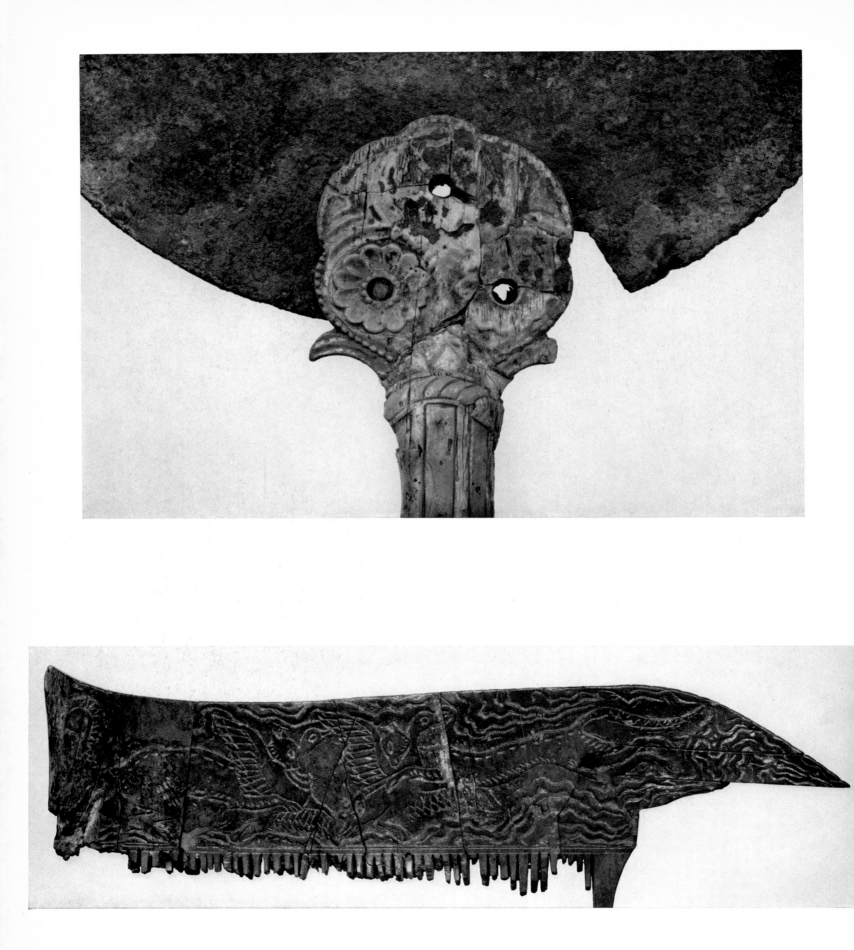

222   Above – Ivory handle of a bronze mirror, with rosettes. Below – Ivory comb: cats hunting wild ducks.
Both from Rutsi near Pylos

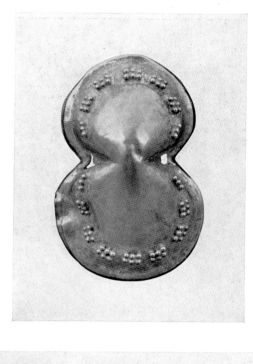

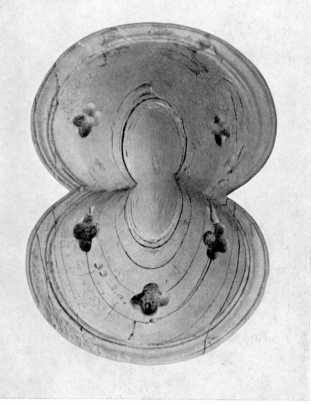

223   Left – Ivory pyxis with spiral decoration. From Rutsi near Pylos. About life size c. 1500 B.C.
Right – Miniature shields of gold from Pylos, and of ivory from Mycenae

224   Lead figure of a youth. Height 12 cm. From a grave at Kampos, Laconia. See plate 225

225   Lead figure of a youth. Height 12 cm. From a grave at Kampos, Laconia. See plate 224

226 Fragmentary fresco depicting a women's procession. Height about 30 cm. From the Palace of Tiryns

227   Tall vase with three handles, decorated with nautili. Height 78 cm. From Kakovatos, Triphylia

228   Tall vase with three handles, decorated with palms. Height about 45 cm. From Deiras in the Argolid

229   Tall jug with stylised ivy branches. Height 33 cm. Citadel of Mycenae, grave I

230 Above – Beaked jug. Height 31 cm. Below – Spouted vase. Height about 21.5 cm. Both from Rutsi near Pylos

231 Above – Small three-handled jar. Height 24.5 cm.
Below – Spouted vase with three handles. Height without handles 28.5 cm. Both from Prosymna in the Argolid

232   Crater with soldiers. Side view. Height 41 cm. From the Citadel of Mycenae. About 1200 B.C.

233   Crater with soldiers. From the front. Height 41 cm. From the Citadel of Mycenae. About 1200 B.C.

234 Vase fragment with warriors in a chariot. From Mycenae

235 Three-legged rhyton decorated with two stag's heads and a bull's head. Height 22.4 cm. From Palaipylos.
In the Chora Museum near Pylos

236 Libation vase in the form of a winged boot. Height about 13 cm. From Voula in Attica

NOTES ON THE PLATES

The scales indicated on text figures are marked in metres and multiples of metres

MAP OF CRETE showing the main sites.

114

CRETE

Unless otherwise stated all objects are in the Archaeological Museum of Heraklion

I

THE MASSIF OF IDA seen from Phaistos

In the foreground is part of the Messara plain with its groves of olives. The twin peak of Ida is 8179 ft. high; behind it lies the plateau Nida, which retains its ancient name. Below the peak on the right is the cave of Kamares, where the so-called Kamares ware was first found. Out of sight on the north flank is the Idaean Cave, the famous cult-place in which the child-god Zeus was said to have been brought up, hidden from his father Kronos, and nursed by the goat Amaltheia.

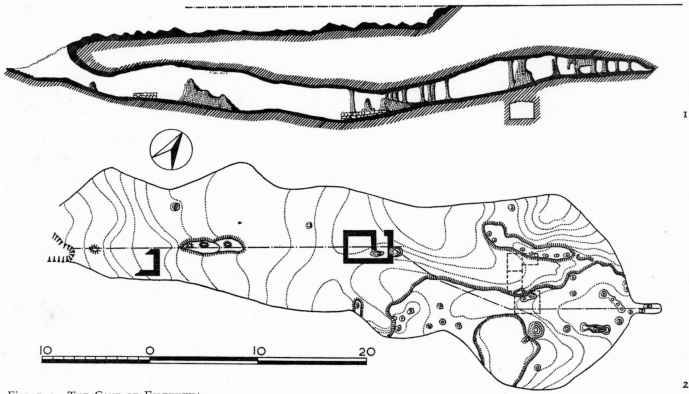

1

2

Figs. 1, 2   THE CAVE OF EILEITHYIA.
1 Section, with the entrance to the left and the present ground surface over the cave shown above; at the right is the hypogaeum.
2, Ground plan. After *Marinatos*.

1; Figs. 1–2

CAVE OF EILEITHYIA AT AMNISOS

The cave had long ago been suspected by J. Hazzidakis but it was first excavated and identified in 1929-30. It is 4 miles east of Heraklion and easily accessible. Its length from east to west is 62.3 m., its breadth up to 12 m. It contains stalactites which bear doubtful traces of ritual attention. The only finds were of pottery which offers an unbroken sequence from the Neolithic to the Early Christian periods. In front of the cave are remains of cult-buildings and simple structures of the early Greek period.

The plates show, above: the centre of the cave, seen from the west, with two stalagmites which had been walled off (the wall is visible at the left); below: two stalactites at the limit of the cave, beneath which there is a narrow entrance to an area which was found to be full of pottery.

Praktika 1929, p. 94, and 1930, p. 91—Nilsson, *Minoan-Mycenaean Religion*, 2nd edition, p. 58.—*Archäologischer Anzeiger* 1930, p. 157, fig. 32.

THE PERIOD BEFORE THE GREAT PALACES

NEOLITHIC (5000–3100 B.C.), SUB-NEOLITHIC (3100–2800 B.C.) AND EARLY MINOAN (2800–2000 B.C.)

2 above

CLAY FIGURE. From Knossos. Height 9.3 cm. Late Neolithic.

The Neolithic finds at Knossos are from the deep, partially excavated levels beneath the palace courts. The fabric is grey, sometimes yellowish or blackish, with incised decoration. There is no painting.

2 below

CUP WITH INCISED DECORATION. From Knossos. Diam. 20.5 cm. Late Neolithic.

One of the rare pieces preserved intact.

Evans, *Palace of Minos* I, p. 46, fig. 121a–c.

3

TWO EARLY MINOAN CIRCULAR TOMBS AT HAGIA TRIADA

These are among the earliest found and they yielded rich finds, especially the larger one to the east (diam. 9 m., walls up to 2 m. thick). The other is poorer and probably later. This type of grave is typical of the Messara plain and near by. Only a few months ago two new examples were excavated at Leben on the south coast of the island. Xanthoudides saw these tombs as tholoi, but this is hardly likely as they stand above ground and some are exceptionally large (Grave B at Platanos is 18 m. across, including the thickness of the walls). Although the walls do lean inwards their roofs must have been of timber and branches. They were built in the second phase of the Early Minoan period. There is one at Krassi on the north coast which may be older but it is more like the Cycladic graves than those of the Messara. They were used for several generations, into the Kamares period. The largest held hundreds of burials.

Paribeni, in *Monumenti Antichi* 14, 1904, p. 677.—Stefani and Banti, in *Annuario Atene* 13–14, p. 147.—The main source is Xanthoudides, *The Vaulted Tombs of Mesarà*, 1924.

4

TWO HIGH-FOOTED CUPS. Pyrgos style. From the cave-grave at Pyrgos near Nirou Chani in Central Crete. Clay. Height of each 22 cm. Early Minoan I, about 2800–2600 B.C.

The two cups with tall feet are of black clay and were decorated by burnishing. They belong with the earliest types of the Bronze Age. On many of them the decoration seems to be in imitation of wood and we may assume wooden prototypes for the shape.

Xanthoudides, in *Deltion* 4, 1918, p. 159.—Evans, *Palace of Minos* I, p. 59.

5 above

MATT-PAINTED BEAKED JUGS. Hagios Onouphrios style. From the cave-burial at Kyparissi, near ancient Lykastos, Central Crete. Clay. Heights 18.5 and 19 cm. Early Minoan I, about 2700–2500 B.C.

Alexiou, in *Kret. Chronika* 5, 1951, p. 277.

5 below

PAN WITH INCISED DECORATION. Imported from the Cyclades. Provenience unknown. Diam. 12.2 cm. Early Minoan II–III. Giamalakis Collection.

6

LID OF A PYXIS IN GREEN STEATITE. From the island of Mochlos, Gulf of Mirabello, East Crete. Diam. 12 cm. Early Minoan II, about 2400 B.C.

Mochlos is now an island but in antiquity it was a peninsula. The lid lay in Grave 1 where there was no other pottery to which it might have belonged. It is likely then that its box was originally of wood, perhaps replacing a broken stone one. The sleeping dog which serves as a handle is an important example of early minor sculpture. There are four holes in the lid for string or wire fastening it to lugs on the box.

Seager, *Mochlos*, p. 21, fig. 5.—Evans, *Palace of Minos* I, p. 94, fig. 62.

II
EARLY MINOAN STONE VASES

Left: SPOUTED BOWL OF GREY VEINED LIME-STONE. Height 7.2 cm.
Right: JUG OF POLYCHROME STALACTITIC STONE. Height 12 cm.
Both from the island of Mochlos, Gulf of Mirabello, East Crete. Early Minoan II, about 2400 B.C.

Mochlos is the most important source of these fine polychrome stone vases.

Seager, *Mochlos*, pls. 4-5.

7
SCHIST PYXIS. From the cave-grave at Maronia, East Crete. Diam. 17 cm. Early Minoan II, about 2500 B.C.

The pyxis is made in three parts, the lower two for the bi-conical body, the third for the lid. On the lower part are incised triangles such as we see, more deeply cut, on the lid from Mochlos (plate 6). The upper part and lid are decorated with running spirals in imitation of gold filigree. Four holes in the lid are for fastening the handle. The pyxis was found in the course of blasting for road-building in a small cave which must have been a tomb. This might well be an import from the Cyclades, but it is not certainly so.

Marinatos, in *Archäologischer Anzeiger* 1937, p. 228, fig. 7.

8 above
'TEA-POT' WITH FIRE-MOTTLED DECORA-TION.
Vasiliki style. From Vasiliki, East Crete. Height 14.5 cm. Early Minoan II, about 2500 B.C.

The 'tea-pots' are innovations of oriental origin. Characteristic is the combination of mottled decoration on the body and painted decoration on the spout of the vase.

Seager, *Vassiliki*, p. 10, pl. 34, 6.—Evans, *Palace of Minos* I, pl. 77.

8 below
JUG WITH WHITE-PAINTED DECORATION.
From the island of Mochlos, Gulf of Mirabello, East Crete. Height 19 cm. Early Minoan III, about 2200 B.C.

This shows the beginning of the light-on-dark style. The spiral decoration is probably inspired by the Cyclades.

Seager, *Mochlos*, p. 46, fig. 19.—Evans, *Palace of Minos* I, p. 109, fig. 76.

III
BEAKED JUG WITH MOTTLED DECORATION.

Height 33.5 cm. Vasiliki style. From Vasiliki, East Crete. Early Minoan II, about 2500–2400 B.C.

The jug has a modelled 'eye' on the shoulder at either side of the handle-attachment. Compare the vases in plates 21 and VIII.

Seager, *Vassiliki*, p. 10, pl. 34.

9
CULT VASE IN THE FORM OF THREE DOVES. Clay. Provenience unknown. Height 12 cm. Early Minoan III. Giamalakis Collection.

The clay is not well-fired and there are traces of black paint.

10 above
CLAY RHYTON IN THE FORM OF A BUST. From the island of Mochlos, Gulf of Mirabello, East Crete. Height 17.5 cm. Early Minoan III.

Its white paint led its discoverer, and Evans, to call the figure female. The features, slight, breast-like nipples and headdress (compare Seager, *Mochlos*, p. 49, fig. 21, which is male) suggest that this cannot be true, however surprising.

Seager, *Mochlos*, p. 64, figs. 32, 34.—Evans, *Palace of Minos* I, p. 116, fig. 84.

10 below
CLAY SHIP. From the island of Mochlos, Gulf of Mirabello, East Crete. Length 20 cm. Early Minoan III.

Its shape and four rudder-posts show that this type of vessel could change direction without turning.

American Journal of Archaeology 1909, p. 279, fig. 2.—Marinatos, in *Bull. Corr. Hellénique* 57, 1933, p. 173, no. 20.

11
EARLY CYCLADIC IDOLS
Left: from a find at Teke, north of Knossos. Heights, above 5 cm., below 8.3 cm.
Right: from the circular tomb at Koumasa, south Central Crete. Height 23.5 cm.
Both Early Minoan II, about 2400–2200 B.C.

Several marble idols and vases were imported from the nearby Cyclades. They have been found in the circular tombs of the Messara, and some had already been repaired in antiquity. An exceptional find is that at Teke, between Knossos and the sea. Several other idols and bronze daggers were found here with no associated buildings or signs of a tomb. They may have been part of a consignment from the coast to the Messara.

Left: Marinatos, in *Archäologischer Anzeiger* 1933, p. 299, figs. 9–14. Right: Xanthoudides, *The Vaulted Tombs of Mesarà*, pl. 7, 1.

12

IVORY SEAL IN THE FORM OF AN APE. Probably from Lasithi. Height 3.2 cm. Early Minoan III. Giamalakis Collection.

An interesting and typical example of the seal-engraving of the last phase of the Early Minoan period. The time at which it was bought by Dr. Giamalakis and other considerations suggest that it is from the Trapeza cave in Lasithi, although very similar seals have been found in the Messara (e.g. Evans, *Palace of Minos* I, p. 118, fig. 87, 1). The device is of two stylised scorpions with five bands of running spirals below.

Xenaki and Sakellariou, 'Cachets Giamalakis', *Études Crétoises* X, p. 1, no. 2, pl. 1.

13

EARLY MINOAN GOLD JEWELLERY

Above left: LEAFY SPRAY AND BLOSSOMS. From the island of Mochlos, Gulf of Mirabello, East Crete. About 1 ½ times life-size. Early Minoan II.

Above right: FROG WITH GRANULATION AND BEAD WITH SPIRALS. From the circular tomb at Koumasa, and from Kalathiana, Messara. Both 3 ½ times life-size. Early Minoan II–III.

Below: PENDANT IN THE FORM OF TWO HORNETS, holding a granulated honeycomb. From the cemetery at Mallia. Width 4.7 cm. Early Minoan III, about 2000 B.C.

The spray and blossoms are elegant work. The frog and hornets are very early examples of granulation, and there is filigree-work on the hornets and the bead with spirals.

Seager, *Mochlos*, pp. 41–43, and *passim*, figs. 10, 11.—Evans, *Palace of Minos* I, pp. 96–98.—Xanthoudides, *The Vaulted Tombs of Mesarà*, pl. 4, 8.—Demargne, *Mallia* I, p. 54.—Evans, *Palace of Minos* IV, p. 75, fig. 48.

THE PERIOD OF THE OLD PALACES

MIDDLE MINOAN I AND II (2000–1700 B.C.)

14 above
CLAY ANIMAL. From a circular tomb at Porti, Messara. Height 19.5 cm. Middle Minoan I.

The creature cannot be certainly identified. The tail and muzzle show that it is no wild goat, as is often suggested. It is more likely a greyhound. The long ears are found on contemporary Egyptian representations of Saluki hounds.

Xanthoudides, *The Vaulted Tombs of Mesarà*, p. 62, no. 5114.

14 below
CLAY RHYTON IN THE FORM OF A BULL WITH ACROBATS. From a circular tomb at Porti, Messara. Length 16 cm. Middle Minoan I.

This is a scene from the life of the Messara herdsmen, and perhaps a forerunner of the later, more elaborate representations of the bull-games. Several other examples are known, from Porti and Koumasa, including another such with three acrobats.

Xanthoudides, *The Vaulted Tombs of Mesarà*, p. 62, no. 5052.—Evans, *Palace of Minos* I, p. 189, fig. 137, 137d.

15
CLAY FIGURES from the mountain sanctuary at Petsofa and the oval house at Chamaizi in Sitia, East Crete. Height of the largest 23 cm. Middle Minoan I.

The most important series of clay figures of men and animals are from East Crete, especially the mountain sanctuaries. The human figures, men and women, are worshippers; the animals are votive. Representations of human limbs, from Petsofa, represent prayers for healing. The statuettes give us a valuable picture of contemporary costume and are not without artistic interest. The largest shown is from the famous oval house at Chamaizi, a Middle Minoan mansion which seems to have had its private chapel.

Myres, in *British School Annual* 9, 1902/3, pl. 8, p. 10 (Petsofa).—Xanthoudides, in *Ephemeris* 1906, p. 138, fig. 4 (Chamaizi).

HEADS FROM FIGURES OF WOMEN. Clay. Heights, top left and centre 12 cm., right 13 cm.
CLAY FIGURE OF A PRAYING WOMAN. Height 26.4 cm. Both from Piskokephalo in Sitia, East Crete. Middle Minoan I–II.

The head shown in profile at the left and frontal in the centre is a recent find, illustrated here for the first time. The head on the right has been known longer. These, with the worshipper, are from the mountain sanctuary at Piskokephalo and should be Middle Minoan I–II, although the recent excavator of the shrine takes them for Middle Minoan III.

Platon, in *Kret. Chronika* 5, 1951, pl. 4, 1 and 6, 1, 4. The head on the right: Müller, *Der Polos*, pl. 1, pp. 1–2.—Bossert, *Altkreta*, 3rd edition, fig. 286.

18

MIDDLE MINOAN OFFERINGS
Above: CLAY BOWL WITH SHEPHERD AND FLOCK. Diam. 19.5 cm.
Below: CLAY BOWL WITH A FLYING BIRD. Diam. 11.3 cm.
Both from Palaikastro, East Crete. Middle Minoan I.

Bowls with modelled clay figures of animals within, as the dove here, are known from chance finds, from graves (the 'Bone-Enclosure' at Palaikastro) and sanctuaries. The upper bowl is unique. Of it Rodenwaldt suggested that the shepherd who offered this representation of himself and his flock had perhaps been saved from a heavy storm. It could as readily, of course, be a prayer for the well-being of the man himself and his 200-odd sheep. Human figures in the typical pose of worshippers are also found in some simple bowls, either as thank-offerings or appeals for help. The last are certainly of about 1600 B.C. if not later.

Bosanquet, in *British School Annual* 8, 1901/2, p. 294.—Evans, *Palace of Minos* I, p. 180, fig. 130.—Rodenwaldt, in *Essays in Aegean Archaeology in honour of Sir Arthur Evans*, 1927, p. 100, pl. 17.

IV

EARLY MIDDLE MINOAN POLYCHROME POTTERY
Above: SPOUTED JUG DECORATED WITH FISH. Earliest Kamares style. From Vasiliki, East Crete. Height 10.5 cm. Middle Minoan I, about 2000 B.C.

Simple natural forms, as of fish, were particularly favoured as decoration at this time.

Seager, *Vassiliki* (Transactions of University of Pennsylvania, 1907, II, 2), p. 125, pl. 30b.—Evans, *Palace of Minos* I, p. 182, fig. 131.

Below left: SMALL JUG WITH MOTTLED DECORATION. Vasiliki style. From Gournia, East Crete. Height 12.2 cm. Early Minoan III—Middle Minoan I.

Gournia, 38, pl. 6, 1.

Below right: DOUBLE-HANDLED JUG. Barbotine style. From Hagia Triada. Height 16.5 cm. Late Middle Minoan I.

On vases of this style the surface is modelled in dots or waves and the painted decoration often polychrome, as on this, one of the best preserved examples.

Banti, in *Annuario Atene* 13–14, pl. 17c.

19

MIDDLE MINOAN OFFERINGS
Above: BELL-SHAPED CULT OBJECT WITH 'HORNS'. From a votive pit at the ancient Harbour of Knossos. Faience. Height 8 cm. Middle Minoan I.
This new find is the first bell-shaped example of a class of object, certainly of some religious significance, which has been found in the circular tomb at Vorou. On this a human face is painted, which the excavator took for a mask.

Centre and below: CLAY CATTLE, painted. Kamares style. From the Old Palace of Phaistos. Height of each 21 cm. Middle Minoan II.

The painted decoration on the animals is in white.

Platon, in *Revue Archéologique* 1949 (Mélanges Picard), p. 835, fig. 1.—On its significance: Marinatos, in *Deltion* 13, 1930/31, p. 158, fig. 21.—Nilsson, *Minoan-Mycenaean Religion*, 2nd edition, p. 191 and addenda on p. XXIII.

20

KAMARES VASES
Above: SPOUTED VASE WITH PAINTED DAISIES. From the Kamares Cave on Ida. Height 12 cm.
Below: CUP. From the Old Palace of Phaistos. Height 16.2 cm. Both Middle Minoan II

The upper vase, from the Kamares cave itself, is interesting for the painted daisies which are almost identical with those on a Kamares vase found in an unplundered tomb at Abydos in Egypt. With this were cylinder-seals bearing the cartouches of Sesostris III (1878–1841) and Amenemhet III (1842–1797). The dates are an important indication for the date of the developed Kamares style of Middle Minoan II.

Dawkins and Laistner, in *British School Annual* 19, 1912/13, pl. 2, 1.—Evans, *Palace of Minos* I, p. 268, fig. 199 and pl. 4.

21

WHITE-PAINTED BEAKED JUG. Kamares style. From the Old Palace of Phaistos. Height 27 cm. Middle Minoan II.

This jug is similar to that on plate VIII in having modelled 'eyes' at the handle-attachment, but it is simpler and only painted white. The two carefully painted, daisy-like stars associate the piece closely with the finest Kamares vases.

Pernier, *Festòs* I, p. 254, fig. 134, etc.

22

VASE WITH STRAINER AND FEEDING SPOUT. Kamares style. From the Old Palace of Phaistos. Clay. Height 13.8 cm. Middle Minoan II.

The wavy rim with the floral decoration suggests that this elaborate vase was modelled after a metal original. Liquid filtered through the sieve could be drunk through the pipe-like mouthpiece. The differently set handles and the oblique spout facilitated feeding.

Pernier, *Festòs* I, colour pl. 34.

V

SPOUTED JAR. Kamares style. From the Old Palace of Phaistos. Height 12.5 cm. Middle Minoan II.

An exceptionally fine and well-preserved vase.

Levi, in *Bolletino d'Arte* II, 1955, colour pl. opposite p. 144.

VI above
Left: SMALL CUP. Height 5 cm.
Right: EGG-SHELL CUP. Height 7.5 cm.

Both of the Kamares style. From the Old Palaces of Phaistos (left) and Knossos (right). Middle Minoan II. In the Kamares period there are small vases with walls as thin as egg-shells. The finest were made in the potteries at Knossos, as the example on the right here which Evans describes as 'admirable in the harmony of its design and hues, on which shell-like sprays, creamy white and crimson-veined, are linked with rosettes reserved in the lustrous black ground'.

Evans, *Palace of Minos* I, pp. 241–242, colour pl. 2a.—Pernier, *Festòs* I, p. 305, fig. 180.

VI below
SPOUTED VASE. Kamares style. From the Old Palace of Knossos. Height 18 cm. Middle Minoan II.

The especial charm of this vase springs from the lustre of the red and white paint over the black, and the contrast of the floral decoration with the linear zigzags.

VII

SPOUTED JAR. Kamares style. From the Old Palace of Knossos. Height 23.5 cm. Middle Minoan II.

This famous vase, which has long—until the recent finds at Phaistos—been counted the most 'artistic' of the Kamares vases, is certainly one of the finest products of the Knossian potteries. The decoration in white and orange lies on a black ground. It is composed of linked medallions with rosettes, and florals which seem to anticipate Greek *anthemia*.

Evans, *Palace of Minos* I, pp. 246–247, fig. 181, colour pl. 3, etc.

VIII

BEAKED JUG. Kamares style. From the Old Palace of Phaistos. Height 27 cm. Middle Minoan II.

This is exceptionally well-preserved. There are two warts or 'eyes' on the spout (compare plates III and 21). The decoration is of double spirals and double 'feathers' set in arcs. The floral element is expressed in a fully linear style.

Levi, in *Nuova Anthologia*, June 1956, pl. 4, 1.

IX

SPOUTED PITHOS WITH THREE HANDLES. Kamares style. From the Old Palace of Phaistos. Clay. Height 69 cm. Middle Minoan II.

Three zones of large running spirals, in white paint, encircle the vase.

Levi, in *Annuario Atene* 33–34, 1955/56, p. 296, fig. 11, 2.

X

THREE-HANDLED PITHOS. Kamares style. From the Old Palace of Phaistos. Height 45.5 cm. Middle Minoan II.

Linear patterns of stylised plants mainly in white with some yellowish orange.

Levi, in *Annuario Atene* 33–34, 1955/56, p. 296, fig. 11, 1.

XI

THREE-HANDLED PITHOS DECORATED WITH FISH. Kamares style. From the Old Palace of Phaistos. Height 50 cm. Middle Minoan II.

Spirals over wavy lines in white paint on the black ground. Above them a large fish, in yellowish-brown paint, swims over the mesh of a net.

Levi, in *Annuario Atene* 33–34, 1955/56, pl. 3.

XII

CRATER WITH MODELLED BLOSSOMS. Kamares style. From the Old Palace of Phaistos. Height 45.5 cm. Middle Minoan II.

The only example of this type yet found. It is from the most recent excavations. This surprising piece is a true crater, like those most common in later Greek times. The chain (most of which is missing), which hangs from the rim, and the seven lily-like blossoms suggest a metal prototype.

Apart from the chequer the decoration imitates breccia, and it is perhaps a stone vase with metal—perhaps silver—chains and blossoms that is being copied. A ladle would have hung from the chain.

Levi, in *Bolletino d'Arte* III, 1956, p. 249, colour pl. 2 opposite p. 246.

23, XIII

FOOTED BOWL. Kamares style. From the Old Palace of Phaistos. Diam. 54 cm. Middle Minoan II.

One of the many interesting finds in the lower levels recently excavated in the Old Palace of Phaistos. A harmonious composition of notched spirals and floral and branch-like motifs, both inside and outside.

Levi, in *Bolletino d'Arte* III, 1956, p. 248, colour pl. 2.

24

PITHOS. Kamares style. From Magazine XXXII in the Old Palace of Phaistos. Height 1.10 m. Middle Minoan II.

Two rows of handles. Red-brown drop-like motifs on the yellowish ground. Within each another 'drop' and a circle making the whole a unique and individual pattern.

Pernier, *Festòs* I, pl. 37.

25 above

PORTRAIT OF A CHILD. Clay seal-impression. From the Old Palace of Knossos. Middle Minoan II, about 1800 B.C.

This interesting piece from the 'Hieroglyphic Deposit' at Knossos was found together with the portrait of an older man, the 'father'. Perhaps they are indeed father and son, king and prince. The youth's face seems drawn and weakly.

Evans, *Palace of Minos* I, pp. 271–272, fig. 201b.

25 below

CHEST-SARCOPHAGUS (Larnax). From a circular tomb at Vorou at the north edge of the Messara, Central Crete. Clay. Length 74 cm. Middle Minoan I–II.
One of the earliest examples of this class. Notice the knobs and loops for the ropes which would have fastened the lid to the chest. There are similar knobs on wooden chests which have been found in Egypt. Odysseus tells us of the complicated knots which Circe herself is supposed to have invented, and which may have served for fastening such sarcophagi (cf. *Odyssey* VII, 447–448). In Minoan Crete a seal might have been used for this purpose but the great king of the *Odyssey* secured his property with knots alone.

Marinatos, in *Deltion* 13, 1930/31, p. 147, fig. 10.

PALACES, MANSIONS AND VILLAS

26–41; XIV–XVII; Figs. 3–6
THE PALACE OF KNOSSOS

To a newcomer the sight of Knossos today makes a profound impression and he feels, as did the ancients, that he dare not enter its ruins without a guide. A clear path through the maze can be picked out once the strict orientation of the palace around its central court is understood. As was inevitable for so large a building the palace had entrances on each of its four sides, but most traffic passed through the main gates at the north and south. The visitor today approaches from the guardian's house into the West Court from which he can reach either main entrance. The interior is best approached from the South Propylon. The original west façade is faced with great orthostats of gypsum, as are the west sides of most palaces and mansions, and with as few openings as possible. At the south-west corner of the palace is the West Porch which gives into the long and celebrated Corridor of the Procession. The entrance portico had at its façade a wooden column 1.20 m. thick, and on the inside a room for the gate-keeper and a waiting-room. There was a relief fresco of plaster with bull-games on the wall to

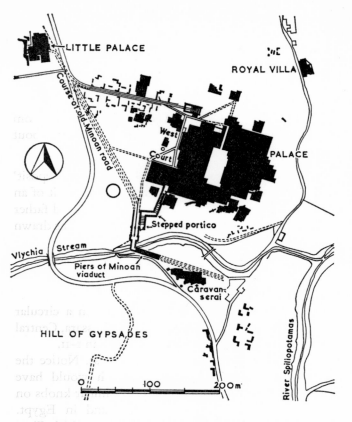

Fig. 3 PALACE OF KNOSSOS AND SURROUNDING AREA. Centre, the Palace itself surrounded by smaller Minoan buildings. Top left, the so-called Little Palace; top right, the so-called Royal Villa. After *Pendlebury*.

the left of the visitor. The long corridor turns a right angle to the east and after some 24 m. reaches the South Propylaeum from which there is a monumental stair-case to the upper Propylon. Beyond this are the cult-rooms and other apartments of the first floor, the Piano Nobile (the central state-room in plate 40). There is also a continuation of the Corridor of the Procession which turns north into the Central Court (Fig. 5). The Corridor and the Propylon were decorated with two registers of frescoes of life-size figures, youths and girls carrying valuable offerings. Only the rhyton-carrier (plate xv) is fully preserved, and the lower parts of some other figures. There were originally more than 500 figures, probably forming a cult-procession; or they may be tribute-bearers from other parts of Crete or the islands. If the last we must remember that there was no form of taxation but that the tribute would be offered as though a spontaneous gift; and the frescoes in the entrance corridor would have served as a re-minder to the visitors of their obligations and of the general practice.

The north entrance (plate 30) was designed for access from the harbour installations north of the palace, at the mouth of the Kairatos and at Amnisos, the main harbour and arsenal. A small Propylon leads to a Pillar Hall from whose south-west corner begins the Northern Entrance Passage. This rises without steps so that it can be traversed by animals and carts. The porticos on either side with relief frescoes of bulls were a later addition; from them is the head of the bellowing bull (plate xiv). These scenes were probably still visible long after the fall of the palace and could have inspired the story of the Minotaur. Theseus, arriving from the port of Amnisos, would certainly have entered the palace through this door, and some say that his victory was won before the 'Door of the Labyrinth' (Plutarch, *Theseus* xix, citing Kleidemos).

The long axis of the Central Court, the heart of the palace life, runs almost exactly north to south. It divides the palace into two wings, each of which is divided by a corridor into two quarters. In the west wing a north-south corridor divides the magazines in the west from the complex of cult-rooms opening into the Central Court. An east–west corridor in the east wing leaves the living quarters to its south, the workshops to its north.

There are twenty-two long, thin magazines lying against the massive west wall of the palace. The three at the south were not in use when the palace fell, and the one at the north was divided up into a sort of office. The other eighteen were full of great pithoi and some also contained stone-lined pits.

The complex for religious ceremonies had a monumen-tal façade facing the Central Court. The Throne Room and its anteroom are the best known today (plate 33). Before entering them you see to the right the rounded corner which survives from the plan of the Old Palace. Within it are winding stairs up to the first floor. A great porphyry bowl in the anteroom was for the ritual purification required before entering the Throne Room. The Throne Room itself presented a vivid picture of the moment when the place was destroyed, for it seems to have been in use at the very moment that the disaster befell. The suddenness of this disaster is reflected in what was found on the floor by the excavators: large, flat alabastra of stone and the remains of a great pithos which certainly did not normally stand there but had been hurried in for libations and prayers in the face of the danger which threatened. The frescoes in the room were preserved right to their tops. They are now in Heraklion Museum and in their place are reli-able copies.

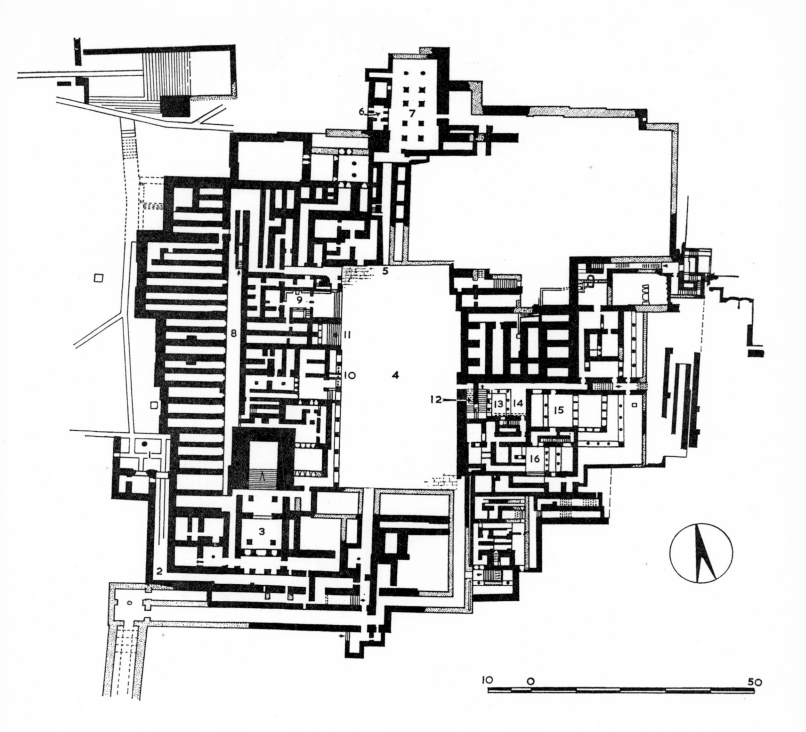

Fig. 4 THE PALACE OF KNOSSOS. Ground plan of the Palace at the level of the Central Court. Entrances: (1) West Porch, adjoining (2) the Corridor of the Procession, which extends from the West Porch along the southern half of the west wing, then leads to (3) the South Propylon (see fig. 6) and on to the south-west corner of (4) the Central Court. (5) North entrance between (6) the North Propylon and (7) the Pillar Hall, leading to the north end of the Central Court. Wings of the Palace—west wing: to the west of the north-to-south corridor are (8) the magazines, to the east (9) the Throne Room, (10) the Palace shrine, the lower verandahs and (11) the Stepped Porch leading to the first floor; east wing: centre, the east-to-west corridor. North of it, artists' and workmen's rooms, to the south the living quarters. At its end (12) the Grand Staircase with (13) Light Area and (14) Hall of the Colonnade. Before it to the east (15) Hall of the Double Axes, the principal reception room. Beside it (16) the rooms of the Queen's Megaron.
After *Pendlebury*.

5

6

Figs. 5, 6 THE PALACE OF KNOSSOS. 5 Conjectural restoration of the façade of the west wing, facing the Central Court, showing (from left to right) the portico, the shrine, the Stepped Porch and the anteroom to the Throne Room, with the Piano Nobile above. Compare Plate 32.
After *Hood*.
6 Restoration of the South Propylon with the Procession fresco of the rhyton-bearers and other gift-bearers in two registers and, in the background, the stairway to the main floor in the west wing.
After *Evans*.

124

Large griffins are seen seated on either side of the Throne. These frescoes belong to the last phase of the palace. The Throne itself is of alabaster but certainly copies a wooden form. There may have been some cult reason for making it of stone, of material born of Earth herself. Was it then for the king, protected by the deity, or if not for the king or queen might it have been for the god himself, bidden to take part in the ceremonies? We find thrones of stone elsewhere, and there are places in which a bed or table is prepared in a sanctuary for the deity (cf. what has already been said of the Throne in the Royal Villa, p. 58). Around the walls of the Throne Room are alabaster benches, and opposite the Throne a balustrade is preserved up to the bases of its wooden columns, which have been restored. This overlooks a small room reached by a few steps down, which served as an underground chapel from which the god could be sought by prayer. It may be that it is an artificial, though artistic, substitute for the Cretan grottoes wherein the gods had been served for millennia. Such rooms have generally been called 'lustral basins', and are met elsewhere, especially in the Old Palaces. A private altar with various cult objects is reached from the Throne Room through a door which could be secured.

South of the complex with the Throne Room is a stairway from the Central Court up to the first floor (plates 26, 32) whose large apartments could also be reached from the South Propylon, as we have seen. The rooms of this Piano Nobile were exclusively ceremonial: a porch with a central column, a vestibule and then the room with three pillars and three columns (see plate 40). To the west is a corridor, over that serving the magazines, but it had no roof and afforded light and air to the rooms along it.

West of this corridor are two large rooms: over the central part of the magazines, one to the south with two columns; and adjoining it to the north another with six pillars (Sanctuary Hall). In the latter was found the fragment of fresco with the 'Parisienne' (plate XVI.)

A number of smaller rooms are attached to the Central Tri-columnar Hall, beside which there is a broad verandah overlooking the Central Court. A continuation of the stairway from the court (plates 26, 32) is represented by a lesser flight which seems to have led to a second story. South of the same stairway from the Central Court there are traces which suggest a tripartite chapel facing the court. The rooms behind were certainly sacred: one contained benches and the two famous stone-lined pits in which the snake-goddesses (plates 70, XXIV) were found with the rest of their treasure, as well

as the two no less famous pillars with the runnels for liquid offerings and incised double axes behind Palace shrine on the plan). It should be remarked here that there is no very good ground for deriving the name 'Labyrinth', by which the palace was called in myth, from the double-axe signs. In Lydian the double axe is called 'labrys', so the Labyrinth might be the house of the double axe, the involved ruins of the palace which the Greeks knew and associated with the story of Ariadne and her thread.

South of the Pillar Crypts a broad verandah stretched along the court to its south-west corner. A few paces to the east was the southern entrance to the Central Court, at the end of the Corridor of the Procession. The main road from the south approached the palace via the monumental viaduct (Fig. 3). Crossing the court we are at the centre point of the east wing, where it is divided by the east-west corridor—or corridors, for they appear on each floor as they did in the west wing, although here the corridor on the first floor was not roofed. Unfortunately we know nothing of the appearance of the façade on to the court, but it is clear that the east wing had several floors.

The complex north of the east-west corridor is of buildings belonging to various periods and with little of interest for the visitor. It seems always to have been the quarter of the artists and artisans whose work won such renown for the palace. In the story of Daidalos we read of the last phase in the artistic life of Knossos. The workshops can still be picked out in which the royal potters of the Old Palace made the superb egg-shell vases and other Kamares pottery. There are still traces of the magazines of the Old Palace and the colossal pithoi, over 2 m. tall, stand here still. These more than man-size jars remind us of the story of Glaukos, a son Minos, who fell into a pithos full of honey and was drowned. The somewhat later pithoi, though still Middle Minoan, in other magazines in this quarter are known as 'medallion' pithoi. Evidence from another room shows that here stone vases were fashioned. This is of the last days of the palace and many fine vases were left on its floor half-finished when the palace fell. In one small room lumps of the raw material were found: 'lapis lacedaemonius', the hard green stone which is still only to be found at Krokeai, near Sparta, and is now known as 'verde antico'.

The living quarter lay south of the east-west corridor, whose west end was formed by the Grand Staircase (plates 34 left, 35–37). Here the colonnades and flights are incredibly well-preserved. Only the columns, whose carbonised remains alone were found, have been replaced by stone. Four of the flights of stairs and part of a fifth are preserved. The Grand Staircase has been most carefully restored to its present form. Evans' work of restoration here has been much criticised but without it neither this stairway nor many other parts of the palace could be seen today; they would have collapsed immediately after excavation.

To accommodate the living quarters east of the Central Court a cutting had been made into the side of the hill even in the period of the Old Palace. At the same time the rooms were orientated north to south on both the ground and the first floors so that they lay within the cutting and could enjoy natural protection from cold in winter and heat in summer. The floor of the second story was on the level of the Central Court, and it is to this floor that the fifth flight of the staircase, already mentioned, led (foreground in plate 32). It is not clear whether there were other floors above.

The steps on the staircase are broad and comfortable. They lend a ceremonial and monumental air to the whole complex, and this was enhanced by the frescoes on each floor of the east-west corridors and by the colonnades. An unroofed area to the east of the stairs (plate 37) is one of the many light-wells, which gave light and air to the close-set rooms. These are like small open courts running up through all the floors of the quarter. Being thus exposed they were generally built most carefully of great ashlar blocks of poros. Evans named several of the apartments after the masons' marks which appear on some of the blocks.

On the ground floor, beside the lowest east-west corridor and the light-well, we find the Hall of the Colonnade. A second light-well to the east indicates that a particularly important apartment is near by, and this, perhaps the most monumental room in the palace, we know as the Hall of the Double Axes from the masons' marks on its walls (plate 39). These elegant rooms, which are found in the best positions in all the palaces, must have been reception rooms rather than private apartments. At Phaistos and Mallia they lie at the north-west corner of the palace to face the cooling winds during the long and scorching summer months. The south-east corner was chosen at Knossos because this part was protected by the cutting into the hillside.

The Hall, with a light-well at its west side, contained a wooden throne and canopy against its north wall. The room is not very large but to the east it has an anteroom, reached through four doors, and this in turn has four and three doors in its east and south walls, so that the rooms could be joined into one if need arose: a notable feature of Minoan architecture. Finally there is an open colonnaded verandah to the east and south which afforded air and light, as well as protection from the direct sunlight. There were frescoes on all the walls but only traces are preserved.

From the throne-room of this complex a twisting corridor leads to a smaller apartment at the south, known as the Queen's Megaron (plates 34 right, 38). Here there is a small private stair to the upper floors. The main room was decorated with frescoes at various periods (plate 38 below) and was furnished with benches. At the east was a small light-well and to the west a small bath-room with a single column. To the south was another light-well and a rather longer corridor which led to a water-closet which is surprisingly modern in its sanitary appointments. Even in the Old Palace the water-supply and drainage were carefully planned. Clay pipes brought drinking water into the palace, and the rain water was led away through ducts into drains as high as a man. The main sewer, roughly oval in section, lies beneath the living quarter, and with its subsidiary drains runs into the eastern arm of the Kairatos.

North-west of the Queen's Megaron, leaving the light-well known as the Court of the Distaffs on the left, a corridor with two bends in it leads us back to the Hall of the Colonnade and the Grand Staircase. On the way a small stairway runs to the west up to the rooms of the first floor which correspond to the Queen's Megaron below.

There is another important complex south of the Queen's Megaron where were the magazines of the early period of the New Palace in which the lily-vases were found (plate xxv). A bath-tub painted with reeds is still to be seen in situ. To the south again lay the shrine of the dove-goddess. This was always a sacred area as the find of a ritual basin there proves. In the last Minoan period, after the palace was in ruins, the small shrine of the dove-goddess was built, barely one metre square. This is especially important because in it there were found in place, left just as the last worshippers saw them, the figures of the goddesses, of the worshipper, the sacred horns and small double axe, the offering table and votive vessels. Here too the disaster which overtook the shrine must have been sudden and unexpected.

Less of interest is preserved in the west court. This was the focal point of several roads of which the most important was the Sacred Way for processions to the Little Palace. At the north end is the Theatral Area with its two flights of steps against the north-west corner of the palace (plate 29). Here the Sacred Way ended. There can be no doubt that the area served for religious ceremonies. On the 'Royal Box' (see below, on plate 29) there may well have been a small triple shrine like that which probably faced the Central Court. We can get some idea of its shape from the fragments of a miniature fresco which decorated the north room on the upper floor of the west wing.

26 The main part of the palace from the hill, Hagios Elias, to the east.

Beyond the palace is the modern town of Knossos, and to the right some of the houses of Fortetsa where there is a cemetery of the Geometric and Archaic periods. In the foreground is the stream Kairatos. Of the palace we see first the living quarters in the east wing, then the central Court with the north entrance to the right, the South Propylon to the left. In the centre of the far side of the Central Court are the four doors into the Throne Room and by them the stairway up to the Piano Nobile in the west wing.

27 Two general views of the palace.

Above: From the east, showing Knossos, Fortetsa and the modern Sanatorium, the construction of which uncovered many important Minoan remains.
Below: South part of the palace from the hill Gypsades, on which there was a thickly populated quarter of the ancient town.

28 The Sacred Way at the north edge of the palace and the steps of the Theatral Area, seen from the east.

The road links the palace with the so-called Little Palace, a building which held many cult-rooms. It was carefully laid and clearly intended for use on ceremonial occasions. We find similar sacred ways elsewhere: the avenues of sphinxes in Egypt, the road of Marduk at Babylon, and, of course, the Sacred Way at Athens.
The Sacred Way at Knossos is 230 m. long and runs due west to a point before the south-east corner of the Little Palace where there was probably a monumental entrance.
The construction of the road is elaborate. The bedding is a layer of rough stones set in clay, above are mortared stones, then another level of clay; and then the surface where there are two rows of stone slabs at the centre and a paved way at either side. The central rows are 1.40 m. wide, the side paths each 1.20 m., giving an overall width of nearly 4 m. Along the south edge runs a drain. It is notable that in the Roman period another road was built on the line of the old one but 2 m. higher.

It seems that the Minoan Sacred Way was remembered to the end of antiquity.

Evans, *Palace of Minos* II, pp. 572 ff., for the account of the discovery of the road and its description.

29 The Theatral Area seen from the Sacred Way.

The two flights of steps are set at right angles. Where they meet there is an elevated platform known as the Royal Box, which may in fact have supported a shrine of light construction, like the façades we see on frescoes and gold plaques (as that from Mycenae, plate 205 centre). The whole complex may have survived as a festal area into later times, and be the fine dancing-place of Knossos which Homer says was built by Daidalos (*Iliad* XIX, 590 ff.).

Description of the Theatral Area in Evans, *Palace of Minos* II, pp. 578 ff.

30 North entrance to the palace. To the left the Pillar Hall, to the right the partly restored portico with the bull-relief.

In the earlier period of the palace the entrance way was broader but it became narrower with the encroachment of buildings in the New Palace.

31 North entrance to the palace, seen from the Central Court.

The main drain of the palace, man-high, runs beneath the paved road.

32 View from the top of the main staircase in the east wing across the Central Court to the west wing. On the left the verandah of the palace shrine, the stairway of the west wing (Stepped Porch), the anteroom to the Throne Room, and at the extreme right the portico by the north entrance. Compare the reconstruction in Fig. 5.

33 The Throne Room of the palace.

This belongs to the last period of the palace. The throne and benches are made of alabaster.

34 View from the west-south-west of the pillared well of the Grand Staircase in the east wing (left), of the Queen's apartments and the floor below. On the right, behind the south-east corner of the colonnade, is the Hall of the Double Axes.

35–37 The Grand Staircase in the living quarters of the east wing.

Four flights of stairs and the beginning of a fifth are preserved. The wooden columns were found in a carbonised condition and have been replaced by stone. Plate 36 shows the upper and plate 37 the lower part of the stair and light-well. Compare also plates 32 and 34, which show the top of the stairway.

38 Above: Queen's Megaron with colonnade and light-well.
Below: Fresco fragment with a dancer from one of the pillars in the Queen's Megaron.

The figure in the fresco is half life-size; good work of little before 1500 B.C.

Evans, *Palace of Minos* III, pp. 70–71, fig. 40 and pp. 370–371, colour pl. xxv.

39 East wing: the anteroom to the Hall of the Double Axes, from outside and inside.

The Hall is the largest room in the living quarters; it contained a throne, and had a colonnaded anteroom at the east. The wooden throne and the shield reliefs in the lower picture are restorations.

40 Central state-room with three columns and three pillars on the main floor of the west wing. Before it the gallery.

There were large reception rooms all over the Piano Nobile of the west wing. They were reached by the great staircase through the South Propylon and, from the east, by the stairway from the Central Court beside the Throne Room (plates 26 and 32). They were lit from the east through the verandahs overlooking the Central Court (plates 26 and 32), and from the west from the north–south corridor by the magazines, which was not roofed.

41 Part of the west magazine with large pithoi in situ.

Some of the magazines are here visible, and beyond them part of the west court. The pithoi still in position are of various forms, all Late Minoan. Beneath the floors of the magazines are stone-lined pits (*kaselles*), and there are some also beneath the corridor.

XIV–XVII
FRESCOES FROM THE PALACE OF KNOSSOS

XIV Head of a bull from the painted plaster relief in the portico by the north entrance. Early period of the New Palaces. Middle Minoan III, about 1600 B.C.

The life-size, lowered head of a bull belongs to a large composition by the north entrance of the New Palace. On other fragments there are rocks, olive branches and part of a woman's leg. Evans thought the whole scene was of the bull-games, but the composition is nearer that on a gem from Vaphio on which the bull is attacked by a lion, and this may be how we should restore the relief fresco. The head is the best preserved and most effective work we have of about 1600 B.C.

Evans, *Palace of Minos* III, p. 172.—Marinatos, in *Archäologischer Anzeiger* 1928, p. 102.

XV Rhyton-carrier from the Procession fresco in the South Propylon of the palace. Later period of the New Palaces. Late Minoan I, about 1500–1450 B.C.

One of the many figures ranged in two registers on the Procession fresco. Notice the stiff pose, noble profile, arm-bands, frontlet and belt of silver, the gems at the left wrist and the youth's ceremonial loin-cloth. The great conical rhyton which he carries was probably of silver inlaid with gold. The clouds above show that the procession was in the open air. The whole series must have included over 500 figures if we add the youths and women in the Corridor of the Procession. These are of the late phase of the New Palaces, not earlier than 1500 B.C.

Evans, *Palace of Minos* II, p. 706 is the Procession fresco; reconstructed in Suppl. pls. xxv–xxvii.

XVI A woman's head, the so-called Parisienne. From the six-columned hall. Late Minoan I, about 1500–1450 B.C.

This was found with other fragments of the same composition over the west magazines, and is from the Sanctuary Hall on the upper floor. There were many figures of young people, mainly youths, set in rows one above the other. At least nine of the twelve figures preserved were shown seated on folding stools which have slim, perhaps metal, legs, and cushions and rugs on them; whence the title for the picture—the Camp Stool Fresco. The 'Parisienne's' bodice seems to be made of a thin, transparent material, which is also used for the great knot at the back of her neck; this is more likely a matter of fashion than a 'sacral knot'. The men and women wear long, colourful robes with short sleeves. Some of the men have wing-like appendages of cloth or fur over their shoulders, and some even wear red gloves. This will be the earliest representation of gloves, *pace* Erman and Ranke (*Ägypte*, vol. II, p. 136) who cite the gloves of Eje at Amarna as the earliest known. One carries in his hands a silver, high-footed cup, and another a similar vessel of gold. Evans explained the scene as a religious version of the passing of a Loving Cup, but these high-footed vases are such as were in everyday use. Analogous pictures in New Kingdom Egypt suggest that this may be a drinking party held, as the folding stools show, in the open air. Although children were generally kept away from adult parties this is still better taken as a secular feast than as a ritual involving children.

Full illustration in Evans, *Palace of Minos* IV, p. 381, with colour reproductions of the most important fragments.

XVII The bull-games. From a small court in the east wing of the palace in which there were scenes of various episodes in the games. Late Minoan I, just before 1500 B.C.

The frieze, from which this is one scene, was 80 cm. high, including the borders. It was in a room over the Court of the Stone Spout in the east wing of the New Palace. There were other panels with scenes from the games. The drawing and material are unusually fine. The borders imitate variegated stones.

In each scene the background was painted alternately yellow and blue. The convention for frescoes was that male flesh was painted red and female white, so that we can tell for certain from these scenes that both youths and girls took part in the bull-games. We can see that the young sportswomen wore several pairs of armlets, necklaces, two-coloured loin-cloths and often blue and red frontlets. Their hair was carefully dressed. It is interesting that the girls should indulge in this mortal sport so fully adorned, and they were perhaps princesses. Many of them—here, the one behind the bull, and even more clearly in another scene of the series (Evans, *Palace of Minos* III, p. 232, fig. 164b)— have slightly tip-tilted noses, like the Parisienne. The same feature is seen on the crowned, presumably regal figure of a woman on the Hagia Triada sarcophagus. This was perhaps a family characteristic in the Cretan royal house for it appears repeatedly over about a hundred years, in the 15th century.

We cannot be sure whether it is the same person represented in the scene in three different positions: grasping the horns of the raging bull, leaping over its back, and safely on the ground behind it after the 'salto mortale'. We have still much to understand about the Cretan bull-games. No weapons seem to have been used and the death of the animal is never portrayed; it was no doubt a sacred beast. (The many scenes in which the Minoan 'matador' thrusts his sword into the bull's neck are certainly from forgeries.)

The sequence of the leap is probably as follows. As soon

as the leaper can seize the horns of the bull he hangs on to them for a short while; the bull is momentarily surprised and unable to get free, and in this instant the leaper must execute his jump over the creature's back. On rings and gems we see episodes in the leap; in the fresco the whole process is shown. It has been noted that the girl is hanging on to the left horn of the bull with two right hands! The agony of the moment and the intense strain of the girl is well expressed in her upturned and half-closed eyes.

The fresco was painted before rather than after 1500 B.C.

Evans, *Palace of Minos* III, pp. 209 ff., fig. 114 etc.

Fig. 7 THE LITTLE PALACE north-west of the Palace of Knossos. Ground plan of the main floor, incorporating at A the plan of the floor below. To the east lie the reception rooms; next (1) the Entrance Hall adjoining (2) the Peristyle with eight columns, then (3) the Great Megaron with two rooms linked with each other and with the Peristyle by (4) four doorways, and opening by means of (5) three doors upon a portico to the east.
Below (on the plan), to the south of the Entrance Hall are situated (6, 7) a pair of pillar crypts, with two and three pillars respectively, which probably served for cult purposes, while in the south-west corner there is (8) a third pillar room in which was found a deposit of ritual vessels and the base for a double axe. To the west, adjoining the Peristyle, (9) a staircase. West of the Megaron are (10) the Cult-rooms.
After *Pendlebury*.

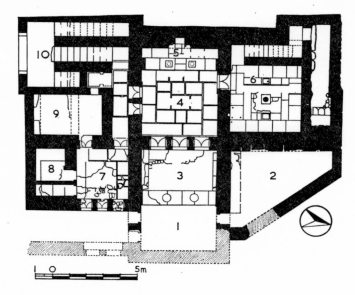

42–43; Fig. 7
KNOSSOS, THE SO-CALLED LITTLE PALACE

The Little Palace contains a number of interesting cult-rooms, including three Pillar Rooms with ritual furniture and a lustral basin with the usual columns, here five in number, fluted and of wood (the right hand shrine in the plan). The plan of this sacred room was later altered by a plaster wall which rose from the sunken basin over the balustrade to enclose the three wooden columns on the east (plate 42). Of these we see only the impressions of their flutes. This formed the so-called Fetish Shrine where natural stone formations were worshipped as cult-images.

The whole building (plate 43) is 45 m. long and nearly 28 m. wide. It had at least one upper floor. The assembly rooms which lie on the east (in plate 43 right) are spacious. Among the valuable cult-objects found in its ruins is the bull's-head rhyton of steatite (plate 98).

The Little Palace lies only 250 yards from the Theatral Area of the main palace, with which it is linked by the finely paved Sacred Way which has already been described. The line of the road was remembered still in Roman times, perhaps together with its religious function and significance. It was the exploration of the road which led the excavators to their discovery of the Little Palace.

Evans, *Palace of Minos* II, pp. 513 ff.

44–45; Fig. 8
KNOSSOS, THE SO-CALLED ROYAL VILLA

This unique building is perhaps no more than a simple private residence for all the originality of its plan. Lack of room necessitated a cutting into the hillside, such as was made for the living quarters of the palace itself. This also meant that the building could only expand in an upwards direction. There are two entrances, one to the ground floor in the east (plate 44 above), and the other to the upper floor on the south from the higher level of the hillside.

44 Above: Inner hall with a view of the anteroom and light-well.
Below: The same with the balustrade and the niche for the throne. At the right is the entrance to the Pillar Crypt, see plate 45 below.

45 Above: Stairs in the south-west quarter.
Below: The Pillar Crypt seen from the corridor to the inner hall.

Fig. 8 THE ROYAL VILLA north-east of the Palace of Knossos. Ground plan. (1) Light-well connecting with (2) an open yard. (3) Anteroom entered through two pillars connecting by means of three doors with (4) the inner hall at the rear of which (5) a throne stands behind a balustrade. To the north is (6) a pillar crypt with a central pillar on a gypsum base flanked east and west by two pits. Adjoining the anteroom to the south (7) a second hall is entered through three doors connecting with (8) a possible bathroom and closet. To the west is (9) another light-well, while in the south-west corner (10) a staircase leads up to a landing where it divides in two.
After *Pendlebury*.

46–47; Figs. 9–10
KNOSSOS, THE TEMPLE TOMB

46 View from the entrance hall over the forecourt towards the inner hall and the Pillar Crypt.

47 View from the hill to the west; the upper pillared hall with the Pillar Crypt below; in the background the forecourt and entrance hall.
For a general discussion see the Introduction, pp. 56–58.

48
PHAISTOS, GROUP OF HOUSES from the period before the construction of the Old Palace, mainly Middle Minoan I.

The levelling of the hill for the Old Palace led to the destruction of a number of houses where the west court was to stand. These close-set houses on the south-west slope of the hill have now been excavated. They belong to the earlier part of the Middle Minoan period. Bottom right is part of a wall with a 'fish-bone' masonry pattern. In many places there are traces of later buildings, of the Geometric period.

49–51; XVIII; Fig. 11
THE PALACE OF PHAISTOS

At Phaistos we can get some idea of the Old Palace because the west court, in its present state, is of that period. The west façade still stands one metre high, while the façade of the New Palace is set back about 7 m. to the east. A shrine with four small rooms and the great steps (plates 50 below and 51 centre) which embrace the whole north side of the court, can be associated with the earlier façade. This side is 25 m. long. A paved way leads to it across the whole Theatral Area.

Where it meets the steps they are made somewhat higher. Here there may have been some sort of altar or throne, or even a small shrine abutting on to the supporting wall behind the steps. The path would have been a Sacred Way for processions. The small shrine of the Old Palace which lay at the east end of the steps (plan; VIII–X); is cut into the rock. At its centre is a hole for libations. Its main room is surrounded by benches and had a clay offering-table set in the plaster of the floor (it is now in Heraklion Museum). Various cult objects were scattered about it. The shrine was within the original west façade, but outside the façade were three other tiny rooms with flimsy walls (plan; V–VII) which must be later additions. Behind the shrine a small stair (plates 50 below and 51 below) led up to a slightly higher terrace which could have accommodated spectators of the ceremonies.

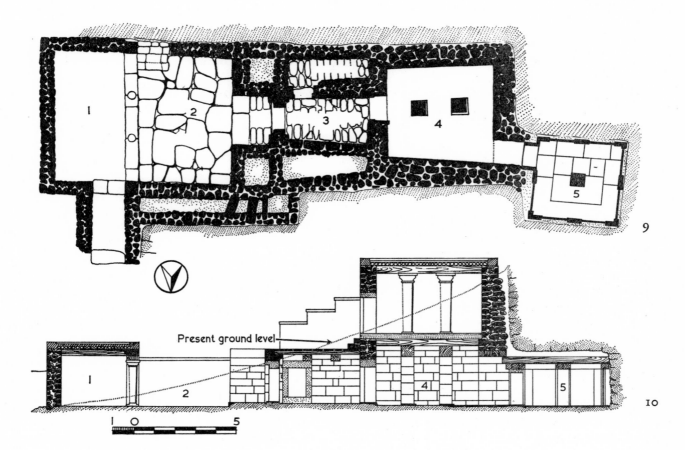

Figs. 9, 10   THE TEMPLE TOMB, south of the Palace of Knossos. 9 Ground plan. 10 Section. To the east (1) an entrance hall (Pavilion), then (2) a small court, from which one reaches (3) the Inner Hall and from there (4) the Pillar Crypt. Adjoining this, carved out of the rock, is (5) the Sepulchral Chamber.
After *Evans* and *Pendlebury*.

The west part of the palace even today impresses with its monumentality. A third stairway (plates 50, 51 above and XVIII) runs from before the shrine and at right angles to the steps in the Theatral Area, to the Propylon of the New Palace. There was no such stairway in the Old Palace, but when the new one, with its Propylon, was built the level of the west court was raised by about one metre. In this way the orthostats of the old west façade, the shrine, and the steps of the Theatral Area (except for the upper four) were buried beneath the new, higher floor of the west court. The west façade of the Old Palace and the Theatral Area were the first parts of the palace to be uncovered by the Italian excavators whose care was rewarded by these fine structures. The Sacred Way to the Theatral Area runs from the south where, from the shape of the hill, the main entrance to the palace must have been. Later Greeks built a temple over it, and the bronze shields dedicated in it suggest that it was for Magna Mater or Rhea, the same goddess to whom the temple and sacred grove over the Palace at Knossos were consecrated. The Sacred Way disappears now at a point in the west court where traces of the monumental entrance to the Old Palace have been found. This was similar to the West Porch at Knossos with a great wooden column in the centre (plan; 11). The column base is of polychrome stone, a characteristic material in the Old Palace, and is about 1.25 m. across. A corridor, like the Corridor of the Procession at Knossos but much shorter, led to the Central Court which was as we see it today (plate 49), remaining unaltered during the building of the New Palace. Some steps in the corridor show that the west porch was at a slightly lower level than the Central Court.

It is not easy to pick out this main corridor of the Old Palace because it is overlaid by the foundations of the New Palace and by a stairway belonging to a later, Greek house. On either side of it were magazines and work-rooms. In one can be seen the fine, bellying relief pithoi of the Old Palace. These rooms now lie beneath the floor of the entrance corridor of the New Palace, which was twice as broad as its predecessor but in about the same place. Also of the Old Palace is a series of small magazines (plan; XXXIV) which were found under the later court of the propylon and left accessible by the excavators. They were full of Kamares pithoi (plate 24) which had contained various agricultural products. Although they were set close together in dark and narrow cellars, virtually buried, they were brightly decorated as though they were show-pieces. Beside these magazines is another lustral basin, also of the Old

Palace. The excavators dated the fall of the Old Palace to about 1650 B.C., but we cannot be sure of the exact date.

We have already noted that the west façade of the New Palace lay 7 m. farther to the east making the west court more spacious. Its floor was plastered, but this was removed by the excavators to lay bare the original floor of the court of the Old Palace.

The Propylon of the New Palace at the north-east corner of the west court (plan; 68, 69) is one of the most ambitious Minoan architectural conceptions. A monumental stairway (plate XVIII and 51 above) with twelve low steps about 13.60 m. broad led to the Propylon. In their centre was a single column, 1.30 m. thick at its base, which, with the projecting antae at either side, supported the roof. The area behind was broad and quite deep. From it two doors led into a room of the same size which gave on to the open court behind through a screen of three columns. Below this area was found the magazine of the Old Palace (plan; XXXIV). The whole complex made a truly royal entrance way. The column-bases are of red stone or variegated breccia, the floors of gypsum slabs. In Knossos the South Propylon led to the state-rooms of the Piano Nobile in the west wing, and in the east wing the Grand Staircase led to the Hall of the Colonnade and the adjacent reception rooms, but there is nothing at Phaistos to match these apartments. There were certainly here also large and well-appointed rooms but they were reached by various minor stairways and entrances.

The finest part of the palace, set high in the open air, was the Central Court with its porticos at the east and west sides (plate 49). Cult ceremonies might have been held in its north-west corner where there was an altar. A stairway links it with the north-west quarter which lies somewhat lower and, as we shall see, was the most elegant part of the palace. It could only be reached from the Central Court by two roundabout ways. The primary entrance to the residential quarter lay through the Propylon in the west court, and this was the Propylon's main function. That its steps also served as a stand for spectators of ceremonies in the Theatral Area was of secondary importance.

A second entrance to the palace was the west–east corridor that we have already mentioned, which ran from the middle of the west façade to the Central Court. It was certainly roofed. Along its south side were rooms which can only have served for the domestic staff or as work-rooms, apart from two lustral basins. The hillside falls away to the south at this point and this must have been the one part of the palace which was the least

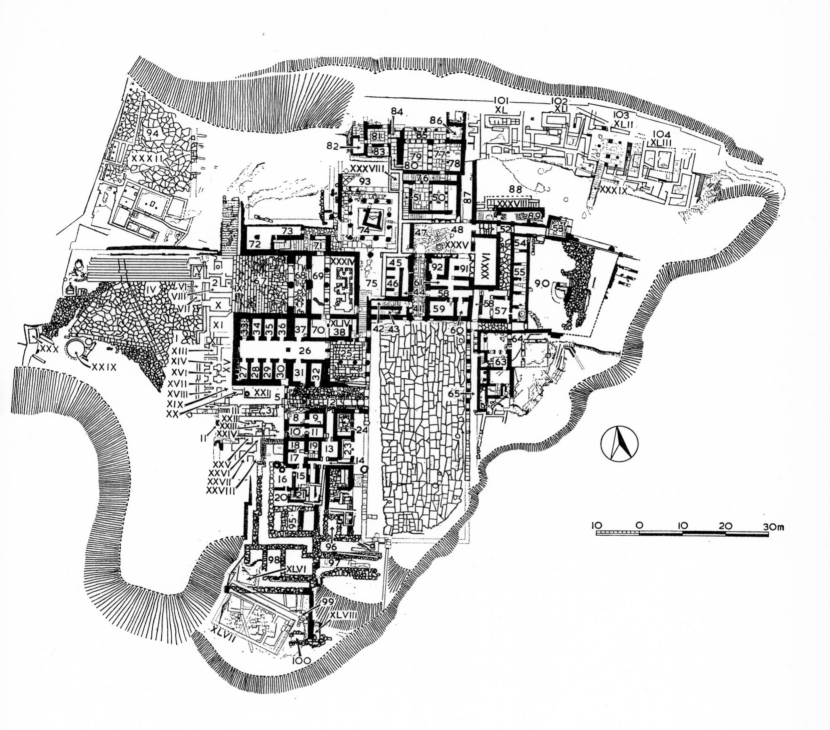

Fig. 11   THE PALACE OF PHAISTOS. Ground plan. The walls of the Old Palace are unhatched and its rooms numbered with Roman numerals; in black are the walls of the New Palace, its rooms numbered with Arabic numerals. The outlined walls at the north-west, north-east
and south are buildings of the later Greek period. At the southern limit is the site of a temple of the Hellenistic period. The original
pavement of the courts and open spaces is shown. For separate items see the descriptions in the text.
After *Pernier*.

sheltered from the summer heat. Along the north side of the corridor is the double row of magazines of the New Palace (plan; 27 to 37). We can better appreciate the care with which they were laid out now that the decipherment of the tablets has given us an idea of the complicated administration and the daily rationing of essentials.

The magazines are enclosed in a rectangular building with massive walls. A west–east corridor (plan; 26) divides them into two rows (plan; 27–32, 33–37). Each magazine has a door on to the corridor, and only the eastern rooms have their doors into the palace itself (plan; 31, 32). These must have been the administrative offices. The second of the easterly rooms has a door on to each corridor and must have served for the store-keeper.

The end of the magazines is closed by a portico (plan; 25) which opens on to the Central Court. Its roof was supported by two inner columns, and the portico on to the court is formed by three pillars and a column with a somewhat elliptical section. This design is continued south of the west–east corridor by the verandah-like structure in front of rooms 24, 23 and XLV in the south-west quarter.

The south-east corner of the Central Court has fallen away, but we cannot assume that the whole east wing of the palace suffered the same fate. The remains suggest that the east wing was never in fact erected in the space allotted for it. At the north-east corner of the court is an important, though small, house with a colonnaded court and salon (plan; 63, 63a–d, 64). This might have been the home of a high palace official. There is a magnificent vista today over the great stone-paved Central Court with the porticos on its long sides (plate 49, and see also plate 1). The whole area measures some 23 by 46 m. To the north the massif of Ida is visible unobscured by buildings, its sides covered with snow in the winter and the slopes at its foot dotted with villages here and there. The larger towns lie more thickly in the south east before the lower range of Asterousia. The view in plate XVIII from a higher point at the north-west of the palace, and that in plate 50, give the same landscape background as is seen from the south-east corner of the Central Court. To the east the eye ranges over the full extent of the Messara plain, framed by the range of Dicte some 25 miles away. The lush green of the plain, flecked with the bright colours of its many flowers, is a vivid token of the land's riches. To the east and north of the hill on which Phaistos stands runs the stream Electra (now called Geropotamos, 'the old stream'), which is the largest in Crete and runs on to

the west, through the plain below Hagia Triada, to empty itself soon in the Libyan Sea.

In considering the position of the Palace of Phaistos we must not forget that we are already as far south as the 35th parallel, farther south than Algiers and Tunis, and that the summer's heat would be unbearable were it not for the north-west wind which in mid-summer blows from about midday—Homer's Zephyros, blessed by the ancients, bringing coolness and moisture to both men and animals. We can understand then why the best living quarters in the palace lay in the north-west where the first breath of the north-west wind was felt. Even the gods felt the need of Zephyros' blessing. It is no chance that Rhadamanthys, King of Phaistos, ruled the Land of the Blessed where 'the sea carried the breath of Zephyros to refresh men'; thus it is described in *Odyssey* IV, 565 ff., where Proteus is describing Elysium to Menelaus. There may be reason too in thinking that the ship offered to the dead man on the Hagia Triada sarcophagus (plates XXVII, XXIX) was to serve him for his voyage to the Islands of the Blessed (see Nilsson, *Minoan-Mycenaean Religion*, 2nd edition, 1950, pp. 619ff.). The importance of the rooms in the north part of the palace is shown by the elegant treatment of the north side of the Central Court which was also the south façade of the living quarters. Before it, in the north-west corner of the court, lay a great stepped altar built of stone.

A north–south corridor, with a large two-leaved door, led direct from the court into the north quarter. The door shows that the corridor was roofed. Before its jambs were half-columns whose bases are still preserved. Two rectangular niches, which might have held double axes or something of the sort, stand beside the jambs and were decorated with linear frescoes. Passing through the door in the corridor we find ourselves at once in a planned complex of rooms. At the left is a stair to the Peristyle (plan; 74) and to a group of what may be storerooms. At the right a small corridor leads to various rooms whose pillars and bases seem to belong to the period of the Old Palaces. Beyond is an inner court (plan; XXXV). This may have been a separate apartment for the women of the palace (plan; 58–61, 91, 92 and XXXVI). Over all was a well-appointed upper floor whose façade overlooking the Central Court repeated the architectural features of the façade of the ground floor. The last and most artistically planned part of the palace is formed by the reception and audience chambers in the king's private quarters. The principal approaches to this complex were from the north or through the Peristyle already mentioned (plan; 74), but there was also a small doorway into the women's apartments. We first reach a small group of rooms comprising a room with benches, a court to the east, and a portico farther to the east. From its four columns, two in the east and two in the west, this has been compared with the Etruscan atrium. The walls are faced with gypsum slabs, as are the benches in the small room and its floor. The more northern complex is more luxurious (plan; 77–79) and can be matched in the Hall of the Double Axes at Knossos. At the very north is a portico (plan; 85), then a *polythyron* or salon with four doors in both its north and east walls (plan; 79), to the east another portico with two doors to the north and a court to the east beyond two columns (plan 77, 78). The columns and the salon lend the room a peculiar charm. As through a trellis the range of Ida can be glimpsed in the golden light of evening or with the dark shadows of clouds on a brilliant summer's day. And each midday the royal apartment was freshened by the comforting breeze which swept down from Ida.

Part of these rooms has been restored by the excavators. The new gypsum slabs are from the same quarry near Hagia Triada which was used in antiquity. Originally the door-jambs, pillars, walls and floors were covered with plaques of fine variegated alabaster and gypsum, from whose polished crystalline surfaces the light played and sparkled.

A door and corridor west of the main room (plan; 80) led to the lustral basin and private rooms, and a stairway led to the great Peristyle which could be reached direct from the staterooms which we have just described.

There is no more to say of the main part of the palace. A quarter at the north-east corner is formed by buildings of many different periods. Most are of the Old Palace (plan; XL–XLIII). The rooms lie lower than the palace, like annexes. A Pillar Room of unusual plan (plan; XLII) is linked with the north-east corner of the palace by a stepped way and platform. Farther west are two long rooms set at right angles (plan; XL). Here the Phaistos disc was found (plates 72, 73). This whole quarter may have served as temporary accommodation while the New Palace was being built.

XVIII   West façade and part of the west court. In the foreground ruins of houses of the Greek period; in the background the range of Asterousia.

The upper terrace, north of the west court, was partly built over with the houses of the Greek town whose ruins are visible. Behind them, to the right, is part of the paved west court, and to its left the foundation of the west façade of the Old Palace; beyond this the façade of the New Palace with the monumental stair to the Propylon.

49   View from the south across the Central Court. In the background the massif of Mount Ida.

The paving of rectangular poros slabs is largely preserved. The excavations proved that there were colonnades along both long sides of the court.

50   Above: The palace with the stairway to the Propylon and the Central Court from the north-west.

Below: The west court with the shrine of the Old Palace, Theatral Area (left) and stairway, as well as the smaller stair to the upper terrace of the New Palace. Before it is the raised processional way which divides in front of the steps.

51   The ruins of the west part of the palace.

Above: The stairway and Propylon, beyond them the Central Court and, below right, part of the west façade of the Old Palace which was covered by the New Palace but has been laid bare again by excavation.

Centre: In the right foreground the four small rooms of the Old Palace shrine. Beside them the steps of the Theatral Area with their supporting wall to the north. The characteristic jogs in the wall are clearly visible. The higher steps where the processional way ends can also be seen.

Below: The metre-high part of the west façade of the Old Palace which has been uncovered, beyond it the west wing and magazines of the New Palace and to their right the entrance corridor to the Central Court.

52–55; XIX; Fig. 12
THE PALACE OF HAGIA TRIADA

52   View from the north-east over the main part of the palace. This shows the north front of the original palace and the 'rampa del mare', as the excavators called it, in front. At the centre are the steps which lead to the Phaistos road. In the background the chapel of Hagios Georgios.

XIX   View from the great court towards the massif of Mount Ida.

Fig. 12 THE PALACE OF HAGIA TRIADA. (1) Main court, the focal point of public and religious life. To the west, the principal living-quarters with large inter-connecting reception rooms (2), *polythyron* and apartment (by 3). (4) Office and Palace Archives. (5) Magazines (6) Other living-rooms with three *polythyra*. (7) Corridor with magazines full of relief pithoi. (8) Two Late Minoan shrines. (9) Servants' quarters. (10) The Market. Eight magazines (probably originally two-storied), in front of them the great hall, with a row of alternating columns and pillars on its north-west side. In front of them is the settlement.
After *Banti*.

At the foot of the ruins runs the stream Electra, the largest in Crete.

53 View from the south east.
In the foreground the main part of the palace.

Behind, the valley of the Electra, and beyond it the western spur of Ida, Kentros, 6000 ft. high, and here covered with cloud. To the left the shore of the Libyan Sea and the Bay of Timbaki.

54 View from the north-north-east over the so-called market and magazines.

The eight magazines opening into a portico on the west are a unique example of a Minoan market.

55 Above: View from the south-west across the palace.

This is a general view of the ruins with the court of the shrines to the right. Below is the stream Electra. To the left the houses of the town, and to the right the market with its portico. Behind is Kentros.

Below: View from the servants' quarters to the portico of the market with its alternating columns and pillars, and the magazines.

56–59; XX; Fig. 13
THE PALACE OF MALLIA

56 Above: The north entrance. In the centre is the end of the stone-paved street leading to the palace. This leads to the north court, and through a corridor beyond it (plan; XXI) to the Central Court. Rooms XXIII 1 and 2 which block the way are later additions. The pithoi visible in the picture are Middle Minoan.

Below: The kernos found in position at the south-west corner of the palace. The depressions on it were to hold the offerings of first-fruits. The larger hole at the centre may have been for a lamp.

XX The palace seen from the west.

The characteristic red earth of this area is clearly shown. The visible part of the palace contains the magazines east of the Central Court.

57 Above: The central part of the palace from the west. There is a deep setback in the façade and beside it the entrance to the palace.

Below: View of the north end of the Central Court with the north portico and adjacent Pillar Room.

58 Above: South part of the Central Court with the Theatral Area.

At the south-west corner of the court, at the centre of the picture, is the south entrance to the palace, and in the right corner the theatral steps and the kernos (see plate 56).

Below: The central part of the west wing; in the foreground the Central Court with the altar (*eschara*).
At the right is another stairway and the loggia for official receptions. In the room beside it the mace-head (plate 68) and ceremonial sword were discovered. The *eschara* or altar of the palace is found in this form only at Mallia.

59 Above: North-west part of the Central Court with the north portico and adjacent Pillar Room.

Below: View of the Central Court with the altar. To the right the east portico with alternating pillars and columns.

In the north portico it can be seen how the space between the columns is occupied by rectangular bases. These might have been for a sort of balustrade between the columns. By contrast the east portico has regularly alternating columns and pillars. This is a common feature in Minoan architecture, here repeated for a stretch of over 30 m.

Chapouthier and Demargne, *Fouilles executées à Mallia*, IIème *Rapport: Exploration du Palais*, 1942.

60–62; XXI
THE MANSION AT VATHYPETRO, south of Knossos. Late Minoan I, 16th century B.C.

60 Above: At the right below is part of the north façade, and above it the pillared magazine (roofed). At the left the wine-press and weaver's shop (also roofed).

Below: The east court seen from the south. At the left the main room with three columns at the façade. At the right the tripartite shrine which was less solidly constructed.

XXI General view from the north. The great mansion was never completed but was destroyed soon after 1550 and abandoned. The most important parts were built

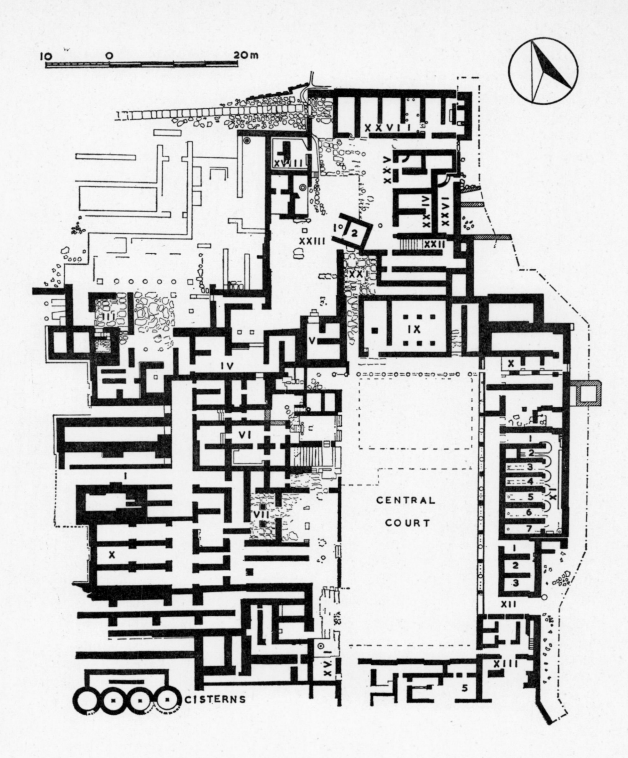

Fig. 13 THE PALACE OF MALLIA. Ground plan. Top left, the north entrance, whence, via the north court and corridor XXI, to the Central Court. (IX) The Pillar Room. The south entrance to the court lay at its south-west corner. Beside it are the steps of the Theatral Area, then a loggia and another stair. There are magazines in the west side of the west wing and in rooms XI 1–7 and XII 1–3 in the smaller east wing. As there was no spring the Palace had no comprehensive water-system. Therefore in the south-west corner of the Palace there were eight large round stone-lined cisterns, which together formed a kind of reservoir, four of which are shown on the plan. After *Chapouthier*.

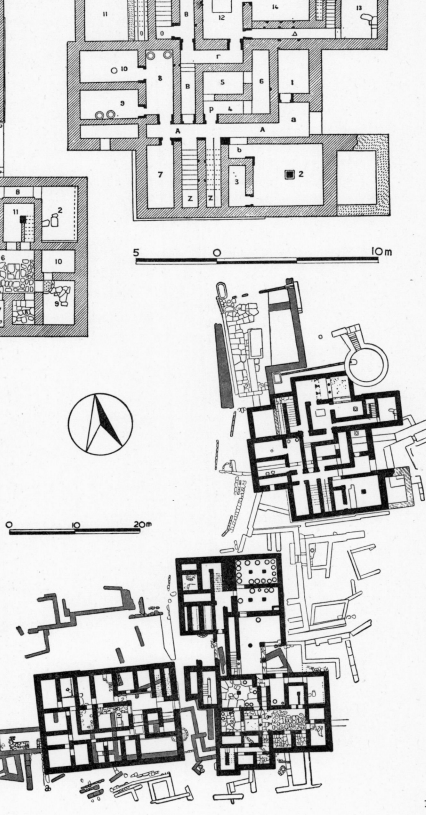

Figs. 14–16 Mansions at Tylissos.
14 General plan. House A (fig. 15) below
right; House B below left; House C (fig.
16) above. The black walls of the mansions are Late Minoan I. The shaded walls
are of earlier buildings. The walls and
buildings of later periods are shown in
outline.

15 House A. ψ/ω Door. (b) Vestibule.
(1, 2) Rooms linked by corridor B. A,
Corridor to the south wing. φ light-well.
(3–5) Rooms used as magazines. (6) Main
room (Megaron) with three doors
opening on to corridor A and light-well.
φ. (11) Stairs up. (15) Large room, supported by a stout wooden column, adjoining
the vestibule. (16, 17) Magazines, each
with two pillars and containing pithoi.

16 House C. (a) Vestibule to east entrance.
A Adjoining east-to-west corridor. Z
Stairs with two flights. B North-to-
south corridor. (7) Room with frescoes.
(8–10) Magazines. θ Second stair, with
room (11) reached beneath its second
flight. (12) Vestibule with central shrine
and access to rooms (13, 14), corridor Δ
and the third stair H. (15) Megaron with
three doors on to a porch and light-well
(stippled).
After *Hazzidakis*.

15

16

14

of poros ashlars, the column bases of variegated conglomerate, and the drains of black limestone quarried on Mount Juktas near by.

61 Above left: The east-west corridor seen from the east. To the left before it the wine-press and weaver's shop (roofed). At the east end of the corridor the pottery and kilns were found.

Above right: The south entrance with its pillars, and to the left the wine-press and weaver's shop.

Below: The west court and façade.

62 Above: The wine-press in situ, as it was found. There is a broad shallow clay bowl for crushing the grapes, a great pithos, three-quarters buried, to receive the must, and beside it another pithos. Embedded in the paved floor are a stone basin and stone drain.

Below: The olive-press in the west court. The olives were crushed by a great boulder. The mush was then packed into sacks and pressed under wooden levers weighted with stones.

63; Figs. 14–16
THE MANSIONS OF TYLISSOS

Three large houses have been excavated in Tylissos, which must have been one of the more important Minoan towns. The southernmost, B (in the background of the upper picture), is the smallest and has no state-rooms, but it was carefully planned and built. The middle house, A (in the foreground), is the largest, with important rooms and two Pillar Rooms full of pithoi. Here the Pillar Rooms served also as magazines, as at Vathypetro. The northern house, C (in the lower picture), is the most luxurious, with several stairs to its upper floor, walls faced with gypsum, and a round fountain-house with steps which was built somewhat later (on the right). This seems to have been a cult-place right into the Greek period when Artemis was worshipped here. The houses belong to the first phase of the Late Minoan period.

Hazzidakis, 'Tylissos', *Études Crétoises* III, 1934.—*Ephemeris* 1912, pp. 197ff.

64
AMNISOS, VILLA WITH THE LILY-FRESCOES

Strabo says that Minos used Amnisos as his harbour town. Its long sandy beach makes it a fine landing place.

It is mentioned in the Odyssey although not as being well-sheltered. Excavations have shown that there had been a Middle Minoan settlement on the small hill at the centre of the coastal strip (to the left in the upper picture). To its west a shrine of Zeus Thenatas was uncovered and found to overlie Minoan levels and buildings. On the north side of the hill by the sea were Minoan buildings and a spring-house, not yet fully excavated. To the east were the ruins of the villa shown in this plate. It had two stories, a verandah overlooking the sea (to the right above, to the left below) and a large two-columned hall, repeated on the first floor and decorated with frescoes. These are of Middle Minoan III and represent one of the earlier styles of Cretan painting. The best-preserved fresco is shown on plate XXII.

Marinatos, in *Archäologischer Anzeiger* 1935, p. 290, figs. 1–4.

XXII
WHITE LILIES IN A FLOWER GARDEN. Fresco from the villa at Amnisos (plate 64). Height about 180 cm. Middle Minoan III, about 1600 B.C.

This, the largest and best preserved, is from the upper floor of the villa. Groups of three lilies—a scheme we often meet—are shown on two frescoes. The white lilies stand out in the dark red ground whose stepped frame suggests the enclosure of a garden or park. The flowers are somewhat sunken in the field of the picture and painted with a thicker white paint to make an elegant though simple composition. The fresco shown was painted about 1600 B.C. and is one of our earliest monuments of major painting. Vase decoration was probably influenced by the fresco patterns, as the lilies on the vase shown in plate XXV. The lilies on both fresco and vase are the madonna lilies (*lilium candidum L.*) and not the pancratium lily which we see often elsewhere.

Illustrated, together with the 'flower-pots' from the same room by Evans in *Palace of Minos* IV, Suppl. pl. 67a–b. An early photograph appears in *Archäologischer Anzeiger* 1933, p. 291, fig. 2, and ibid. fig. 1 shows a provisional plan of the villa and drawings of some other fresco-fragments. On the symbolism of the frescoes, *British School Annual* XLVI, 1951, p. 102, and in general on the identification of Minoan representations of flowers Möbius in *Jahrb. Deutsch. Inst.* 48, 1933, pp. 1–39.

65; Fig. 17
NIROU CHANI, VILLA OF A HIGH PRIEST. Late Minoan I. Above, seen from the east; below, from the west.

This is a neat and carefully built establishment some 8 miles east of Heraklion and on the coast. The walls of the main rooms were faced with gypsum slabs and the floors paved. The reception room has a bench of gypsum in its corner. The court is paved with slate and leads to an entrance with two columns between antae; thence there are four doors to the interior (plan; 2) and the corridor decorated with frescoes (plan; 11); this is all seen in the upper picture. At the south side of the court steps lead to an annex in which part of some stone horns of consecration was found, which shows that this was the cult-place. Many cult-objects were found in the megaron.

Xanthoudides, in *Ephemeris* 1922, pp. 1 ff.—Evans, *Palace of Minos* ii, pp. 279 ff., figs. 166–168.

66–67; XXIII
RUINS OF THE TOWN OF GOURNIA, Gulf of Mirabello, East Crete.

66 above and XXIII: General view from the east.
66 below: Road in the north part of the town.
67 above: View of the west part of the town from the south; on the right the palace with its court and theatre.
67 below: Part of the circuit road in the west part of the town.

The town stands on a hill near the sea with the small palace and its ceremonial court at the top. Around it and to the north was the main part of the town, but there were groups of houses also down on to the plain. The site gives an interesting picture of Minoan town life, with its small close-set houses, the usual narrow streets, the workshops and small palace.

Boyd-Hawes, *Gournia*, 1908.

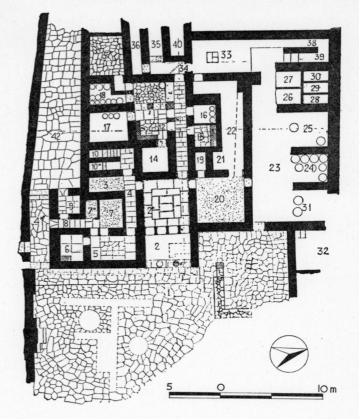

Fig. 17 HIGH PRIEST'S HOUSE AT NIROU CHANI. Ground plan. (1) East court; on the south side a building with three steps and Horns of Consecration, a kind of exedra for those attending religious functions. (2) Propylon. (2a) Megaron. (3, 14) Rooms without natural lighting. (7) Shrine with four double axes and (7a) side chamber. (17–18) Magazines. (24–32) Magazines reached across the open area (23). (33–36) Minor apartments. After *Xanthoudides*.

THE EARLY PERIOD OF THE NEW PALACES
MIDDLE MINOAN III (1700–1550 B.C.)

68

MACE-HEAD IN THE FORM OF A LEOPARD. From the Palace of Mallia. Grey schist. Length 14.8 cm. Middle Minoan III, about 1650–1600 B.C.

The mace-head, which ends in a battle-axe, was found in the Loggia of the west wing of the palace together with a dagger and long sword, both with golden hilts, the sword having an amethyst pommel. Evans and other scholars have dated the find to Middle Minoan IA

but this does not seem possible in view of the length of the sword, if nothing else, which cannot be paralleled so early. The modelling of the leopard's head and its forelegs stretched out in the 'flying gallop', as well as the spiral pattern on its body which is so common on vases of the end of the Middle Minoan period, suggest rather a date about 1650–1600 B.C.

Chapouthier and Charbonneaux, *Mallia* I, pl. 32, 1.—Evans, *Palace o Minos* ii, p. 274.

69

GOLD COVERING OF THE POMMEL OF A BRONZE SWORD. From the Palace of Mallia. Diam. 7 cm. Middle Minoan III, about 1600 B.C.

The ceremonial sword was found, with another, at the north-west corner of the palace where the royal apartments lay. Both are of the type of short rapier with broad haft which belongs to the years about 1600 B.C. On the disc we see in low relief the arched body of a youth wearing a belt and loin-cloth. Similar representations in Crete and Egypt show him to be an acrobat.

Chapouthier, *Mallia*, 1938.—*Études Crétoises* v.

70

EARTH-GODDESS WITH SNAKES. From the underground treasury of the central sanctuary of the Palace of Knossos. Faience. Height 34.2 cm. Middle Minoan III, about 1600 B.C.

The figure was found with a second, smaller snake-goddess and other rich offerings, in two stone-lined pits. Apart from the later clay idols with upraised hands it is the largest extant example of Minoan sculpture in the round. The later figures, sometimes holding snakes as attributes, are certainly goddesses, and this is likely then to be true also of the faience figures. It is still, of course, possible that they represent a queen or priestess in divine dress, but the intimacy with snakes seems improbable for a mortal. The first snake, whose head is held in the goddess' right hand, tail in her left, and body wrapped around her shoulders and back, is an exceptionally large creature. The two other snakes are knotted around the girdle of the figure and one of them raises its head above the goddess' headdress like an Egyptian uraeus. Only divine skill could control them thus. The goddess has the generous proportions and large, bare breasts of a Mother-goddess. We cannot say whether the large ears and rather terrifying expression were deliberate.

Evans, *Palace of Minos* I, p. 500.—Nilsson, *Minoan-Mycenaean Religion*, 2nd edition, p. 84 and *passim*.—Matz, *Göttererscheinung und Kultbild im minoischen Kreta* (Abhandlungen der Akademie Mainz, 1958, no. 7) p. 412.

XXIV

EARTH-GODDESS WITH SNAKES. From the underground treasury of the central sanctuary in the Palace of Knossos. Faience. Height 29.5 cm. Middle Minoan III, about 1600–1580 B.C.

This smaller figure has only two snakes. Her attribute,

the wild creature on her headdress, designates her as a goddess. Her breasts are yet fuller than those of the larger figure; she wears a similar apron and belt, with a flounced skirt. Neither shows the feet, and this might be taken as another indication that they are cult-idols and not representations of mortals, although this feature is not, of course, decisive.

Bibliography as for 70.

71

FAIENCE RELIEFS WITH ANIMALS SUCKLING. From the underground treasury of the central sanctuary of the Palace of Knossos. The bases are each 19 cm. wide. Middle Minoan III, about 1600 B.C.

These small reliefs with a goat and a cow suckling their young were found with other fragments of reliefs and with the two snake-goddesses. They would have decorated some cult-object, and may have been inlaid in wood. In style and date they are close to the goddesses. The wild goat is shown in its natural setting of rough boulders; the cow and calf, a favourite Egyptian motif, is set on a more formal base. It is likely that both reflect some more monumental work of art.

Evans, *Palace of Minos* I, p. 510.

72–73

THE DISC OF PHAISTOS. Fired clay. Diam. 16 cm. Middle Minoan III, after 1600 B.C.

This is one of the most remarkable inscribed objects to be found in Crete. The disc has a hieroglyphic inscription arranged in a spiral on both sides, the symbols being individually stamped, an anticipation of true printing. The disc has been known for half a century but it remains undeciphered. Meanwhile two other works with a similar script on them have been found: a bronze double axe from the cave of Arkalochori and a stone object from Mallia. This shows that the disc is no foreign product as had long been thought. Perhaps the Egyptian practice had suggested the retention of the use of hieroglyphs for religious documents after the linear script had been developed for everyday usage. The two finds mentioned are of about 1600, and the excavators date the disc a little later. This is the period of Linear A.

First published by its finder, Pernier, in *Ausonia* 3, 1909, p. 255, and then in *Festòs* I, p. 419 with full bibliography up to 1931. See also Ipsen's monograph, *Indogermanische Forschungen*, 1929. More recently, since Ventris' decipherment of Linear B, Schwartz in *Journal of Near Eastern Studies* 18, 1959, pp. 105 and 222. For Arkalochori see Marinatos in *Archäologischer Anzeiger*, 1935, p. 253; Mallia, *ibid.* 1937, p. 230.

74

TWO-HANDLED BELLIED JAR DECORATED WITH PALM TREES. Last phase of the Kamares style. From the Palace of Knossos. Height 57 cm. Middle Minoan II–III.

There are fragments of this important vase also in Oxford. It demonstrates the intrusion of naturalistic elements at the end of the main period of a purely decorative style. Groups of three realistic palm-trees rise from an irregular ground line on either side of the vase; they are painted white with red details, the central one of each group being the tallest. The arrangement, which we meet again on the lily-vases and the Amnisos frescoes, is typically Egyptian.

The pictures are of the side of the vase, with the smaller palms of each group visible, to show the original and un-restored part only.

Evans, *Palace of Minos* I, pp. 253–254, fig. 190.

XXV

VASE DECORATED WITH LILIES. From the Palace of Knossos. Height 27 cm. Middle Minoan III, about 1600–1580 B.C.

South of the living quarter of the palace was a sacred room with a lustral basin, which, at the very end of the Minoan period, was converted into the 'Shrine of the Double Axes'. The small store-room beside it probably served some religious function, and it was in it that were found the elegant vases of which one is shown here. Their technique is purely Middle Minoan, with white paint over lilac and brown. The three-lily groups may have had some symbolic importance, as has been suggested for their forerunners, on the Amnisos frescoes (plate XXII). The vases are rather later than 1600 B.C. and there may be some religious conservatism behind their decoration.

Evans, *Palace of Minos* I, pp. 578 and 603, fig. 347. See also the remarks on the Amnisos lily-frescoes, plate XXII.

75

JUG DECORATED WITH BIRDS. Imported from Melos. From the treasury of the palace sanctuary at Knossos. Height 58 cm. Middle Minoan III, about 1600 B.C.

A typical example of the matt-painted Melian style of Middle Cycladic III. In style and date it corresponds to the matt-painted Middle Helladic III vases such as were found in the shaft-graves at Mycenae. This jug was found in the same stone-lined pits as the snake-goddesses and the reliefs with suckling animals, and it affords a useful dating point. The back-tilted spout is such as one finds on eastern water-skins.

Evans, *Palace of Minos* I, pp. 556 ff., figs. 404–405.

76

TWO-HANDLED VASE. From Zakro, East Crete. Height 22 cm. Middle Minoan III, about 1560–1550 B.C.

A combination of linear decoration with a frieze of wind-stirred star-anemones painted white on a dark ground. It belongs to the advanced Floral style but the technique is still Middle Minoan. The flowers show Minoan art at its most charming.

Hogarth, in *Journal of Hellenic Studies* 22, 1902, pp. 333 ff.—Evans *Palace of Minos* II, p. 472, fig. 279. On the plants see Möbius, in *Jahrb. Deutsch. Arch. Inst.* 48, 1933, pp. 25 f.

THE LATE PERIOD OF THE NEW PALACES

LATE MINOAN I AND II (1550–1400 B.C.)

77

BEAKED JUG. From the Palace of Knossos. Height 31.5 cm. Late Minoan I. About 1550 B.C.

Typical naturalistic decoration of Late Minoan IA, particularly with the 'eye-spirals' with their thick outer bands and central discs.

Evans, *Palace of Minos* IV, p. 264, fig. 195.

78

MUGS AND CUPS. From the New Palace of Knossos. Heights, above 6.8 and 6.4 cm.; centre 12.3 cm.; below 7.5 and 6.5 cm. Late Minoan I, about 1550–1520 B.C.

The Floral style of about 1550 is characterised by patterns of upright or oblique grasses, olive branches, broken wavy lines which imitate the surface-appearance of metal vases, 'rippling' (common since Middle Minoan II) and the 'eye-spirals' (see plate 77). Plain, handleless mugs have been found in Crete by the thousand; they are less common in Mycenaean Greece.

Evans, *Palace of Minos* II, p. 475, fig. 282.

79
BEAKED JUG WITH DECORATION OF GRASSES
From the New Palace of Phaistos. Height 29 cm. Late Minoan I, about 1550–1520 B.C.

Typical of the developed, naturalistic Floral style with its close-set grasses. The wavy ground-line with moustache-like pendants is met on Mycenaean vases of about 1500 and later.

Pernier and Banti, *Festòs* II, p. 175, fig. 106 and pl. 2.

80
PITHOS DECORATED WITH SPIRALS. From the island of Pseira, Gulf of Mirabello, East Crete. Height 98 cm. Late Minoan I, about 1550–1520 B.C.

The whole surface of the pithos is covered with spirals, and it has two rows of handles. The outer bands and discs of the 'eyes' carry white dots. Between them are small dotted circles. A similar pithos was found in the North-east House at Knossos.

Seager, *Excavations on the island of Pseira*, p. 27.—Evans, *Palace of Minos* II, p. 422, fig. 245.

81
CULT-VASE WITH DOUBLE AXES AND BULLS' HEADS. From the island of Pseira, Gulf of Mirabello, East Crete. Height 77 cm. Late Minoan I, about 1550 B.C.

The red-on-white bulls' heads, double axes between ivy branches, 'sacral' ivy or lily frieze, and the figure-of-eight shield handle, all suggest that this is a cult-vase. The 'eye-spirals' appear again at the base.

Seager, *Pseira*, p. 26, pl. 7.—Evans, *Palace of Minos*, II, p. 484; fig. 284 on p. 476.

82 left
JUG WITH DOUBLE AXE AND SACRED KNOTS. From the Palace of Hagia Triada. Height 28.5 cm. Late Minoan I.

The main pattern is of double axes with, in the place of shafts, loop-pendants which Evans identified as sacred knots (*Palace of Minos* I, p. 432, and III, p. 140). Their similarity to the *ankh* (an earlier explanation of them by Evans), or the Isis-knots, cannot be gainsaid. The

tooth-pattern below (Evans' 'adder mark', *Palace of Minos* IV, pp. 178ff.) appears often on cult-objects and is painted on Mycenaean hearths.

Halbherr, *Memorie R. Istituto Lombardo*, p. 21, pl. 6, fig. 13.—Nilsson, *Minoan-Mycenaean Religion*, 2nd edition, 1950, p. 210 (wrongly dated).

82 right
JUG WITH STYLISED PAPYRUS. From Palaikastro, East Crete. Height 24.5 cm. Late Minoan I.

The papyrus stalks are grouped heraldically in threes, with the familiar wavy ground-line and moustache motifs.

Bosanquet and Dawkins, 'The Unpublished Objects from Palaikastro' *British School Annual*: Suppl. Paper I, 1923, colour pl. 18b.

XXVI
SPOUTED VASE WITH TWO HANDLES. From the Palace of Hagia Triada. Height 16.5 cm. Late Minoan I, about 1500 B.C.

In the style of the late Floral vases, close to the new Palace style. The artist now deliberately uses thicker paint for parts of the foliage to give some impression of depth and structure.

Pernier and Banti, *Festòs* II, fig. 293, 2.

83 above
JUG. From Palaikastro, East Crete. Height, 24.5 cm. Late Minoan I, about 1500 B.C.

The main pattern is of a branch rolled into a great spiral. It is very like the famous Marseilles jug which probably came from Egypt but is certainly Cretan. Palaikastro might well have been the place from which it was sent to Egypt. Both this and the Marseilles jug have heavy high-swung handles, and could be from the same workshop.

Bosanquet and Dawkins, 'The Unpublished Objects from Palaikastro,' *British School Annual*: Suppl. Paper I, p. 46, fig. 35 ('Late Minoan II'). For the Marseilles jug see Matz, *Kreta-Mykene-Troja*, fig. 73.

83 below
BEAKED JUG AND CUP with sacred symbols (double axe and sacred knots). From the New Palace of Phaistos. Heights 26.8 and 14.5 cm. (without handle). Late Minoan I, about 1500 B.C.

The jug carries wavy lines, stripes, lily-patterns and grasses on the neck. The cup is of a typical shape for this period.

Pernier, in *Monumenti Antichi* 12, 1900–1901, pl. 8.—Pernier and Banti, *Festòs* II, p. 271, fig. 171.—Evans, *Palace of Minos* IV, p. 184, fig. 145b.

84 above

DOUBLE JUG. From Gournia, East Crete. Height 26 cm. Late Minoan I, about 1500 B.C.

Probably a cult-vase. The nautili with their striped shells appear also on the Pylos dagger (plates XXXVIII and 171).

Boyd-Hawes, *Gournia*, pl. J.

84 below

HANDLED JAR AND VASE IN THE FORM OF A BASKET. From the island of Pseira, Gulf of Mirabello, East Crete. Heights 14.5 and 20 cm. Late Minoan I, about 1500 B.C.

The small cylindrical vase has waz-lily patterns; the other imitates a plaited basket. It is decorated with rows of double axes between rock-like motifs, such as decorate altars. At Arkalochori double axes and a rock-like object of gold were discovered (*Archäologischer Anzeiger* 1935, p. 248, fig. 3).

Seager, *Pseira*, figs. 11–12. For a side view of the basket-vase see Evans, *Palace of Minos* IV, p. 290, fig. 226.

85

RHYTON DECORATED WITH NAUTILI. From the New Palace of Phaistos. Height 20.2 cm. Late Minoan I, about 1500 B.C.

This type of rhyton is evolved from the ostrich-egg vases. The final, elongated form is seen in plate 86. On our vase the centre part is prominent and there is a funnel-shaped termination below. Fully developed Marine style.

Pernier and Banti, *Festòs* II, p. 173, pl. 2, fig. 103.

86

TWO RHYTONS IN THE EAST CRETAN MARINE STYLE

Left: RHYTON WITH DOLPHINS. From the island of Pseira, Gulf of Mirabello, East Crete. Height 32 cm. Late Minoan I, about 1500 B.C.
A calm, sun-lit sea-scape with dolphins. The waves are shown by a scale-pattern.

Right: RHYTON WITH STARFISH AND SEA SHELLS. From Zakro, East Crete. Height 33 cm. Late Minoan I, about 1500 B.C.
This was found with 16 others stored in a house, no doubt ready for export.

These show the last stage of the ostrich-egg form; see plate 85.

Evans, *Palace of Minos* II, pp. 222 ff., fig. 129 (for the shape), pp. 508 ff., fig. 312 (for shape and decoration).—*Journal of Hellenic Studies* 22, pl. 12.

87

LENTOID FLASK WITH OCTOPUSES. From Palaikastro, East Crete. Height 28 cm. Late Minoan I, about 1500 B.C.

This, with the related stirrup-vase from Gournia, is one of the most ambitious examples of the Marine Style.

Bosanquet and Dawkins, 'The Unpublished Objects from Palaikastro', *British School Annual: Suppl. Paper* I, p. 47, colour pl. 18.—Evans, *Palace of Minos* II, p. 509, fig. 312d.

88

DOUBLE CULT-VASE WITH A VOTARY. Height 16 cm. Late Minoan II, about 1400 B.C. Giamalakis Collection.

A feeding-bottle, θηλάστριον. The figure which stands at the handle junction with its hands held before its chest may be male.

89

RHYTON WITH A GOAT'S HEAD. From Palaikastro, East Crete. Height 29 cm. Late Minoan I, about 1530 B.C.

Unusual for the number of handles, one of which is formed by the goat's horns. The painting is of early Late Minoan IA.

Dawkins, 'Palaikastro III', in *British School Annual* 10, 1903/4.—Evans, *Palace of Minos* II, p. 537, fig. 34.

90

TWO RHYTONS IN THE FORM OF BULLS. From the island of Pseira, Gulf of Mirabello, East Crete. Length 25.5 and 26 cm. Late Minoan I, about 1520 B.C.

Above: A bull in yellowish clay with no painting to distract the eye from the fine modelling.
Below: A plumper beast painted with a net-pattern. The net may have been woollen, and, as in the other scenes in which it appears, may have some religious significance.

Seager, *Pseira*, pp. 22–23, fig. 7, pl. 9.—Evans, *Palace of Minos* III, p. 206, fig. 139b on p. 204.

91

THREE-HANDLED JAR WITH PAPYRUS DECORATION. Palace style. From the Palace of Knossos. Height 70 cm. Late Minoan II, about 1425 B.C.

Typical of the last palace period. The decoration is related to the triple groups as on the Amnisos frescoes (plate XXII). The added two stalks with buds also appear on the irises of the Amnisos frescoes.

Evans, *Palace of Minos* IV, p. 328, fig. 271.

92

THREE - HANDLED JAR WITH PAPYRUS DECORATION. Palace style. From Knossos. Height 78 cm. Late Minoan II, about 1430 B.C.

The pattern on the neck is still of the Floral style, but the papyrus is in the full Palace style, a form which influences all other floral representations of the period. The 'sandy' filling ornament is also a commonplace.

93

PITHOS WITH A PAPYRUS IN LOW RELIEF. From the Royal Villa at Knossos. Height 97 cm. Late Minoan II, about 1425 B.C.

Early, developed Palace style. It stood on the landing of the main staircase as a decorative piece simply. The papyri are painted and in low relief. The wavy lines suggest water.

Evans, *Palace of Minos* II, p. 300, fig. 231.

94

THREE-HANDLED JAR. From a grave near the mouth of the Kairatos, in the harbour area of Knossos. Height 47.5 cm. Late Minoan II, about 1425–1400 B.C.

Still of the Palace style. The helmets are of the type covered with boars' tusks, with horse-tail crests and cheek-pieces.

Alexiou, in *Antiquity* XXVIII, no. 112, Dec. 1954, p. 211, pl. 8.

95

NARROW NECKED JUG WITH RELIEF DECORATION. From a grave near the mouth of the Kairatos in the harbour area of Knossos. Height 49.5 cm. Late Minoan II, about 1400 B.C.

Technically this is an unusual piece with its plastic spikes, relief figure-of-eight shield and fine red paint. The papyrus and nautilus provide the main patterns. The decoration is of the earliest Palace style. It was found with an alabaster vase which bore the cartouche of Thutmosis III (1504–1450 B.C.).

Alexiou, in *Kretika Chronika* 6, 1952, pp. 25 ff., colour pl. A.

96–97

BULL-JUMPER. From the Palace of Knossos. Ivory. The man is 29.9 cm. long, his head 4.5 cm. high. Early in Late Minoan I, about 1550 B.C.

This small masterpiece—part of a group showing the bull-games—was found beneath a minor stairway in the living quarters. There were fragments of several jumpers, each made in separate pieces. Gilt bronze wire would have been added for the wind-swept locks. The pose is that we see in the frescoes and on seals. We cannot tell whether the figure was attached to the bull. Of the creature there is only part of a faience head with gold-lined holes for the horns. The movement, bold pose and working of detail all command admiration. Fingers, finger-nails, veins and muscles are modelled or incised with precision, while, as in other plastic works of the best period, the features are summarily and almost poorly rendered. We see the same on the bronze statuettes of worshippers, on gold rings and seals. The general lines of the head remind one of the snake-goddesses despite the softer treatment.

Evans, *Palace of Minos* III, p. 428 and passim.

98

RHYTON IN THE FORM OF A BULL'S HEAD. From the Little Palace at Knossos. Black steatite. Length of the head without horns 20.6 cm. Late Minoan I, about 1550–1500 B.C.

The Little Palace was certainly a cult building of some sort. There are at least three fine cult-rooms and the South-west Pillar Room where the fragments of this fine rhyton were found. The head is of black steatite. The neck is hollowed and a lid of the same material closed the opening. On the lid a bull's head is incised. The aperture for filling is in the neck and the spout is formed by a small hole in the muzzle. The ears of steatite, and the horns, no doubt of gold leaf but they are now missing, were made separately. The eyes—only that on the right in the picture is preserved—are of rock crystal, the iris painted black and the pupil red. The muzzle was inlaid, with tridacna shell, it seems. The hair between the horns is worked in relief and incised lines portray the mottled hide. The horns and part of the left side of the head (invisible in the picture) are restored.

Evans, *Palace of Minos* II, p. 527.

99

RHYTON IN THE FORM OF A LIONESS' HEAD.

From the Palace of Knossos. White limestone. Diameter at rear 16.6 cm. Late Minoan I, about 1550–1500 B.C.

This cult-vase is from the portico of the central sanctuary in the west wing. There were two rhytons among the many cult-objects found here: a fragmentary one in the form of a lion's head, and that shown here which is nearly intact but for its lid and the inlays from the eyes and nose. The material is a fine-grained, marble-like stone with a yellowish tint, like the finest marble of Paros, lychnites. Fragments of similar rhytons of the same material were found in the lowest levels of the sanctuary at Delphi, and must have been made in the same place; whether this was Knossos or some Mycenaean centre remains unresolved. There are traces of the inlay of red jasper on the nose and in the eyes. The eye-sockets were lined with jasper, the eyes themselves no doubt being of rock crystal. This is of the best period, an imitation of the more expensive metal rhytons.

Evans, *Palace of Minos* II, p. 827.

100–102

THE CHIEFTAIN'S CUP. From the Palace of Hagia Triada. Steatite. Upper diam. 9.9 cm. Late Minoan I, about 1550–1500 B.C.

The cup is almost complete and probably shows children at play. One figure stands stiffly before what may be a door-post. He is richly dressed with a necklace and arm-bands, something like a dagger at his belt and a staff or sceptre in his right hand. He is the Chieftain or Prince. Before him is his 'Officer' with what may be a sword over his right shoulder—no scabbard is visible—and what seems to be a crook in his left hand. Some have seen in this a cult-sprinkler, aspergillum, and others would have the officer helmeted. Behind him are three 'soldiers'. We can only see their heads—and only one of these is preserved—for their bodies are covered by things which have been variously called cloaks, shields and elephant skins. The cup is worked with the skill met on the other stone vases from Hagia Triada. Closer inspection reveals some awkwardness in the composition. The Prince is too stiff, the Officer like a puppet. Comparison with the other vases of this type shows that the features are those of children, and children are of course fond of playing grown-ups. Minoan art affords many representations of the very young.

The relief vases from Hagia Triada were studied in detail by K. Müller, in *Jahrb. Deutsch. Arch. Inst.* 1915, pp. 242 ff.—Evans, *Palace of Minos* II, pp. 742 ff., 790 ff. etc.

103–105

THE SO-CALLED HARVESTERS' VASE. From the Palace of Hagia Triada. Black steatite. Greatest diam. 11.5 cm. Late Minoan I, about 1550–1500 B.C.

The stone rhyton is in the form of an ostrich-egg vase. It was made in three pieces of which the lowest is missing. The scene on it is not readily explained. An elderly man, perhaps the landlord, leads the procession to the right. He wears what may be ceremonial dress and holds a staff with a hooked end over his right shoulder. Behind him follow his workmen in pairs and in step; they are the usual slim Minoan figures and although they are all clean-shaven the artist has succeeded in suggesting their varying ages. They carry over their left shoulders—thus not obscuring their features—peculiar instruments which seem to be combinations of a sickle and a fork. They may have been used in threshing or for the olive harvest.

In the procession there is a group of three singers (104 below) led by a man who holds a sistrum in his right hand while he keeps time with his left. His lungs are so full that we can count his ribs as he sings lustily with wide open mouth. The youth before the last two pairs has tumbled over and his companion laughs at him. The whole scene has been conceived with the greatest skill and lively humour. Despite much discussion it is still not clear whether this is a religious procession or some more secular festival; or even a mixture of the two. We may remark that a clay potter's wheel has been found at Vathypetro with a double axe and a sickle-fork implement, like that carried on the rhyton, incised on it.

Savignoni, in *Monumenti Antichi* 13, 1903, pls. 1–3.—*Jahrb. Deutsch. Inst.* 30, 1915, p. 242.—Evans, *Palace of Minos* IV, p. 218; II, p. 47 about the sistrum and dance; the reconstruction of the lower part by Gillieron, *ibid.* pl. 18, is unhappy as the legs, especially of the leader, seem neither to dance nor to march.—Matz, 'Die Agais', in *Handbuch der Archäologie* IV, p. 256, pl. 20, 1.

106–107

FUNNEL-SHAPED RHYTON. From the Palace of Hagia Triada. Black steatite. Height without handle 46.5 cm. Restored. Late Minoan I, about 1550–1500 B.C.

The size, draughtsmanship and subjects of this piece make it of especial importance. Its handle is made separately and its fitting partially obscures the figures of two wrestlers. The uppermost of the four registers shows wrestling scenes, the second bull-games, the third and fourth boxing by helmeted and unhelmeted athletes. The bull-games are familiar from many other representations but here for the first time we see boxing and wrestling. The 'pillars' with their capitals decorated with discs are not readily explained. Very similar 'pillars' are seen on the Miniature Frescoes at Knossos. That they are no ordinary pillars is shown by the fact that they appear in both instances in the open, and by the way they narrow towards the top unlike the usual Minoan architectural supports. They are perhaps standards or banners raised for festal occasions, like those we see in the east, on the stela of Gudea on which there is a pole decorated with many discs as well as other festal symbols (Unger, *Sumerische und Akkadische Kunst*, fig. 45).

Jahrb. Deutsch. Inst. 1915, p. 247.—Evans, *Palace of Minos* IV, pp. 20-21 (for the 'pillars'); III, p. 224 (for the bull-games) I, p. 668 (for the athletes).—Matz, *Die Ägäis*. p. 257.

108
BRONZE STATUETTE OF A MAN PRAYING.
From Tylissos. Height 15.2 cm. Late Minoan I, about 1500 B.C.

The pose is the customary one. The surface is rendered in a rough, impressionistic manner, as on the figurine in Berlin and other contemporary works.

Hazzidakis, 'Les villas minoennes de Tylissos', in *Études Crétoises* III, 1934, p. 95, pl. 26.

109 above
IVORY PLAQUE WITH A SUPERNATURAL BIRD. From Palaikastro, East Crete. Height 7 cm. Late Minoan I.

Palaikastro is a rich source of fine ivories. This must have been one of a series of plaque inlays. The bird rising from rocks into the clouds is a cross between a heron and a pheasant.

Dawkins, in *British School Annual* II, p. 284, fig. 14a.

109 below
IVORY SQUATTING CHILD. From Palaikastro, East Crete. Height 4 cm. Late Minoan I.

The child's head and body are rendered with understanding and accuracy. He may have been playing with knucklebones; another, found with him, was standing upright. It has been wrongly suggested that these are not Cretan work, for East Crete has yielded similar figurines, some in clay. For other scenes with children playing with knucklebones see the fresco in Evans, *Palace of Minos* III, p. 25.

Bosanquet and Dawkins, 'The Unpublished Objects from Palaikastro', *British School Annual Suppl. Pager* I, p. 125, pl. 27. An Egyptian origin is argued by Pendlebury, *Aegyptiaca*, pp. 32-33, pl. 3 (as XII Dynasty).

110 above
GOLD DOUBLE AXE. From the cave at Arkalochori, Central Crete. Width 8.6 cm. Late Minoan I.

Works in precious metals are rare in Crete but more than two dozen gold double axes were found in the cave at Arkalochori, some with golden shafts, like that shown here. At the end of the shaft of one is a ring which shows that these axes might have been hung up. Many have incised or chased decoration.

The finds from Arkalochori are still not published. Pictures in *Archäologischer Anzeiger* 1934, p. 250, fig. 3, and Evans, *Palace of Minos* IV, p. 346, fig. 290.

110 below
GOLD PENDANTS. Left BULL'S HEAD. Height 2.5 cm. Right LION. Width 2.7 cm. From a grave near the palace of Hagia Triada. Late Minoan I.

The modelling here is cursory but other gold objects from Hagia Triada are worked with delicate filigree and granulation.

Paribeni, in *Monumenti Antichi* 14, 1905, p. 730, figs. 28-30.

111 above
GOLD SIGNET RINGS. From various graves in Crete. Enlarged four times. Late Minoan I and II.

Not many rings have been found in Crete. Of the four here the first is both the earliest—of the end of Late Minoan I—and the most interesting. It is from the tomb at Isopata near Knossos and shows an ecstatic dance of women with, in the heavens, a divine epiphany. The two smaller and later rings are rather worn. They are from the cemetery at Kalyvia near Phaistos. One has a column, symbolising a sanctuary, with a female figure, the goddess, before it. She seems to be naked but there must be some doubt about this as nakedness is quite un-Minoan. To the right is a dog-headed creature in a pose of adoration and another woman. The other ring illustrates the tree-cult and is one of several representations of the uprooting of the sacred tree. This symbolises the death of the year's vegetation, and with it the deeper truth that death is defeated by death and is itself the source of new life. A ring from Mycenae (plate 206, left in the second row) has a more explicit scene of the uprooting.
The fourth ring was in a private collection which was given to the Heraklion Museum and has been often illustrated and discussed. Its style is rather stiff. Another

ring with the same scene, but for slight differences in dress and pose, is in the National Museum in Athens.

Evans, in *Archaeologia* 65, 1914, p. 10, fig. 16.—*Monumenti Antichi* 14, p. 578, figs. 51 and 13, p. 43. fig. 37.—Nilsson, *Minoan-Mycenaean Religion*, 2nd edition, p. 267, fig. 131.—Hogarth, in *Journal of Hellenic Studies* 22, 1902, pp. 82–83, figs. 16–17.

111 below
CLAY SEAL-IMPRESSIONS. Enlarged three times. Late Minoan I, about 1550–1530 B.C.

These were made by metal finger-rings, the signets of officials with wide jurisdiction in the island.

Left: A bull gallops to the left. Impressions have been found in Gournia (*Gournia*, p. 54, fig. 30, 4). Hagia Triada (Levi, in *Annuario Atene* 8–9, p. 101, no. 54, fig. 71) and Sklavokampos (Marinatos, in *Ephemeris* 1939–41, p. 88, no. 2).
Right: A chariot with two horses; the charioteer, who is holding a whip, is leaning forward. Impressions found in Hagia Triada (Levi, *op.cit.* no. 117, fig. 133) and Sklavokampos (Marinatos, *op.cit.* p. 90, no. 8, pl. 4, 8). Both are clear impressions of fine intaglios.

112, 113 above; Fig. 19
GOLD HANDLE OF A BRONZE SWORD. From grave 36 in the Zapher Papoura cemetery at Knossos. Diam. of the agate pommel 4.4 cm. Length of the sword 61 cm. Late Minoan II.

The decipherment of the clay tablets has shown us that the Knossian graves dating from 1450 and later were of the Achaean warrior-lords.
The sword lay with another, of the 'horned' type and 94.5 cm. long, by the body in the 'Chieftain's Grave'. The pommel is of variegated, partly translucent agate. On the gold plates over the hilt there are lions chasing goats; at the upper end the quarry has been caught and is being mauled.

Evans, *Palace of Minos* IV, pp. 863 ff., fig. 851.

113 below
BRONZE HELMET WITH CHEEK-PIECES. From an Achaean grave near Knossos. Overall height 38.6 cm. Late Minoan II.

The holes at the edge of the helmet show that it had been lined with leather or felt, and was not simply worn over a felt cap as was the practice later in Greece; this we see on vases. There is a curved forward edge to the cheekpieces and a knob at the crown.

Hood and de Jong, in *British School Annual* 47, 1952, p. 256, pl. 50.

114
WORK IN STONE
Above: FRIEZE FROM THE NORTH-WEST GATEWAY OF THE NEW PALACE OF KNOSSOS. Limestone. Height 19 cm. Late Minoan I–II.

The 'triglyph and half-rosette' frieze is also popular in Mycenaean Greece, as on the doorway of the Treasury of Atreus at Mycenae (now in the British Museum). This is a finely carved block of greenish limestone.

Evans, *Palace of Minos* II, pp. 590 ff., fig. 368.

Below left: UPPER PART OF A LAMP WITH PAPYRUS DECORATION. From the New Palace of Knossos, north of the Central Court. Middle Minoan III–Late Minoan I.

The quadruple shafts of the lamp-stands in red porphyry-like alabaster copy Egyptian models. The papyrus pattern decorates the bowl above.

Evans, *Palace of Minos* II, p. 523, fig. 325.

Below right: PART OF A LAMP WITH IVY DECORATION. From the South-east House at Knossos. Middle Minoan III—Late Minoan I.

Probably from a lamp-stand with a spiral-fluted column on which is the relief pattern of ivy motifs.

Evans, *Palace of Minos* II, p. 481, fig. 228; I, pp. 344 ff., fig. 249.

115
WORK IN STONE
Above: LAMP. From the Palace of Hagia Triada. Dark limestone. Diam. 12 cm. Late Minoan I–II.

There are small spiral knobs on the lip as on the relief ceiling decoration with spirals from Knossos (Evans, *Palace of Minos* III, colour pl. 15). There are similar motifs on Minoan and Mycenaean bronze vases.

Below: ALABASTER TRITON SHELL. From the cemetery at Kalyvia near Phaistos. Length 30 cm. Late Minoan II.

Scenes on gems tell us that shells were used as rhytons, and originals of this shape as well as stone copies have been found. There is a similar piece from Knossos.

Evans, *Palace of Minos* II. p. 823, fig. 539.

116 above
WRITING TABLETS OF CLAY. Life size.
Right: LINEAR A. From Hagia Triada. Late Minoan I.
Left: LINEAR B. From Knossos. Late Minoan II.

Typical examples of the two different scripts and—as we now know them to be—languages. The Linear A tablets are generally small and rectangular with short texts. The Linear B tablets may also be rectangular, and of some size, as here, or more elongated and leaf-shaped.

116 below
Left and centre: FRAGMENTS OF A STEATITE VASE WITH LINEAR A INSCRIPTION. From Apodoulou, west of Phaistos, where traces of a mansion have been found. About 1550 B.C.

Right: VASE-FRAGMENT WITH LINEAR B IN-SCRIPTION. Found in the living quarters at Knossos. From a clay vase bearing Mycenaean decoration, so this must be an import from the mainland of Greece. After 1400 B.C.

Evans and Myres, *Scripta Minoa* II, pl. 95, no. 813.—Evans, *Palace of Minos* IV. pp. 656–657, fig. 642, p. 738, fig. 722.—Marinatos, in *Archäologischer Anzeiger* 1935, p. 247, fig. 2.

117
SEAL-STONES FROM VARIOUS SITES IN CRETE. Late Minoan I–III. Views of the originals and of plaster impressions, three and a half times life size.

The seals, of various semi-precious stones, are generally lentoid or amygdaloid in shape. Only one illustrated here, on plate 118 above right, is of the earlier flattened cylinder form.

Above: Onyx. From the Phaistos cemetery. Two lions attack a bull. Impression and original.

Monumenti Antichi 14, 1905, p. 621, pl. 40, figs. 14–15.

Centre: From the Dictaean Cave. Another of the common scenes of two lions attacking a bull. Original and impression.

Below: Yellow agate. From Praisos. Bull and acrobat. Impression.

British School Annual 8, p. 252, fig. 25.

118–119
SEAL-STONES FROM VARIOUS SITES IN CRETE. Late Minoan I–III. Views of the original stones, three times life size.

118 left above: From the Lasithi area. Recumbent lion. A typical late motif.

118 centre left: Meteorite. From Vatheia, Central Crete. Figure in Asiatic (?) dress with a Syro-Hittite axe over his shoulder. The weapon, in this form, is often represented in Crete, and on the mainland once, in a grave at Vaphio where an original weapon of the same type was found.

Evans, *Palace of Minos* IV, p. 414, fig. 343, and p. 946, fig. 914 bis.

118 below left: Steatite. From the Little Palace of Knossos. A singing priest; probably a portrait.

Evans, *Palace of Minos* IV, p. 218, fig. 167.—Biesantz, in *Marburger Winckelmann-Programm* 1958, pp. 13 ff., pl. 10, no. 3.

118 above right: Steatite. From Knossos. Giamalakis Collection. Female monster with a bird's head and wings.

Xenaki Sakellariou, 'Les cachets minoens de la Collection Giamalakis', in *Études Crétoises* X, 1958, p. 62, no. 373.

118 centre right: Chalcedony. From Knossos. Giamalakis Collection. Bull and acrobat.

Xenaki Sakellariou, *op. cit.*, p. 58, no. 357.

118 below right: Chalcedony. Unknown provenience. Giamalakis Collection. Two pigs; a common motif.

Xenaki Sakellariou, *op. cit.* p. 46, no. 302.

119 above: From Monastiraki near Knossos. Lioness (with mane!) attacking a bull. About 1400 B.C. or later.

119 centre, left to right: From Tylissos. A goat struck by a spear. About 1500 B.C.

Hazzidakis, *Tylissos à l'époque minoenne*, 1921, p. 44, pl. 3f.

From Phaistos. Meteorite. Giamalakis Collection. Minotaur. About 1500 B.C. or a little later.

Xenaki Sakellariou, *op. cit.* p. 63, no. 379.

Unknown provenience. A cervine.

119 below: Two sides of a prism seal. From one of the Sanatorium graves near Knossos. About 1450 B.C. Left: A bull resting by a tree. Right: A lion.

Hood and de Jong, in *British School Annual* 47, 1952, fig. 10, III, 22.

THE PERIOD AFTER THE GREAT PALACES

LATE MINOAN III (1400–1100 B.C.) AND SUB-MINOAN (1100 TO AFTER 1000 B.C.)

120

GOLD JEWELLERY. From the Zapher Papoura graves near Knossos and the cemetery at Kalyvia near Phaistos. Late Minoan III, just after 1400 B.C.

Necklaces were worn by both men and women. The commonest motifs on them are lilies (as worn by the prince in the Knossos fresco), papyrus, rosettes, and two nautili conjoined (the last type is not met in the shaft-graves at Mycenae).
The earring looks like a cross between a bucranium and a bunch of grapes, and is a form known since 1600 B.C. The granulation on these pieces reminds us of Homer's epithet for earrings, μορόεις—like a mulberry.

Evans, in *Archaeologia* 59, 1906, p. 129, fig. 119.—*Palace of Minos* IV, p. 862, fig. 845.—*British School Annual* 28, 1926/1927, pl. 18 for the earring (from the Mavro Spelio cemetery at Knossos).

121

BRONZE STATUETTE OF A YOUTH. From Griviglia near Rethymnon. Height 29 cm. Late Minoan III, about 1200 B.C.

This, one of the largest extant examples of the type, is a recent find in the Rethymnon area of West Crete, where there is much evidence for the influence of the latest Minoan products. The nervous and stiff pose is here more relaxed, and the hand is not raised to the head. The quieter composition and the long thighs of the figure anticipate Greek Geometric art.

Bulletin de Correspondance Hellénique 76, 1952, p. 240, pl. 10b.

122

CLAY ALABASTRON WITH WATER-BIRDS Height 23 cm.

123

CLAY ALABASTRON WITH WATER-BIRDS AND FISH. Height 28.5 cm. Both from the cemetery at Kalyvia near Phaistos. Late Minoan III, about 1300 B.C. or later.

These tall pear-shaped alabastra with linear decoration and stylised animals are typical of the period.

Savignoni, in *Monumenti Antichi* 14, pl. 1, 1.

124

JEWEL-BOX DECORATED WITH BIRDS. From a chamber-tomb at Pachyammos, Gulf of Mirabello, East Crete. Height 10.3 cm. Late Minoan III.

Partridges are pecking at full poppy-heads; a scene of some elegance and humour despite the formal treatment which is typical of the late period.

Alexiou, in *Kretika Chronika* 8, 1954, 404ff., pl. 6.

125

MIXING-BOWL. From a late chamber-tomb at Amnisos. Height 24.5 cm. Late Minoan III.

This shape for a clay mixing bowl is commonly met in the last years of the Minoan civilisation. The decoration of this example reflects some woven pattern.

Marinatos, in *Deltion* 11, 1927 1928, p. 80, fig. 5, pl. 1, 3.

XXVII–XXX

POROS STONE SARCOPHAGUS WITH FRESCO PAINTINGS. From a chamber-tomb near the Palace of Hagia Triada. Length 137 cm. Early in Late Minoan III, about 1400 B.C.

This famous piece, of the utmost importance for our understanding of Minoan religion, was decorated long after the main period of Cretan painting. It is nevertheless a work of high quality and even though it is later than 1400 B.C. it at least shows us that at Hagia Triada the tradition of fine painting long survived. All four sides of the sarcophagus are painted, and the preservation of the scenes is good but for a patch missing on one of the long sides. Individually the scenes are intelligible but the explanation of them as a group is far from clear. No other Minoan find can have been so much discussed and still so little really understood.
On one of the long sides the colour of the background changes to differentiate three scenes (plates XXVII, XXIX above). To the left, on a light ground, we see three liquids being poured into a mixing bowl which stands raised between two double axes, on each of which a bird is perched. The first large vase is being poured by a woman dressed in an animal skin. The woman behind her with the two other libation vases may be an at-

tendant, but she wears a crown, such as is worn only by divine beings, like sphinxes, or the Priest-King at Knossos. She should then be a queen or princess. Third comes a lyre-player. The background now becomes a greenish-blue. Three youths move to the right carrying two calves and a boat. On the light ground of the last scene we see the probable recipient of these offerings. A mantle of skins covers this figure hiding his arms. He stands erect before a building, his 'grave', and before him and to his side are a tree and a stepped altar. The figure of the dead man is to be thought of as an unseen witness of the rites summoning him back to life.

The colours of the background on the other long side (plate xxviii) divide it into four fields. Left, on a yellowish ground, four women move to the right. The foremost, the only one completely preserved, stretches out her arms. This is the same crowned figure which we saw on the other long side, and it may be that these are meant to be successive scenes of one ritual ceremony. On a light ground a bull is sacrificed to the music of double pipes. Next, on a greenish-blue ground, a woman dressed in an animal skin lays offerings on an altar. On it is a double-beaked jug and a basket with apples and figs. Behind the altar is a double axe with a bird. Finally, on a light ground again, is the sanctuary crowned with horns of consecration and the sacred tree.

One of the two short sides (plate xxix below) shows a chariot drawn by two heavy figures of horses, on a light ground. On the chariot are two women. Above can be seen feet, from some other unfinished or worked-over scene.

The other short side (plate xxx) shows another chariot with two women, this time on a dark red ground, and the chariot drawn by two griffins with large colourful wings. A supernatural bird hovers before the women.

Do these individual scenes form a unity? If so, what of the simpler but otherwise similar decorated clay sarcophagi which have been found? The main objection to the belief that this shows a sequence of scenes is the mixture of divine and mortal subjects. Perhaps this is a resurrection symbolic of the seasons; perhaps it is the Underworld and Elysium. We do not know.

Paribeni, in *Monumenti Antichi* 19, 1 ff.—Nilsson, *Minoan-Mycenaean Religion*, 2nd edition, p. 426.—Matz, *Göttererscheinung und Kultbild im minoischen Kreta*, 1958.

126–127
LATE MINOAN SARCOPHAGI

The Cretans did not use true sarcophagi of the Egyptian type. When the bodies were not simply laid in an earth grave they were buried in some piece of household furniture, like a pithos or bath, and children in smaller vases. Wooden coffins or clay imitations of them were for the well-to-do. When cremation was adopted at the very end of the Minoan period the ashes were deposited in a clay or bronze vase. Real cremation-urns came to be used only very gradually. In the Mycenaean world baths and chests were very seldom used for burials. The baths, like the pithoi, had first been in use in the house, but many of the clay chest-sarcophagi were deliberately made for burials. The finds at Vathypetro have shown that both wooden and clay chests were also in use domestically. The baths are generally decorated with the usual vase-painters' patterns, but the chests may carry religious or symbolic scenes referring to their use as coffins. The trouble taken with the clay imitations make it clear that the wooden chests must have been in general use as coffins before. One piece of evidence for them is the find of parts of a wooden coffin painted blue in the harbour town of Knossos (Alexiou, in *Kretika Chronika* 6, 1952, p. 11).

126 above
BATH-SARCOPHAGUS WITH AN OCTOPUS AND STYLISED PAPYRUS. From Pachyammos. Upper length 121 cm. Late Minoan III, about 1400–1350 B.C.

The front shows an octopus, scale pattern—which, in the terminology of the Pylos tablets, we know as *pitirowesa/ptiloessa*, 'feather-decoration'—and three papyrus plants. Inside three dolphins are painted, to remind us of the bath's original function.

Alexiou, in *Kretika Chronika* 8, 1954, p. 402.

126 below
CHEST-SARCOPHAGUS WITH A LID. From Vasilika Anogeia, Central Crete. Late Minoan III, about 1400–1350 B.C.

Crude decoration of water-birds, fish and papyri stylised like water-plants.

Orsi, 'Urne funebri cretese', in *Monumenti Antichi*, 1890, pl. 1–2.

127 above
CHEST-SARCOPHAGUS WITH GABLED LID. From Palaikastro, East Crete. Upper length 123 cm. Late Minoan III, about 1400 B.C.

Elaborately decorated with religious symbols; the

double axe, horns of consecration and winged griffin, with lily-like patterns.

Bosanquet, in *British School Annual* 8, 1901–1902, pl. 18.—Nilsson, *Minoan-Mycenaean Religion*, 2nd edition, pl. 170, fig. 71.

127 below
BATH-SARCOPHAGUS WITH CATTLE. From Gournia. Upper length 117 cm. Late Minoan III.

A cow with a suckling calf and a bellowing bull.

Boyd-Hawes, *Gournia*, pl. 10, 44.

128–131
FEMALE IDOLS FROM GAZI. Clay. Heights 52 cm. (plates 128, 129) and 77.5 cm. (plates 130, 131). Late Minoan III.

These are the largest and most important of the late clay idols to have been found. They were excavated in a sanctuary or cult-room at Gazi, four miles west of Heraklion, in 1936. In all there are five figures (one headless), and with them were found vases and cult-objects.

The goddess on plates 128, 129 is painted in red and has on her head two doves and the so-called horns of consecration. She is perhaps the earliest of the Gazi figures with these symbols. The goddess in plates 130, 131 is the tallest. She has become known as the Poppy-goddess for the three poppyheads (*papaverum somniferum*) in her crown, which make us think rather of a healing or fertility goddess. We may note that the poppy-heads are cut in the same way that they are today to extract opium, before they ripen. The deduction is that the women of Crete understood the effect of opium which they tended, as a mystery of their goddess, and dispensed in cases of suffering or despair. In the *Odyssey* (IV, 220 ff.) we read that Helen, to comfort Menelaus and Telemachus, mixed in their wine a physic which would still grief and banish grudges; and here we think naturally of opium.

Marinatos, in *Ephemeris* 1937, 1, p. 278.—Nilsson, *Minoan-Mycenaean Religion*, 2nd edition, p. 100 and *passim.*—Alexiou in *Kretika Chronika* 12, 1958, pp. 179–294.

NOTE: The reference to this figure as a Moon Goddess in the illustration caption is not correct.

132 above
THREE WOMEN IN A CHAIN DANCE, WITH A LYRE-PLAYER. From Palaikastro, East Crete. Height of the figures 13.1 cm. Late Minoan III.

We cannot say whether this is a cult-dance or simple entertainment. It is not certain that the bird belongs with the group.

'The Unpublished Objects from Palaikastro', *British School Annual Suppl. Paper* 1, p. 88, fig. 71.—Nilsson, *Minoan-Mycenaean Religion*, 2nd. edition, pp. 109–610, fig. 30.

132 below
GODDESS WITH DOVES AND VOTARIES. From Knossos. Height of the central figure 21 cm. Late Minoan III.

These were found in the so-called Shrine of the Double Axes, a small cult-room little more than a yard square, of the 'Reoccupation' period.

Nilsson, *Minoan-Mycenaean Religion* 2nd edition, p. 78 ff., fig. 13, with further bibliography.

133 above
CLAY HEAD. From the Cave of Hermes Kranaios, at Patsos near Rethymnon. Height 8.5 cm. Late Minoan III.

This head with round eyes and crown of applied strips, was found in a cave on the west side of Ida which in Roman times was dedicated to Hermes Kranaios. We do not know whether the head is of a man or a woman.

Halbherr, 'Santuario di Hermes Craneo', in *Museo Italiano di Antichità Classica* II, 1888, p. 913 ff, and pl. 14.

133 below
RHYTON IN THE FORM OF A HEAD. From the New Palace of Phaistos. Height without handle 15 cm. Late Minoan III or a little earlier.

The head is characterised by its low forehead, high-set nose, and the stippling which suggests side-boards and beard.

Pernier and Banti, *Festòs* II, 1951, p. 507, fig. 288, pl. 1.

134
CLAY ANIMALS. From the New Palace of Phaistos. Heights, above 17 cm., below 37 cm. Late Minoan III.

The animal above is probably a donkey carrying water-jars. The painting on the bull below suggests a saddle. It is somewhat later than the donkey, which can still pretend to some artistic quality.

Pernier, in *Monumenti Antichi* 12, 1900–1901, p. 118, fig. 47.—*Ibid.*, p. 123, fig. 54.

135–137
FEMALE IDOLS. From Karphi on Mt Dicte. Heights 63 and 67 cm. Sub-Minoan, about 1100–1000 B.C.

These were found in a humble sanctuary high on Dicte where Minoan culture and religion seems long to have survived. Of the nine figures recovered five can be completed. It seems that in this late period all feeling for form and proportion had been lost. The heads are ugly, careless work. The goddess wearing the horns of consecration has her dress cut away to show her legs and feet which hang free within.

British School Annual 38, p. 76, pl. 31; a brief description of the first two goddesses to be restored. Further account and bibliography by Alexiou, in *Kretika Chronika* 12, 1958, p. 152 ff., pl. 6, 1.

138–139
CLAY MODEL OF A SMALL SHRINE. From Archanes, Central Crete. Height 22 cm. Sub-Minoan, about 1100–1000 B.C. Giamalakis Collection.

The shrine, found in what had been an important Minoan centre six miles south of Knossos, belongs to the beginning of a new era in the history of Greek art. Minoan still are the goddess with raised hands, though she is seated, and the round shape of the building. We see similar, probably wooden structures, on Minoan gems, but this is the first copy of one in clay. At the front is a removable door which reveals the goddess seated within. The cella has a broad opening in the roof, reminding one of the chimney in the palace of Pylos.

Two men and a quadruped are looking at the goddess from on top of the roof. Their significance, and the objects they held over their heads are not easily explained. The figure within is certainly a cult statue; perhaps a xoanon. Many myths tell of a goddess kidnapped by two companions or freed by her two brothers. Some such story may lie behind this scene, or perhaps some unknown divine triad.

Alexiou, in *Kretika Chronika* 4, 1950, p. 441 ff., and 12, 1958, p. 277 ff., pl. 13, 2.

140
MT IYTTOS (MODERN JUKTAS), THE SACRED MOUNTAIN OF KNOSSOS

The impressive mass of Iyttos lies six miles south of Knossos. The west side, seen in the picture, is steep, but the east falls gently away. At the peak (2745 ft. high) are remains of a mountain-top sanctuary of the early Middle Minoan period with traces of buildings and a Cyclopean circuit wall (Evans, *Palace of Minos* 1, p. 153 ff., figs. 112–114). There were two sacred caves on the mountain, the Chosto Nero and that of Lykastos. Seen from the sea, in the north-west, or the west, as here, the profile is that of a reclining male head, Zeus' head in legend. The grave of Zeus is also said to lie here but this tradition is not an ancient one and we only know the pre-Hellenic name, Iyttos, from an inscription.

MYCENAEAN GREECE

Unless otherwise stated all objects are in the National Museum at Athens

XXXI
VIEW OF MYCENAE FROM THE SOUTH WEST

To the left of the modern road appears the mound which covers the Treasury of Atreus. In this area are many of the chamber-tombs of the 'Cemetery of Kilometer 3' as well as other Mycenaean and later Greek remains. To the right is the ravine of the Chavos and the foot of Mt Zara, which is out of sight. In the middle distance lies the citadel of Mycenae, of which we see the south-west stretch of the Cyclopean wall at whose north-western angle the Lion Gate lies. The palace complex lies at the top of the hill. Behind is Mt Hagios Elias at whose peak traces of Mycenaean building have been found. The topography of the Lower Town of Mycenae has been established by the many years of excavation by Tsountas and Wace (fig. 18). Within

the walls and just inside the Lion Gate is Grave Circle A, which was discovered in 1876, with its six rich shaft-graves (B in fig. 19 and D in fig. 18). Immediately outside the Gate lie three of the nine tholos-tombs of Mycenae; nearest is that of Aigisthos, farther west that of Clytemnestra (fig. 19, C), and north of these the Lion Tomb. Their names are of course conventional. The newly-found Grave Circle B is near the Tomb of Clytemnestra (fig. 19, D), and to its south are three large houses (House of the Shields, House of the Oil Merchant, and House of the Sphinxes) which held the royal archives and housed industries, as that for perfumed oils (fig. 19, E). All this lies to the east of the long spur in which the Treasury of Atreus (another conventional name) was built (fig. 19, H). Outside the citadel, to the north and west, the Mycenaean town

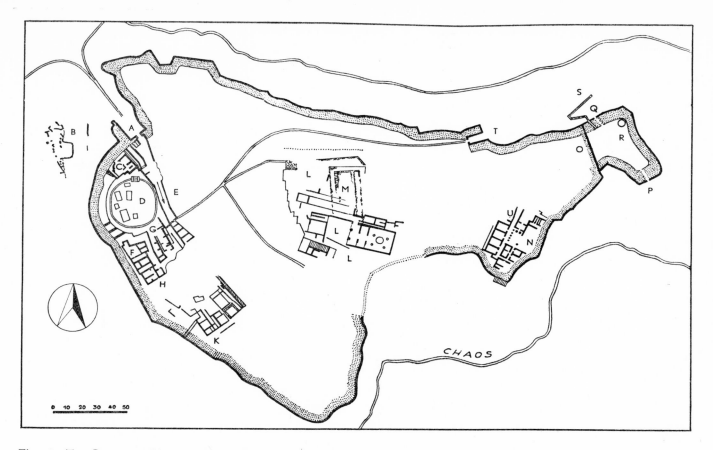

Fig. 18 THE CITADEL OF MYCENAE. (A) Lion Gate. (E) Ramp. (D) Grave Circle A with shaft-graves I–VI in its west half; (C) 'Granary House' of the captain of the guard. (F, G, H, J, K) Houses situated further inside the Acropolis walls: (F) House of the Warrior Vase (Plates 232–233). (G) The Ramp House. (H) The South House. (K) The House of Tsountas. (J) Remains of Hellenistic houses. (L) The Palace. (M) Foundations of temple of classical period. (N) The House of Columns. (T) North Gate. (O) Original east end of the circuit. (P) Sally-port. (Q) Drain. (S) The hidden approach to the fountain 'Perseia'. (R) Hellenistic cistern. (B) Prehistoric cemetery. After *Wace*.

continued, and some hundred metres north of Grave Circle B several interesting houses were found which belong in part, if not wholly, to the palace (fig. 19, F). In them hundreds of vases had been stored ready for export. A similar magazine of vases was found in the palace at Pylos, but at Mycenae the palace lay too high within the citadel and problems of security would have made difficult the free passage to and fro of goods and trade. Thus the royal workshops, which also produced plain vases and prepared spices and other commodities, lay in the Lower Town, though not far from the walls. The other six tholos-tombs and the groups of chamber-tombs of Mycenaean nobles lay farther to the west and north.

141
MYCENAE, THE LION GATE

The picture shows well the new system of fortifications in the Cyclopean circuit wall. The gateway lies at an easy approach to the hill but is strengthened by bastions at either side. At the left the bastion is founded on an outcrop of rock; to the right a rectangular tower was constructed.

The two upper stones to the right of the relief over the gate lay for a long time before the gateway and were replaced only recently. The two stones which covered the relief itself are missing, and the relief is broken away at its top. To restore it we should imagine a dove seated on the capital of the column, as on a seal from Mycenae (Wace, *Mycenae*, fig. 110a) or three flowers, which might better fill the space.

142; Figs. 18–19
THE RUINS OF MYCENAE

Above: Before the Lion Gate. To the left is the rocky bastion crowned by the Cyclopean wall. To the right the ruins of the tower which hides the gateway, and

Fig. 19 MYCENAE, CITADEL AND SURROUNDING AREA. Topographical sketch. (A) Lion Gate. (B) Grave Circle A with shaft-graves I–VI. (G) Palace. (E, F) Groups of houses in the lower town; in (E) the House of the Shields, the House of the Oil Merchant and the House of the Sphinxes; in (F) royal workshops, potteries etc. (C) Tholos tomb of Clytemnestra, to the east that of Aigisthos, and to the north the Lion Tomb. (H) Tholos tomb, the Treasury of Atreus. (D) Grave Circle B.
After *Mylonas*.

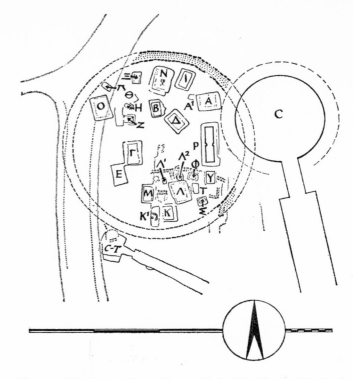

Fig. 20 MYCENAE, GRAVE CIRCLE B, beside (C) the Tomb of Clytemnestra. The 25 graves are lettered A–Φ. The four smallest graves are lettered A^1, K^1, Λ^1 and Λ^2. To the south is (C-T) another chamber-tomb.
After *Mylonas*.

part of a polygonal wall which has been cleared in recent years in the course of restoration work and which is Hellenistic.

Below: Part of the road from the Lion Gate to the palace, which is visible above, to the right. At the centre is part of what may be a Middle Helladic wall belonging to an earlier fortification circuit.
The citadel of Mycenae (fig. 18) is roughly triangular. The walls, about 900 m. long, were built about 1350–1300 B.C. but the eastern part was added later. The Lion Gate (A) was the main entrance. There was another, probably earlier entrance (T), and in the east a postern gate (P) and the famous secret fountain-house (S). Just to the south of the highest point, perhaps to gain some protection in winter, is the palace (L) over which a Greek temple (M) was later built.
The next largest building on the citadel was the House of the Columns (N) for which an isodomic tower had been built on the walls. There are five other houses in the circuit, near the Lion Gate. The first is just behind the gateway (C) at a point of ready access to the walls and with store-rooms, probably for the commander of

the guard. Just within the Lion Gate, as in the north gate (T), there is a small niche. That by the Lion Gate is as big as a small room, and may have been for the watch-dogs. The other houses have been called the Ramp House (G, next to the ramp-approach to the palace), the House of the Warrior Vase (F, where the crater in plates 232–233 was found), the South House (H) and Tsountas' House (K). Grave Circle A (D in fig. 18; B in fig. 19) was sacred ground, as the history of the citadel walls shows. The line of the wall at the west was extended to take in the circle despite the awkward lie of the ground here; it was not simply for the houses (C, E–H). The circle of slabs around the graves was renewed at the time the walls were built, and the circle made somewhat smaller and irregular in shape; its entrance now faced the north and not the west. The stelae were not, however, disturbed, and they remained facing the original entrance in the west.

143
VIEW FROM THE PALACE TO THE SOUTH WEST
At the centre is the inside of the Cyclopean wall at the

156

south-west of the citadel. The Grave Circle, houses (cf. plate 142 below) and inside of the Lion Gate are also visible. In the background is the northern part of the Argive plain and the mountains of Saminthos.

144; Fig. 21
MYCENAE, VIEW FROM THE EAST OVER THE MEGARON AND THE ANTEROOM OF THE PALACE

In the foreground the main room of the megaron with the column-bases and the (covered) surviving half of the circular hearth. Beyond, the anteroom (*promodos*), porch (*aithousa*) and court.

The palace is not well preserved. Its upper parts, near the top of the hill, have completely disappeared and part of the megaron itself had collapsed into the ravine of the Chaos in antiquity. Thus the south wall, throne, one column-base and half of the hearth are missing. There was probably a propylon like that at Tiryns, which has also disappeared. It lay to the north-west facing the older, northern entrance to the citadel. Later, when the Lion Gate was built, there was a new entrance to the south, without a Propylon because the slope is too steep, but with two flights of stairs.

More than forty shallow steps led to a throne-room, probably a guard and waiting-room which was controlled by a trusted official. To the right, in the east, was the palace court, a reconstruction of whose north-west corner appears in fig. 21. To the left, west, in the picture lay the waiting-room, and to the right, north, the great covered east–west corridor of the palace. As the reconstruction shows, there was probably an upper story. What we do not see is the east side of the court with the entrance to the megaron. The floor of the court (12 × 15 m.) was covered with painted plaster, divided into fields variously coloured yellow, blue and red, or marbled and with linear patterns. Around was a dado, shown in the reconstruction, painted with the favourite triglyphs and half-rosettes. The main features of the megaron, which are common to all palaces, have been described in the Introduction, p. 88. The porch (aithousa) opened onto the court through the usual two columns and had a door in its north wall to the corridor. The floor was paved with slabs of gypsum. A single-leaved door led to the Prodomos whose floor was paved around the edges and otherwise covered with painted plaster. Here again there were panels with painted marbling. The main megaron measured

Fig. 21 MYCENAE. Reconstruction of the north-west corner of the palace court, showing indications of plastering at the foot of the walls. After *Wace*.

13 × 12 m. It was paved with gypsum slabs and plaster like the anteroom. The hearth, 3.70 m. in diameter and 15 cm. high, had been re-plastered at least ten times and re-painted always with the same pattern: spirals above and toothed, flame-pattern on the sides and lip. The problems about an upper story over the megaron, its lighting and roof, have been discussed in the Introduction.

When the palace was excavated in 1886 traces of painting were still visible on its walls and floors. From the fragments we can see that a continuous frieze, some 46 m. long, probably ran around the whole megaron. The subject was the storming of a town, such as we see on the silver rhyton from shaft-grave IV (plate 174).

Mycenae and its palace were described by Tsountas and Manatt in *The Mycenaean Age*, 1897, and the place was later explored by Wace and his staff. His discoveries are published in *British School Annual* 24 and 25, and Wace, *Mycenae*, p. 67 ff. For the frieze see Rodenwaldt, *Der Fries der Megarons von Mykenai*, 1921.

145; Figs. 18–19, 22–23
MYCENAE, GRAVE CIRCLE A, WITHIN THE WALLS
At the right is the entrance. The border is formed by

Fig. 23 Reconstruction with the stelae in position, based on early photographs. Schliemann found three stelae over grave V, two over graves I, II and III, and Stamatakis found another over grave I. The stelae faced west and stood over the heads of the bodies, which, with the exception of two in grave IV with their heads to the east, faced west.
After *Wace*.

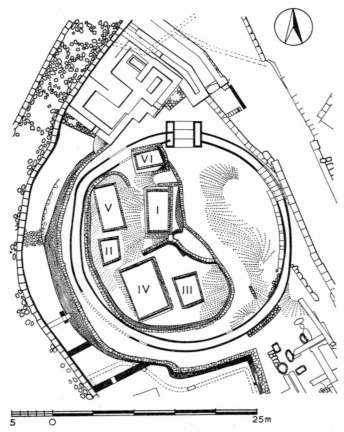

Fig. 22 GRAVE CIRCLE A inside the Citadel of Mycenae.
22 Ground plan. (I–VI) The six shaft-graves.
After *Karo*.

two rows of upright slabs with sinkings in their upper edges for pegs to fasten covering slabs. Within, the left half holds the six shaft-graves, the right is empty. The newly-found Grave Circle B lies outside the walls (fig. 19, D and fig. 20), 130 m. west of the Lion Gate. It is as big as Circle A (diameter 28 m.) but its edge is formed by a wall of simple field-stones about 1.55 m. thick and preserved up to 1.20 m. high. The entrance was again in the west and the stelae orientated as in Circle A.

The Egyptians thought that the dead journeyed to the west. The City of the Dead at Egyptian Thebes lay opposite the town, to the west across the Nile. Grave inscriptions speak of the 'beautiful west' which the souls must reach (Erman and Ranke, *Ägypten*, p. 349). Could this Egyptian belief have been adopted at Mycenae?

In the shaft-graves the bodies lie on pebbles on the earth floor of the pit. They were wrapped in cloths or bandages on which masks, pectorals and other ornaments might be sewn or tied. Schliemann found the skeletons in a good state of preservation but they soon deteriorated after excavation. The bodies in each tomb lay about one metre apart.

There were different numbers of burials in the graves. Graves II, V and VI had only male burials, there was only one body in grave II, three in grave V, of which two wore masks (plates 162–163, XXXIV), and in grave VI at first only one body, but a second was introduced later. Graves I and III each held three women. Only grave IV had bodies of both sexes: three men (with masks, plates 164–166) and two women.

In graves I–III, V and VI the bodies were laid with their heads in the east, facing west. The same is true in grave IV only of the women and the man with the mask shown in plate 166. The other two men lay with their heads to the north.

There were not many offerings in graves I, II and VI, but the women had all their personal jewellery and the men their weapons and other equipment, including two vases in precious metals and some fine painted vases. Graves III, IV and V were, on the other hand, incredibly rich and elegant in their furnishings.

Grave Circle B seems to be somewhat older than Circle A, but not more than a generation at the most. There is more of the matt-painted Middle Helladic pottery here, but this may in part be due to conservatism, the comparative poverty of the burials and the less marked influence of Cretan products.

Circle B (fig. 20) held 25 graves, half of them cist-graves, the rest shaft-graves, the largest of which is about the size of the smallest in Circle A (3.50 × 3 m.). There were also individual cist-graves in Circle A, and the similar graves found in the area, outside the Circles, show that there was a large Middle Helladic cemetery here before the Circles were built.

Mylonas, *Ancient Mycenae, the capital city of Agamemnon*, 1957.

146–147
MYCENAE, TWO GRAVE STELAE OF GRAVE CIRCLE A

Seventeen stelae were found in Circle A of which six were undecorated while the rest had linear patterns or figured scenes on them. Apart from fragments we have three stelae which are fairly well preserved, all of which stood over grave V—Schliemann's 'Grave of Agememnon'. The most complete pair are seen in plates 146 and 147.

146 Stela over grave V. Height 1.12 m., breadth 1.23 m. Inv. no. 1427.
The representation is the most careful of those preserved but not easily explained. It has been thought that there are two episodes: above, an unarmed warrior in a chariot drawn by a horse beneath whose legs is a fallen enemy, apparently helmeted and covered with a figure-of-eight shield; below, a lion is coursing after a deer or

goat; but from its head and long tail the quarry might well be a horse, and the pursuer, from his curly tail, a dog. We see hounds like lions on seals from Knossos, and the Molossian hounds of Epirus could be successfully matched against lions. In Alciphron (3, 11) we read of the 'terrible, roaring Molossian and Knossian hounds', such as a king might gladly rear.

147 Stela over grave V. Height 1.33 m., breadth 1.06 m. Inv. no. 1428.
The figured scene shows a charioteer with a sword and a naked man with what may be a battle-knife, *kopis*, of the sort found in the shaft-graves. The artist was more familiar with representations of bulls than horses, but we may notice that the horses shown in the art of the shaft-grave period are the small, compact, ugly creatures which can still be seen on Pindus and in Skyros. The type was long known in Mycenae and considered the offspring of the man-eating horses of Thracian Diomedes. Heracles brought the horses to Mycenae and Eurystheus dedicated them to Hera. The strain was still alive in the time of Alexander the Great (Diodorus Siculus IV, 15). There may be a grain of truth in this story told at Mycenae of the savage warrior and his equally savage and wild horses and hounds.

Karo, *Schachtgräber von Mykenai*, p. 168, nos. 1427–1428, pls. 7 and 5 with full bibliography.—Mylonas, in *American Journal of Archaeology* 55, 1951, p. 134ff., figs. 6 and 2; he thinks the scenes are of chariot-races.—Wace, *Mycenae*, pl. 79.

148–151; Figs. 24–25
MYCENAE, THE SO-CALLED TREASURY OF ATREUS

This, the most monumental of the tholos-tombs, is built of colossal conglomerate ashlars. The stone-walled dromos faces east and is 6 m. wide and 36 m. long. One of the blocks is 6 m. long and 1.25 m. high. The façade is nearly 10.50 m. high and, like the dromos, 6 m. wide. The doorway is 5.40 m. high; its width 2.70 m. below and 2.45 m. above. The depth of the entrance is 5.50 m. There are two massive lintel blocks of which the inner, larger one weighs some hundred tons. The tholos itself is 14.60 m. across, 13.40 m. high, and has a small side-chamber doorway (2.50 × 1.50 m.), imitating the main door with a massive lintel and relieving triangle. The chamber is almost cubical, with 6 m. sides. It is notable that its sides are quite bare, like a chamber-tomb, but the tholos is so well preserved that any lining it had could hardly have disappeared without trace. It was perhaps never finished, a circumstance which often befell in the great Royal Tombs in Egypt.

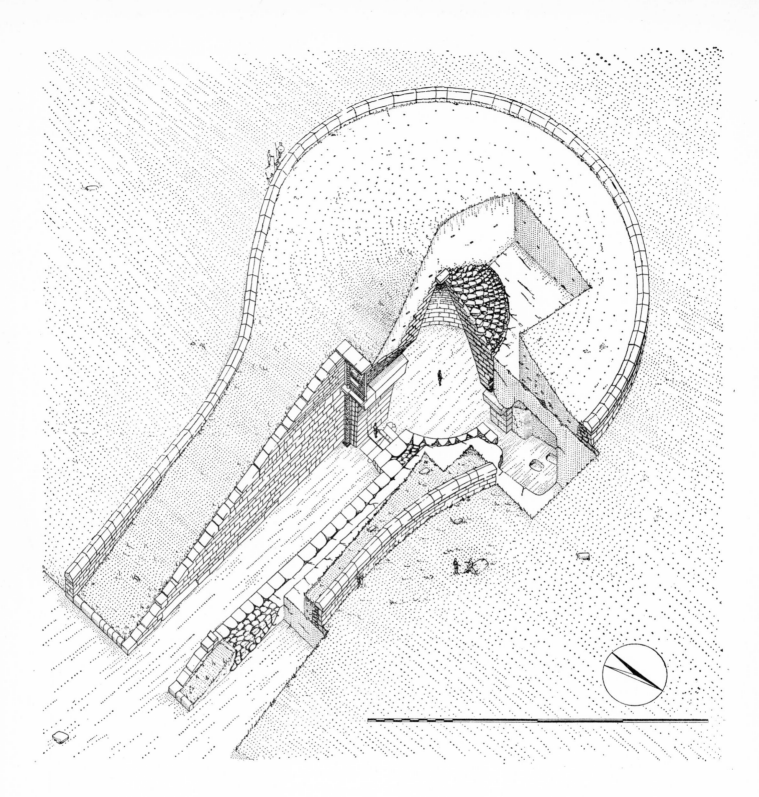

Fig. 24 TREASURY OF ATREUS. Isometric view with reconstruction of the façade and the retaining wall round the base of the mound which covered the dome.
After *Hood*.

The façade carried architectonic decoration in green and red stone. Parts of the plaques and half-columns are now in Mycenae, Athens, and London (plate 149) and there are scraps in other museums. Since the war it has been shown that above the half-columns by the door there was a second, smaller order with half-columns, and that, as on the Tomb of Clytemnestra, there was gypsum decoration also.

The new essay at reconstruction in fig. 25 replaces that in Perrot and Chipiez without, of course, being by any means definitive.

Wace, *Mycenae*, pls. 5, 8–10, 49–50, 51.—Mylonas, *Ancient Mycenae*, fig. 26.—Marinatos, in *Ephemeris* 1953–1954, I, pl. 1.

152–155; Fig. 26
THE CITADEL OF TIRYNS

The colossal fortifications of Tiryns have long excited admiration, and are spoken of with awe by Pausanias. The name, Tiryns, is pre-Greek, as is the other name still applied to the citadel, Licymna. A whole cycle of myths was spun around the castle and the goddess Hera was particularly associated with it. Heracles was from Tiryns; here Proitos and Anteia conspired against the blameless hero Bellerophon; and the only mention of the art of writing in Homer is associated with the city. The southern part of the hill, barely 20 m. high, was occupied by the citadel with the palace and fortifications which are of various periods. The northern part, the lower town, was only fortified as a place of refuge.

The circuit of the walls is 700 m. long, enclosing about 20,000 square metres. The main entrance is in the east, facing inland. Along a ramp (plan; 1), an entrance way in the outer wall (plan; 3) and a narrow corridor, fatal for any attacker, the real gateway was reached. This is comparable with the Lion Gate at Mycenae for its size, construction and appearance. Farther south is another gate (plan; 12) and then an open space (plan; 14). The east galleries (plan; 15) can be reached from here, as well as the first propylon to the palace (plan; 17). The forecourt (plan; 19) is closed by the complicated construction of the south galleries (plan; 20), while to the north lies the second propylon (plan; 21) which leads to the pillared court with a round altar (plan; 22, 23) and the palace itself (plan; 24 etc.).

The palace is better preserved than at Mycenae. Its front is 12.50 m. wide and overall length 25 m. The porch (*aithousa*) of the megaron has the famous alabaster benches which have been wrongly identified with the Homeric *kyanos* frieze. Beyond the ante-room (plan; 24) lies the main megaron, 9.80 × 11.80 m. The hearth and base for the throne are well preserved and in places

the painted floor was found intact. From the fragments of fresco it seems that the walls were decorated with scenes of the boar-hunt. A life-size frieze of standing or walking women was also found in fragments (the most important shown in plates XL and 226). A simpler and smaller megaron (plan; 29) was probably the women's quarters. Another entrance was cut through a bastion on the west (plan; 35–37) to give more ready access to the sea.

The existence of such a strong and well-appointed citadel only 10 miles from Mycenae presents something of a problem. In legend the two towns belonged to the same lord, and it is quite possible that, at least for a while, one and the same king ruled in both citadels.

For *Tiryns, Die Ergebnisse der Ausgrabungen des Deutschen Archäologischen Instituts*, Athens, 1912ff., II: Rodenwaldt, 'Die Fresken'; III: K. Müller and H. Sulze, 'Die Architektur der Burg und des Palastes'.

156; Fig. 27
THE AREA OF PYLOS, WEST MESSENIA

Above: The bay of Bouphras (Voidokoilia), which was smaller in antiquity. Beyond is the broader bay of Pylos-Sphacteria, probably the most secure anchorage in the Peloponnese.

Below: General view of the Palace of Nestor at Englianos, on the border between Messenia and Triphylia (cf. fig. 27); behind is the Aigaleon range.

XXXII
KORYPHASION, THE HOME OF NESTOR

At the centre is the rocky promontory of Koryphasion. The Greek tradition placed Nestor's house and tomb here, no doubt by the Cave of Neleus which appears as a black dot at the centre of the cliff, and, a little farther off, the tomb of his son Thrasymedes. There is no sign now on Koryphasion of Nestor's palace or tomb, but the recently excavated tholos-tomb, seen at the bottom of the picture, may be the alleged Tomb of Thrasymedes.

XXXIII
VIEW FROM KORYPHASION TO THE NORTH

The view is from the entrance to the Cave of Neleus. In the foreground are the green lower slopes of the promontory. In antiquity there were extensive sand-dunes over the lake (to the right here) and part of the bay of Voidokoilia. To the left at the entrance to the bay is the 'Tomb of Thrasymedes' (see plate XXXII). Inland, 3 miles north of the bay, is the 'Palace of Nestor' at Englianos. In the background again the Aigaleon range.

Fig. 25 TREASURY OF ATREUS. Reconstruction of the façade. Compare Plates 148, 149. Scale 1:50.
After *Marinatos.*

GRAVES IN THE PYLOS AREA

Above: The royal tholos-tomb 150 m. north of the palace at Englianos. It was preserved up to its lintel and the roof has been restored.

Below: One of the Early Mycenaean chamber-tombs found at Palaipylos (Volimidia, near Chora in Triphylia). The tomb was found intact. Note the short dromos with straight sides and steep floor with a secondary burial at the left side.

Marinatos, in *Das Altertum* 1, 1955, p. 140 ff., especially p. 145 f. (grave A9).

158–159; Fig. 28
THE ACROPOLIS OF ARNE (GLA) BOEOTIA

158   Above: View from the palace to the east.
Below: Part of the north wall and gate.

159   Above: North-west corner of the wall; on the left the supporting wall of the palace; in the background Lake Copais, now drained.

Below: North gate.

This, the largest Mycenaean fortress, stands on a low hill. The fairly steep north-west side rises about 70 m. above the plain. To the east the hill falls away gently so that the easternmost gate in the north wall is only 12 m. above the plain.

The walls are nearly 3000 metres long and the acropolis occupies about 200,000 square metres. The corresponding measurements of other citadels are:

> Mycenae: 900 m. and 30,000 sq.m.
> Tiryns: 700 m. and 20,000 sq.m.
> Athens: 700 m. and 25,000 sq.m.
> Troy VI: 500 m. and 20,000 sq.m.

Fig. 26   THE CITADEL OF TIRYNS. (1) Ramp to (3) the outer east door. (5) South-west gate to the lower town, and (6) north gate. (9) Inner main door. (10) Dipylon (inner court). (12, 13) Wooden gates. (14) Forecourt. (15) Portico, probably with rooms behind. (16) West casemates. The rooms to the east of the casemates fell in and were buried, and were partially excavated for the first time in 1934. Their outer walls also collapsed in antiquity. (17) Outer Propylon and (19) outer Palace court. (20) South casemates. (21) Inner Propylon. (22) Main inner court with (23) altar. (24) Vestibule to the Megaron; before it the anteroom *(aithousa)* with two columns leading to the main court. Behind it the Megaron proper. (26) Bathroom. (28) Small inner court. (29) West (smaller) megaron with painted floor. (30) East (smallest) megaron. (31) Pillared court. (34) Rear court. (35) Tower of the west bastion. (37) West gate.
The walls are shown here partially restored.
After *Karo*.

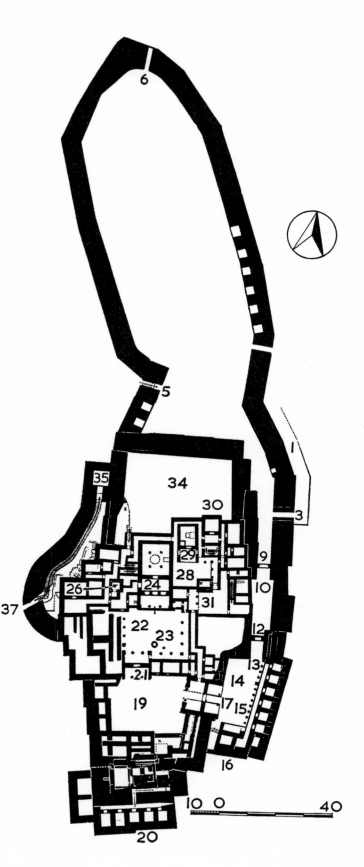

Comparison of these measurements shows that Arne can hardly have been the seat of some powerful king whose name has been completely lost to history, but was rather a refuge-town which served the whole neighbourhood. The fortifications are the work of a league of cities, a communal effort.

Somewhat later the surrounding population (amphiktyones) of Onchestos had their centre in this area. Homer mentions Onchestos together with Arne, the name now associated with the ruins at Gla. The walls are so shattered (see plate 158 below) that they must have been overthrown by an earthquake or an enemy attack. They were literally dismantled stone by stone, although in one or two places they are still preserved to a height of 3 m. They were 6 m. thick and their course is everywhere clear.

Cyclopean walls of Mycenaean citadels are faced, back and front, with large blocks, and filled with field-stones and earth. At Arne the construction is different and relatively larger stones were employed for the full thickness of the wall.

The indented, saw-like profile of the walls is still clearly visible (plate 158 below). This feature is less well attested in Mycenae and Tiryns but appears in the supporting wall behind the Theatral Area at Phaistos (plate 51 centre). Students of Mycenaean architecture had long ago derived this type of construction from the east—there are similar walls in Troy VI—without being able to explain the need for it. The technique of brick construction, as described by Koldewey for Babylon, may help us here. If the inner face of a wall is not laid exactly parallel to the outer face, and the line has to be constantly adjusted, this saw-like plan is the result. The same fashion in brick-walling had no structural significance. Admittedly, the indented walls of Babylon are later than those of Troy VI, Phaistos and Arne, but the tradition may have been deep-seated in Mesopotamia and had its effect overseas at a much earlier date (Koldewey, *Das wieder entstehende Babylon*, 4th edition, p. 108ff., 184, 279, fig. 235).

The walls of Arne are not truly Cyclopean although there are some massive stones in them. They seem to have been built hurriedly. There are no towers, and the great extent of the circuit necessitated four gateways. The main gates are at the north (plate 159 below) and south, and to the east, on the south side, is a double gate. The fourth is in the west. This number of entrances is far from being characteristic of the plans of Mycenaean citadels. Seven-gated Thebes and the Enneapylon Pelargikon at Athens might seem to contradict this, but the description of Thebes might be a later

Fig. 27 THE PALACE OF NESTOR at Englianos near Pylos. (A) The earliest quarter. (10) Large anteroom with three columns. (11) The main room of the Old Palace with four columns and probably an upper floor. (12) Court, which after the completion of Palace B linked the Old with the New Palace. (B) The main Palace, somewhat later than (A). (1) Propylon with a column at either side. (2) Court with a north-east portico. (3–5) Megaron: (3) Aithousa. (4) Prodomos. (5) Main room, the throne-room with central hearth (4.02 m. across and 15–20 cm. high). Four columns around the hearth supported the upper story, probably a gallery. The throne is against the north-east wall and has a libation bowl beside it. (6) Two magazines with oil and wine jars. The rooms to either side of the megaron are divided from it by corridors. (7) The archive room where the clay tablets were found. (8) The Queen's Megaron. (9) Bathroom. (C) The south-east quarter: (13) Altar. (14) Palace shrine.
After *Blegen*.

invention prompted by the story of the Seven against Thebes, and the magic number seven.

As there were no towers, keeps were built beside the gates (see plate 159 below). The main gates, 5 m. wide, are much wider than the Lion Gate. We do not know how they were fastened.

A terrace wall of large blocks (plate 159 above) supported the 'palace'. This is a series of rooms with long connecting corridors, arranged in two wings at right angles to each other. There are insignificant traces of painted decoration. The purpose of a large, enclosed and court-like room south-west of the palace is not clear.

De Ridder, in *Bulletin de Correspondance Hellénique* 18, 1894, p. 271ff.—Frazer, *Commentary on Pausanias* 5, p. 120ff.—Tsountas and Manatt, *The Mycenaean Age*, p. 374ff.—Noack, in *Athenische Mitteilungen* 19, 1894, p. 405.

ORCHOMENOS, THE TREASURY OF MINYAS
The fine great tholos-tomb, which was still intact and admired in Pausanias' day, is now largely destroyed. The roof has collapsed and in recent times the walls of the dromos have been stripped to build a church. Schliemann excavated what remained. The tomb is known as the Treasury of Minyas, 'richest among men'. The Minyans were seafarers, whose fame lived on in the story of the Argonauts, and at the same time engineers who tackled the problems of irrigating the great plain, as is shown by the great 'Minyan canal'. There is evidence for the wealth of Orchomenos and the Minyans in the Early Bronze Age. There were granaries there, like those in Egypt, and indeed Orchomenos was like an Egypt in Greece. The method of irrigating the plain at the times of the periodic high water levels of Lake Copais was similar to that employed in the Nile valley at the time of the annual floods. The memory of this greatness is recorded in Homer (*Iliad* IX, 381–382) where Orchomenos is compared with Egyptian Thebes,

although by Homer's day both great cities had long passed their prime. The only monument of the golden age of Orchomenos is the tholos-tomb, which has with reason been compared with the Treasury of Atreus at Mycenae. The length of the dromos cannot now be determined, but it is 6 m. wide. The entrance is 5.60 m. high and 2.76 m. broad at the base; naturally it was narrower at the top. Only part of the lintel is preserved and all above it is missing. The diameter of the tholos is little more than 14 m., and so very close to that of the Treasury of Atreus. Here too there are bronze pegs around the door to the side chamber, which suggest metal ornaments on its walls.

The side chamber was not cut in the rock as in the Treasury of Atreus but stone-built. Its ceiling is made of the fine-grained greenish limestone which was so popular with Cretan and Mycenaean masons. It measures little less than 3.70 × 2.70 m. and has an all-over relief decoration of spirals and flowers, broken at the centre by a panel-border of two rows of rosettes with an astragal between.

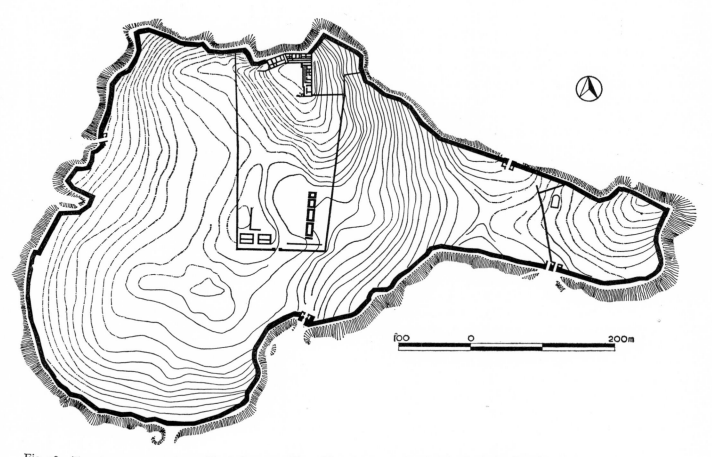

Fig. 28   THE ACROPOLIS OF ARNE (GLA), BOEOTIA. Plan. After the survey by the *Greek Archaeological Service*.

Schliemann said that he found the interior piled with ashes and clinkers which he rightly took to be the remains of burnt offerings. On the analogy of other tholoi and chamber-tombs it would have been the dead who were honoured with offerings, in this case Minyas and the heroes of his line. In the Macedonian and Roman periods the tomb was converted into some sort of shrine. A marble foundation with three sides is still visible at the centre of the tholos and scraps of marble statuary, apparently of Macedonian date, indicate the practice of cult within the tomb in this period.

Tsountas and Manatt, *The Mycenaean Age*, p. 126 ff.—Frazer, *Commentary on Pausanias* 5, pp. 187 ff.—Orlandos, in *Deltion* 1, 1915, Appendix, pp. 51 ff.

162–167; XXXIV
FUNERAL MASKS OF MYCENAEAN PRINCES

162–166; XXXIV Gold masks from the citadel of Mycenae, Grave Circle A, graves IV and V.
162; XXXIV From grave V. The so-called Agamemnon. Height 26 cm. Inv. no. 624.
163 From grave V. Height 31.5 cm. Inv. no. 623.
164 From grave IV. Height 20.5 cm. Inv. no. 253.
165 From grave IV. Height 21.5 cm. Inv. no. 254.
166 From grave IV. Height 30.3 cm. Inv. no. 259.
167 Electrum mask. From grave Gamma in Grave Circle B outside the citadel of Mycenae. Height 22 cm.

Only the men in Grave Circle A wear gold masks, and they were found, as we have remarked, only on the three men in grave IV and two of the three in grave V. There were no masks with the body in grave II and the two burials in grave VI.

There were three burials in grave V. The offerings with the central one had been all robbed. The one to the south is the one that Schliemann called Agamemnon and wore the mask shown in plates XXXIV and 162. The one to the north was the most richly furnished. The body wore a gold necklace of double-eagle pendants (plate 205 above) and the mask shown in plate 163. There may have been some attempt to reproduce the features of the dead in the masks, but they had certainly been made only for some religious purpose. The two in grave V render quite different physiognomies, one with a flat and angular face, the other more rounded. It is difficult to believe that they can represent brothers or close kin.

The three men in grave IV all wore masks. Two (plates 164–165) are like the 'Agamemnon' and are very similar to one other, the third (plate 166) has a round face with protruding eyes. It is rather like the face of the mask from grave V, in plate 163; and perhaps the two dead were related.

Only one mask was found in Grave Circle B, in grave Gamma (plate 167). There were three bodies here, and the mask did not lie over the face but above and to the right of a head. We cannot say whether it was originally set there or had been shifted during a later burial. At all events it has, like the others, holes for fastening behind the ears. It is a small mask and its gold content low. There is an unquestionable resemblance to the smaller masks from grave IV in Circle A (plates 164–165), both in technique and features. All three have meeting eyebrows, and it may be that there was some blood-relationship between the two dead in grave IV and the man in grave Gamma in the other Circle.

It might be argued that only kings were buried with masks, and not lesser members of the royal family. It is an open question whether there were two branches of a single dynasty who occupied the throne alternately, as the tradition as Mycenae told and for which the double kingship at Sparta offers a historical parallel.

Karo, *Schachtgräber von Mykenai*.—Eugen Fischer *ibid.*, p. 320.—Marinatos, *Geras Keramopoullou*, 1953, pp. 61, 78 ff.—Mylonas, *Ancient Mycenae*, p. 107 and *passim*.—Biesantz, *Marburger Winckelmann-Programm* 1958, p. 9 ff.

168
GOLD PECTORAL OF THE SO-CALLED AGAMEMNON. Citadel of Mycenae, grave V. Height 36.5 cm. Inv. no. 625.

The two bodies with masks in grave V also wore pectorals. One was quite plain; the other, that of 'Agamemnon' shown here, is decorated with loops and spirals. The nipples are represented.

Karo, *Schachtgräber von Mykenai*, p. 122, no. 625, pl. 55.

169
TWO GOLD DIADEMS. Citadel of Mycenae, grave III. Both are from a women's grave, and were made as funeral ornaments only, of thin gold plate and with no particular regard for their strength. They appear here as they have been spread out for exhibition. Compare Karo's illustrations of the pieces.

Above: Diadem with blossoms. Width 62 cm. Inv. no. 1. Elliptical with pointed ends. Decorated with beaten circles filled alternately with seven bosses and rosettes. Nine blossoms, each of four leaves, are fastened to the upper border.
Below: Radiate diadem. Width 65 cm. Inv. no. 3.

Again elliptical with pointed ends. Nine bosses with ornamental borders in graduated circles, and similar decoration on the 'rays'.

Above: Karo, *Schachtgräber von Mykenai*, p. 43, no. 1, pls. 11–12.—Below: *Ibid.*, p. 44, nos. 3 and 5, pls. 13–14.

170–171; XXXV–XXXVIII
INLAID BRONZE DAGGERS

We have remarked in the Introduction, p. 104, that inlays of metal in metal are a Mycenaean speciality, particularly for the decoration of ceremonial weapons. The main period of the practice lay in the 16th century, particularly its second half. Only simpler inlay-work is found after 1500 and the latest is of the end of the 15th century, with isolated motifs and not whole scenes, such as the blades from Prosymna (plate XXXVIII below). In Grave Circle A Schliemann found several plain, or slightly decorated blades, as well as five daggers with the very finest inlay decoration. The materials employed were gold, silver and niello. In some instances colour contrasts were obtained by various mixtures of gold and silver, or different preparations of oxydised silver. The inlaid scenes were prepared on a thin bronze strip which was afterwards fastened on to the blade itself. The preparation of the inlay was the task of the goldsmith, its application that of the bronzesmith.

Karo, *Schachtgräber von Mykenai*, pp. 96, 137; for the daggers p. 313 and *passim* for the inlay technique.—Evans, *Palace of Minos* III, p. 113, colour pl. 20 for the Nile scene p. 118 for the lion-hunt; further on inlaying and conservation, Persson, *Dendra*, pp. 48, 134.

170 above: Dagger with gold handle and lily-decoration. Grave V. Length preserved 18 cm. Inv. no. 764. The lilies are hammered into the blade; their petals are of electrum, their stalks gold. The inlay and the decoration of the handle are both of the highest quality.

Karo, *Schachtgräber von Mykenai*, p. 137, no. 764, pls. 91, 92.

170 centre: Bronze blade with gold spiral decoration. Grave V. Length 24.3 cm. Inv. no. 744. An engraved gold strip is inlaid on either side of the blade and decorated skilfully with a complex of spirals and dot-rosettes.

Karo, *Schachtgräber von Mykenai*, p. 135, no. 744, pls. 91, 92.

170 below: Gold handle of a sword decorated with lions and spirals. From Grave Delta in Grave Circle B, outside the citadel of Mycenae. Length of the handle 14 cm.
The blade of the sword is 94.5 cm. long and has griffins engraved on either side. The covering of the handle is decorated with spirals and terminates in two lions heads which appear to bite the blade.

Mylonas, *Ancient Mycenae*, pp. 140 f., fig. 51.

XXXV–XXXVII: Blades of three daggers with gold, silver and niello inlays. Citadel of Mycenae, graves IV and V. About 1570–1550 B.C.
The earliest and most accomplished examples of the inlay technique.

XXXV above and XXXVII below: From grave V. Length 16.3 cm. Inv. no. 765.
Leopards hunting among wild-duck at the edge of a papyrus swamp. Small fish are shown swimming in the wavy strip of water.

XXXV centre and XXXVI: From grave IV. Length 23.8 cm. Inv. no. 394.
On the front a lion-hunt; a common scene in Mycenaean art. The representations of arms and armour are particularly interesting. Four hoplites and an archer attack a lion, while two other lions have turned in flight. The lion at bay has been struck by a spear but has pulled down the nearest of the warriors. On the other side a lion seizes a gazelle while two others leap away.

XXXV below and XXXVII below: From grave IV. Length 21.4 cm. Inv. no. 395.
Three running lions, with clouds and rocks shown above and below.

171; XXXVIII above and centre:
Two daggers from the tholos-tomb at Rutsi near Pylos. About 1500 B.C. The graciously stylised inlays are of the second phase in this art. The circumstances of the find indicate that the weapons belonged to a woman, which need not surprise us in view of the athletic achievements of women in Mycenaean art and legend. We also think of the weapons of Queen Aahhotep in Egypt.

171 above and XXXVIII above:
Swimming nautili in the Cretan Marine style (compare the vase in plate 84 above). The blade is the longest (25 cm.) of those inlaid. At the moment of discovery the niello looked dark blue rather than black, like the deep blue of Greek waters.

171 centre and below; XXXVIII centre:
Dagger with golden handle engraved with spirals.

Length 32 cm. The inlaid blade shows three leopards between rocks, the central one being an exceptionally fine animal representation. On both daggers the scenes are repeated on both sides with only slight differences.

XXXVIII below:
Bronze blade of a dagger with a dolphin. From Prosymna, Argos. Length 18.5 cm. About 1450 B.C.

This is of the third phase in which there no are longer complete scenes but individual figures.

Blegen, *Prosymna* I, p. 330, no. 1.

172–173
CEREMONIAL SWORD FROM STAPHYLOS ON SKOPELOS. Diameter of the pommel 13.8 cm. Length of handle and pommel 24 cm. About 1500 B.C.

Staphylos is the name of an area at the south of the island of Skopelos, ancient Peparethos. A partly destroyed shaft-grave, with only its north-east corner intact, was found here by chance.
The stone lining was preserved at the north for 2.80 m. and at the east for 2.50 m., so the grave must have been unusually large. Staphylos was the name of a Cretan of the time of King Rhadamanthys of Phaistos, and the lord of this small island. This fine weapon may be associated then with the reputed colonists of the island or their successors.
The handle is the largest known of this period. No trace of the blade was found. The art of the shaft-grave period is still apparent in its decoration.
The associated pottery, still not published, is, at the earliest, of about 1500 B.C., at the latest, of about 1400. The grave would have held several burials and the sword might have belonged with one of the earliest as easily as with one of the latest. At all events it had been buried with the dead man by his family as a most precious heirloom.

Bakalakis, VI *Intern. Arch. Kongress*, Berlin, 1939, p. 309 ff.—Platon, in *Kretika Chronika* 3, 1949, p. 534 ff.

174
UPPER PART OF A SILVER FUNNEL-SHAPED RHYTON. Citadel of Mycenae, grave IV. Overall height 22.9 cm., upper diameter 11.2 cm. Inv. no. 481.

The famous rhyton is only partly preserved and has not been well restored; its sides should be straight. The scene shows Mycenaean soldiers disembarking before the walls of a city. Some are attacked by the enemy archers and slingers, others crawl ashore, swim, or are pursued by sea-monsters.

Karo, *Schachtgräber von Mykenai*, p. 106, no. 481, pl. 122.—Marinatos, in *Deltion* 1926, p. 78 ff.—Evans, *Palace of Minos* III, p. 89 ff.

175
SILVER AND GOLD RHYTON IN THE FORM OF A BULL'S HEAD. Citadel of Mycenae, grave IV. Height without the horns 15.5 cm. Inv. no. 384.

Grave IV in Circle A was rich in fine rhytons. This, and the last-mentioned, are of silver, spoiled by oxydisation. It is a technical and artistic masterpiece and must have been the most valuable object in a grave which was certainly the richest of all the shaft-graves at Mycenae. Egyptian sources, among others, tell us that at first silver was more precious than gold. Silver is somewhat more common in the shaft-grave period at Mycenae, and gold is more popular only later. (Erman-Ranke, *Ägypten*, pp. 551–552.)

Karo, *Schachtgräber von Mykenai*, p. 93, no. 384, pls. 119-121.

176; XXXIX
GOLD RHYTON IN THE FORM OF A LION'S HEAD. Citadel of Mycenae, grave IV. Height 20 cm. Inv. no. 273.

This ritual vase was not only a grave offering but had been used, and so had been made of heavy gold sheet. It is an exceptional piece, hammered out of a single sheet of gold. Its art, typical of the 16th century, mixes strength and naturalism in a decorative, symmetrical composition. The ears are simple and almost human. The nostrils are represented by spirals and the inner corners of the eyes are drawn out, as on the lioness-head rhyton from Knossos (plate 99).

Karo, *Schachtgräber von Mykenai*, p. 77, no. 273.

177
RHYTON IN THE FORM OF A STAG. Citadel of Mycenae, grave IV. Base silver. Height to the mouth 16.2 cm. Inv. no. 388.
This has often been taken for an import from the east. In its poor state it is impossible to see whether there was a hole in the creature's mouth, but this is likely in view of the second orifice in the back.

Karo, *Schachtgräber von Mykenai*, p. 94, no. 388, pls. 125-126.

178–185
TWO GOLD CUPS SHOWING THE CAPTURE

OF BULLS. From the tholos-tomb at Vaphio in Laconia. Upper diameters 10.8 cm. About 1500 B.C.

These superbly well preserved cups are from a tholos built at the top of a hill and covered with an immense mound of earth. They carry repoussé scenes of the capture of bulls. Consecutive views of the scenes are shown in plates 178, 179 and 182, 183. Enlargements of some details appear in plates 180, 181 and 184, 185.

Gold Cup I. Capture of a bull with nets, and hunters. 178 above, 180: A bull attacks a hunter and huntress. 179–181: A bull caught in a net. 178 below: The other side to the scene above. A bull in flight. The gold seal from Pylos is a contemporary parallel for the capture of a bull in a net (plate 209). Here the bull is seized by the horns at the moment when he tries to free himself from the net, while on the cup the bull is left in the net (plates 179, 181) while the hunters are occupied with another bull (plates 178 above, 180). One of the figures has bravely seized one of the raging creature's horns and swung his legs around the other. Evans thought this figure was a woman and this seems right when we compare the forelocks of the girl leaping a bull on the Knossos fresco (plate XVII). Women, then, shared the dangers of the bull-hunt.

Gold Cup II. Capture of a bull with a decoy-cow. 182 above: A bull tethered by its hind leg. 182 below, 184, 185: Hunter tethering the bull. Behind him is the decoy-cow with another bull. 183 above, 185: Cow and bull. 183 below: Cautious approach of a third bull.

Tsountas, in *Ephemeris* 1889, p. 129 ff., pl. 9.—Evans, *Palace of Minos* III, p. 180 ff., figs. 123-127, 130.

186
ELECTRUM CUP WITH GOLD AND NIELLO.
Citadel of Mycenae, grave IV. Height 15.5 cm. Inv. no. 390.

The slight amount of gold in the composition of the cup has been sufficient to prevent oxydisation. There are strips of niello at the top and bottom of the lip; the upper one carries a thin gold band, the lower a row of gold discs. Three flower-pots of cut-out gold sheet are hammered on to the upper part of the cup, and dittany plants are shown growing in them. An excellent piece for the subtle colour-contrast of the silver, gold and niello.

Karo, *Schachtgräber von Mykenai*, p. 94, no. 390, pls. 112-113.—Evans, *Palace of Minos* I, pp. 242, 243, fig. 183.

187–194
GOLD VASES FROM THE CITADEL OF MYCENAE

187 Gold cup from grave IV. Height without the handle 15 cm. Inv. no. 351.

This is a heavy vessel, hammered from a single sheet of gold. The beading on the foot, three ridges, and rosettes, are all beaten.

Karo, *Schachtgräber von Mykenai*, p. 91, no. 351.

188 The so-called Cup of Nestor from grave IV. Height without the handle 14.5 cm. Inv. no. 412.

Hammered from a single sheet of gold, but thinner than that usually employed for pieces intended for everyday use. It was perhaps used only for libations. It was at first handleless and taller, but was cut down, hammered open and given two handles. These were given tall supports. Schliemann called the birds seated on the handles doves but they are more probably falcons, and their presence may indicate the ritual character of the vase.

Karo, *Schachtgräber von Mykenai*, p. 100, no. 412, pl. 109.—Marinatos, in *Neue Beiträge zur klassischen Altertumswissenschaft* (Festschrift B. Schweitzer), pp. 11-18.

189 Gold cup with dogs' heads. From the southern edge of Grave Circle A. Height about 15 cm. Inv. no. 957.

Some months after Schliemann's discovery of the shaft-graves, in January 1877, Drossinos found, at the southern edge of the Circle, a hoard of gold objects which seem to have been deposited there by grave-robbers. There were four cups with handles ending in dog's heads; all about 15 cm. high. One is shown complete here, and the detail above is from another of the four. The shape is not met in the shaft-graves and is of somewhat later date. The greyhounds' heads are fine pieces of minor plastic art. The lion in plate 199 above is from the same find and may have served to decorate a vase-handle like the dogs' heads.

Schliemann, *Mykenai*, p. 339 ff., one cup shown under no. 528. On Creto-Mycenaean dogs see Schweitzer, in *Athenische Mitteilungen* 55, 1930, p. 111.

190 above: Gold cup from grave IV. Height 9 cm. Inv. no. 441.

Beaten from thick gold sheet, its only decoration a central ridge. The shape is well known in clay copies.

190 below: Gold cup from grave IV. Height without handle 12.6 cm. Inv. no. 427.
One of the most elegant finds, despite its lack of decoration. Beaten from thick gold sheet and with a high foot.

Karo, *Schachtgräber von Mykenai*, p. 103, no. 441, pls. 107–108 and p. 102, no. 427, pl. 107.

191 above: Gold rouge-vessel from grave IV. Height without handle 12.2 cm. Inv. no. 391.
The lid is fastened by gold wire passing through two holes near its edge.

Karo, *Schachtgräber von Mykenai*, p. 95, no. 391, pl. 114.

191 below: Gold cup from grave IV. Height 7 cm. Inv. no. 442.
Finely decorated with upright, beaten fluting.

Karo, *Schachtgräber von Mykenai*, p. 103, no. 442, pls. 107, 108.—Evans, *Palace of Minos* I, pp. 242–243, fig. 183.

192 above: Gold cup with lions from grave V. Height without handle 12.8 cm. Inv. no. 656.
The high-footed cup is beaten from thick gold sheet. Three rather stylised lions leap around the upper part. Good local work.

Karo, *Schachtgräber von Mykenai*, p. 125, no. 656, pl. 126.

192 below: Gold kantharos from grave IV. Height without handles 9.2 cm. Inv. no. 440.
From heavy gold. A simple but elegant cup.

Karo, *Schachtgräber von Mykenai*, p. 103, no. 440, pl. 108.

193 above: Gold cup from grave IV. Height without handle 6.2 cm. Inv. no. 392.
One of two similar vessels beaten from thin gold sheet. Decorated with parallel, equally spaced ribs.

Karo, *Schachtgräber von Mykenai*, p. 95, nos. 392–393, pl. 104.

193 below: Tall gold cup from grave V. Height without handle 12 cm. Inv. no. 628.
The shape, with a ridge around the middle, is very common in clay vases. This vase has herring-bone pattern below the ridge, and arcades above it. Beaten from fairly thick gold sheet.

Karo, *Schachtgräber von Mykenai*, p. 122, no. 628, pl. 124.—Evans, *Palace of Minos* I, p. 243, fig. 183.

194 above: Gold cup from grave V. Height without handle 11 cm. Inv. no. 629.
A broad ridge with spirals above and below. Beaten from heavy gold sheet.

Karo, *Schachtgräber von Mykenai*, p. 122, no. 629, pl. 125.

194 below: Gold cup from grave IV. Height without handle 8.8 cm. Inv. no. 313.
Also beaten from heavy gold sheet. The seven plants may be dittany.

Karo, *Schachtgräber von Mykenai*, p. 84, no. 313, pl. 110.

195
SILVER JUG. Citadel of Mycenae, grave V. Height 34.5 cm. Inv. no. 885.

Made from two thick sheets of silver, one for the body and one for the neck. At the junction is a heavy roll such as we see on many clay vases. There are horizontal ribs, double arcades with drop-pendants, and spirals above.

Karo, *Schachtgräber von Mykenai*, p. 148, no. 855, pl. 134.—Evans, *Palace of Minos* II, p. 645, fig. 411.

196 above
SILVER CUP with inlaid male heads. From a chamber-tomb at Mycenae. Diam. 16.2 cm. Inv. no. 2489.

Above and below the lip a single and double row of gold and niello leaves. Between are 21 male heads with beards but no moustaches. Compare the similar heads from a vase found at Pylos, plate 204 below.

Tsountas, in *Ephemeris* 1888, pl. 7, 2.—Tsountas and Manatt, *The Mycenaean Age*, pp. 167, 234, fig. 117.

196 below, 197
GOLD CUP. From Midea in the Argolid. Diam. 17.3 cm. Inv. no. 3736.

From an unplundered tholos-tomb. The decoration is hammered, punched and incised, and shows an elaborate scene of swimming dolphins, octopuses and small nautili in disturbed water, the waves being shown as scales. For this representation of the sea compare the rhyton on plate 86 left, from the island of Pseira in East Crete.

Persson, *The Royal Tombs at Dendra near Midea*, frontispiece and pls. 9–11 and p. 43 ff.

198, 199 below
SIX-SIDED WOODEN BOX WITH GOLD PLAQUES. Citadel of Mycenae, grave V. Inv. nos. 808–811.

Six-sided wooden plaques from the floor and lid of a box were found, as well as four gold plaques with spirals, four with a lion chasing a goat to the left and a bucranium above, and four with a lion chasing a stag to the right and palms below. This may be local work. The reconstruction of the plaques in plate 199 below may not be completely accurate.

Karo, *Schachtgräber von Mykenai*, p. 143, nos. 808–811, pls. 143, 144.

199 above
GOLD RECUMBENT LION. Citadel of Mycenae. From a find south of Grave Circle A. About three times life size. Inv. no. 991.

The solid, cast lion on a plinth may be from the handle of a cup like the four with dogs' heads (plate 189) from the same find.

Schliemann, *Mykenae*, p. 410, fig. 532.

200 left
SILVER PIN WITH GOLD DECORATION. Citadel of Mycenae, grave III. Length of the pin 21.5 cm., of the attachment 6.7 cm. Inv. no. 75.

From the women's grave. The top of the pin is bent over so that the attachment hangs from it. It shows a woman, no doubt a goddess, with arms outstretched as though flying. Over her head are two waz-motifs with three papyrus stalks on either side which curve round with hanging blossoms.

Karo, *Schachtgräber von Mykenai*, p. 54, no. 75, pl. 30.—Marinatos, in *British School Annual* 46, 1951, p. 102 ff.

200 right
GOLD ORNAMENTS in the form of stylised nautili. Mycenae, from the dromos of the Tomb of Clytemnestra. Somewhat enlarged. Inv. no. 2795.

The conjoined nautili are a common motif for gold or glass necklaces, and are later stylised almost out of recognition (as in Late Minoan Crete, see plate 120). The motif is not found in the shaft graves at Mycenae.

Wace, *Mycenae*, fig. 57a top left.

201 above
GOLD ARMLET FOR A MAN. Citadel of Mycenae, grave IV. Diam. 9.3 cm. Inv. no. 263.

One of the heaviest pieces of jewellery from the graves. It was made for a man's upper arm. The bow-like ends of the hoop were silvered over and to them attached a gold blossom with a silvered bronze stud at the centre. The gold of the hoop is well preserved but the overlying silver is largely missing. We have already re-marked that silver was more precious than gold in this period.

Karo, *Schachtgräber von Mykenai*, p. 76, no. 263, pl. 42.

201 below
GOLD EARRINGS. Citadel of Mycenae, grave III. Diam. 7.5 cm. Inv. no. 61.

The earrings from the women's grave are of two gold sheets with cut-out star decoration fastened on to gold wire. Spiral rings fastened them to the ears. The earrings, with the pin on plate 200, were probably worn in life by the queen with whom they were buried.

Karo, *Schachtgräber von Mykenai*, p. 62, no. 61, pls. 20, 32.

202
REPOUSSÉ GOLD DISCS. Citadel of Mycenae, grave III. About life-size. Inv. nos. 2, 4, 6, 8–14.

Many of these gold discs were found, cut from thin sheet and stamped with a variety of patterns of which a selection is shown here. Those with holes in them could have been sewn on to the clothes or shroud. We do not know how the others were fastened or what purpose they served, but they were certainly some sort of funerary ornament. Schliemann found 701 discs and noted that many were found around the legs of the bodies.

Karo, *Schachtgräber von Mykenai*, p. 34, nos. 2, 4, 6, 8–14, pls. 27–29.

203 above
GOLD NECKLACES. From Prosymna in the Argolid, grave 41. One-and-a-half times life-size.

The centre-pieces are rosettes, and the beads are in the form of lily-blossoms and papyrus-heads (see the remarks on plate 120).

Blegen, *Prosymna* II, pl. 85, fig. 362 and pl. 83, fig. 359.

203 below
GOLD OWL AND FROG. From Kakovatos near Pylos. Three and a half times life-size.

These are from tholos-tomb A at Kakovatos in Triphylia. The frog has granulated decoration. The owl appears seldom in Creto-Mycenaean art but we may recall that it later became the attribute of Pallas Athena.

K. Müller, in *Athenische Mitteilungen* 1909, p. 271, pl. 13, 27, 28 and pl. 12, 8.

204 above
GOLD ORNAMENTS IN THE FORM OF
OCTOPUSES. Citadel of Mycenae, grave IV. Two-
thirds life-size. Inv. nos. 386, 387.

The octopuses are cut out from thin gold sheet. They
were sewn on to clothing, especially at the hems. The
creatures are unusual in having only seven arms. The
artist was perhaps influenced by the magic properties of
that number.

Karo, *Schachtgräber von Mykenai*, p. 94, nos. 386, 387, pl. 44.

204 below
HEADS OF GOLD AND NIELLO. From the palace
at Englianos near Pylos. About one-and-a-third times
life-size.

They are very similar to the heads from the silver vase
found at Mycenae and their excavator has suggested
that these too decorated a silver vessel.

Blegen, in *American Journal of Archaeology* 59, 1955, p. 32, pl. 23, 3.

205 above
GOLD NECKLACE WITH PAIRS OF EAGLES.
Citadel of Mycenae, grave V. Nine-tenths life-size. Inv.
no. 689.

Found with the body whose mask is shown in plate 163.
From their long tails these are perhaps falcons rather
than eagles.

Karo, *Schachtgräber von Mykenai*, p. 128, no. 689, pl. 66.

205 centre
GOLD ORNAMENTS. Citadel of Mycenae, grave IV.
Nine-tenths life-size. Inv. nos. 243, 242.

Two of these ornaments were found in grave III and
three in grave IV. All are in the same form with the
façade of a shrine like that on the Knossos fresco. At
either side are doves, and at the top three pairs of horns
of consecration, one shown end-on.

Karo, *Schachtgräber von Mykenai*, p. 74, nos. 242–244, pl. 18.

205 below
GOLD ORNAMENTS. Citadel of Mycenae, grave III.
Nine-tenths life-size. Inv. nos. 27, 28, 36.

From the women's grave. There are naked goddesses
with doves, and clothed figures which may not be
divinities.

Karo, *Schachtgräber von Mykenai*, pp. 48–49, nos. 27, 28, 36, pl. 27.

206
GOLD SIGNET RINGS. From chamber-tombs in the
lower town of Mycenae. Views of the originals, three-
and-a-quarter times life-size. Inv. nos. 2970, 3148, 3179,
3180, 2921, 3182, 3181.

Above: Two winged griffins with crests.

Evans, *Palace of Minos* III, p. 511, fig. 360.—Bossert, *Altkreta*, 3rd edition
fig. 395 f.

Second row left: A sanctuary with the sacred tree being
tended by a worshipper. Behind him is a goat and
another tree.

Evans, 'Mycenaean Tree and Pillar Cult', in *Journal of Hellenic Studies* 21,
1901, p. 99 ff.

Second row right: This is a much-discussed piece. A
man is uprooting the sacred tree. A woman is 'wailing
and smiting her thighs', in Homer's expression, and
another bows weeping over an altar.

Evans, op. cit., p. 79 (177), fig. 53.

Third row left: In the centre background is the sanctuary with the sacred tree. Below it is what must be the
plan of the sanctuary, like that recently found at
Vathypetro (plate 60 below).
Two women pray before the shrine, and there are a
tree and three cypresses in the background.

Evans, *op. cit.*, p. 85 (183), fig. 57.

Third row right: The 'sacra conversazione' between a
seated goddess and her young partner. This is the
generally accepted explanation. The scene might be
secular, although the woman is shown so large.

Evans, *op. cit.*, p. 77 (175), fig. 51, and *Palace of Minos* III, p. 464, fig. 324.

Fourth row left: Seated, winged sphinx with a lily-crest.

Bossert, *Altkreta*, 3rd edition, fig. 391c.

Fourth row right: Seated goddess with a winged and
crested female griffin.

Bossert, *op. cit.*, fig. 399e, and Stais, *Collection mycénienne*, no. 3181.

207
TWO GOLD SIGNET RINGS
These valuable rings are the largest preserved of our
period, and perhaps the most interesting. Both are from
grave-robbers' hoards which had been re-buried in
Mycenaean times. One was found in 1915 in the lower
town of Tiryns (*Deltion* 2, 1916, Appendix, p. 13 ff.).
The other was found with the cups (plate 189) and lion

(plate 199 above) found by Drossinos south of Grave Circle A at Mycenae in 1877 and published by Schliemann.

Above: From the lower town at Tiryns, Width 5.6 cm. Weight 78.2 g. Three times life-size. View of the original. Inv. no. 6208.

The goddess sits on a folding stool with a high back and rests her feet on a footstool, the Homeric θρῆνυς. The same word, *taranu*, appears on a Linear B tablet from Pylos together with an ideogram picture of the stool; a striking confirmation of the correctness of the decipherment. Behind the goddess is a bird, like a falcon, and before her an incense-burner. She holds a sacred cup; compare the original shape of the 'Cup of Nestor' (plate 188). Four Ta-urt demons with jugs approach her. In the heavens are sun and moon and four ears of corn. Can this be the month in which thirsty Argos and her cornfields long for rain? The demons often appear watering flowers and plants.

Karo, in *Athenische Mitteilungen* 55, 1930, p. 121, Beil, 30, 2.—Evans, *Palace of Minos* IV, p. 460, fig. 385 and p. 393, fig. 329.

Below: From the treasure found south of Grave Circle A at Mycenae. Width 3.4 cm. View of the original, four times life-size.

The goddess sits beneath a tree with three poppies in her hand. Three female figures, one a child, offer her sacred lilies. These may also be divinities and the lions' masks behind them may be their attributes. Compare the ring from Crete in plate 111 above. The double axe behind indicates the earthly sanctuary. An armed man is appearing from the heavens, so this may represent the moment of conception by the goddess of fertility. The sun and moon may symbolise the beginning and end of a particular lunar month.

Schliemann, *Mykenai*, p. 402, fig. 530.—Evans, *Mycenaean Tree and Pillar Cult*, p. 10 (108), fig. 4, and *Palace of Minos* II, p. 341, fig. 194e.

208
SEALS FROM A NEWLY-FOUND THOLOS-TOMB AT PYLOS
Views of impressions, two-and-a-half times life-size.

Above left: Amethyst. Two flying ducks.
Above right: Carnelian. Two bulls beneath a tree.
Centre left: Carnelian. Dying lion with an arrow in his side.

Centre right: Carnelian. A woman offers lilies before an altar with horns of consecration, and myrtle and olive branches.
Below left: Sardonyx, set in gold. Female winged griffin.
Below right: Carnelian. Lion seizing a calf.

Unpublished; illustrated, with a brief description, in *Illustrated London News*, 27 April 1957, p. 691.

209
GOLD SEALS. From Pylos. Views of the originals, three-and-a-half times life-size.

Above: From the tholos-tomb near the 'Palace of Nestor' at Englianos. A royal gold seal with a net pattern on one side, and, on the other, shown here, a crested griffin.
Centre and below: From tholos-tomb 2 at Rutsi near Pylos.
Centre: Hollow seal, once no doubt filled with wood, with a scale pattern inlaid with blue paste on one side, and on the other a bull struck by a spear in the neck.
Below: A bull caught in a net is being grappled by a hunter. Compare remarks on plates 178 above and 180.

Above: Blegen, In *American Journal of Archaeology* 59, 1954, p. 32, pl. 9, 15.—The others: *Illustrated London News*, 27 April 1957, p. 691.

210
SEAL-STONES. From Midea in the Argolid. Views of impressions, two-and-a-half times life-size.

Above: Agate. Lion and bull.
Centre: Dark agate. A massive lion is trying to break the neck of a bull. The scene is as described in Homer's simile (cf. *Archäologischer Anzeiger* 1928, pp. 110–112), and in fact lions may attack far stronger creatures in this way. The marbling below reflects a pattern of wall-painting.
Below: Agate. Bull or cow attacked by two lions. Later than the best period.

Persson, *Royal Tombs at Dendra*, p. 32, pl. 19 above, centre row.

211
SEAL-STONES. From Vaphio in Laconia. Views of impressions, two-and-a-half times life-size. About 1500 B.C.

The tomb which yielded the two famous gold cups (plates 178–185) also contained a fine collection of seals, the more important for the fact that they can be dated to about 1500 B.C.

There were 38 stones found. The next largest find is from an unplundered tomb at Pylos (5 m. in diameter, against the 10 m. at Vaphio) with 20 seals, some from the same workshop and perhaps hand as seals from Vaphio. Tsountas had noticed at Vaphio that the seals seemed to have been strung onto armlets, and the find at Pylos confirms this. The stones on plate 211 are: Left row. Top: Chalcedony. A *potnia theron* with an attendant subdues an animal. Centre: Chalcedony. A hunter attacks a boar with his spear, in a rocky setting. Below: Agate. Two Ta-urt demons with beaked jugs water plants. Between them a tree, horns of consecration and an offering-bowl (compare the Tiryns signet, plate 207 above).
Centre row. Above: Sardonyx set in gold. Two trotting horses draw a chariot. The charioteer has a spear over his shoulder and from it hangs a sack, or perhaps an animal. Next: Carnelian. Two bulls (compare the seal from Pylos, plate 208 above right).
Next: Sardonyx. Lion. Below: Amethyst. Four rams' heads.
Right row. Above: Jasper. A priest or god in an unusual enveloping cloak is leading a winged griffin. Centre: Carnelian. A woman, perhaps a goddess, in an unusual attitude. Below: Carnelian, set in gold. *Potnia theron* holding a great ram.

Tsountas, in *Ephemeris* 1889, p. 165 ff., pl. 10.

212 above
AMETHYST SEAL-STONE. From grave Gamma in Grave Circle B at Mycenae. View of the original, eight times life-size.

A profile portrait of a man with a most distinctive pointed nose. He has a beard but no moustache, part of his hair is combed over his forehead while the rest hangs down, gathered behind the ears: a Cretan hair-style.

Biesantz, *Marburger Winckelmann-Programm* 1958, p. 9 ff., pl. 10, 4.

212 below
ROCK CRYSTAL BOWL. From grave Omikron in Grave Circle B at Mycenae. Length 13.2 cm.

The handle of this spouted bowl ends in a duck's head. See Introduction, p. 106.

Mylonas, *Ancient Mycenae*, pp. 139, 146, figs. 49, 60, 61.

213
ALABASTER VASE. Citadel of Mycenae, grave IV. Height with the handle 24.3 cm. Inv. no. 389.

The three looped handles were fastened with wire to the body of this elegant vase, which is probably a copy of a metal form.

Karo, *Schachtgräber von Mykenai*, p. 94, no. 389, figs. 138, 139.

214–215
TWO WARRIORS' HEADS WITH BOARS' TUSK HELMETS

214   From a chamber-tomb in the lower town at Mycenae. Ivory. About three times life-size.

The best of many such pieces. The helmet, its cheek- and neck-pieces, are of a well-known type covered by boars' tusks. The spiral locks over the forehead and the tusks at the back of the neck may also be part of the helmet. The knob at the top would have carried the crest.

Tsountas, in *Ephemeris* 1888, pl. 8, 12.—Tsountas and Manatt, *The Mycenaean Age*, p. 197, fig. 85.—Evans, *Palace of Minos* IV, p. 870, fig. 861.

215   From Spata, East Attica. Ivory. About three times life-size.

The features are intelligent. The helmet sits high above the forehead, and the neck-piece is longer than that on plate 214. The cheek-piece is shown schematically. Less careful work but an impressive portrait.

Bulletin de correspondance Hellénique 1878, p. 185 ff.

216
IVORY RELIEF PLAQUES. From Spata, East Attica. About three-and-a-half times life-size. Inv. nos. 2053, 2045.

Above: A sphinx with spread wings, schematic side-locks and crown.
Below: Another conventionalised scene of a lion attacking a bull. Both plaques are, however, well carved and striking pieces.

Bulletin de correspondance Hellénique 1878, p. 185 ff., pl. 17.

217
SEATED GODDESS. From Mycenae. Ivory. About twice life-size. Inv. no. 5879.

This is probably a goddess, seated on a rock. Although the head is missing it is the most complete representation of this interesting Cretan motif. Two reliefs of similar, elaborately dressed figures were found in the island of Pseira in East Crete, and there is another such scene from Knossos.

Journal International d'Archéologie numismatique 1912, p. 181 ff., pl. 1 cf. Evans, *Palace of Minos* III, p. 38 and fig. 27 on p. 45 (Knossos) and p. 28, fig. 15A (Pseira).

218–219
IVORY GROUP OF A DIVINE TRINITY. From Mycenae. Twice life-size. 15th century B.C. Inv. no. 7711.

This was found in 1939 in a Mycenaean shrine below the northern supporting wall of the Greek temple which overlay the palace. It is of the highest importance for its religious significance as much as for its artistic quality.

Two identically dressed, crouching women sharing a single cloak watch over a child playing before them. This is not the first time that we have met such a trinity. We must associate it with the legends of a motherless child-god, rescued, guarded and brought up by two, or sometimes more than two, divine nurses.

Wace, *Mycenae*, p. 83, figs. 101–103.

220–221
IVORY HANDLES FROM TWO BRONZE MIRRORS. From Mycenae, the Tomb of Clytemnestra. About four times, and twice, life-size. After 1500 B.C. Inv. no. 2900.

The burial of a woman was discovered in 1892 in the dromos of the Tomb of Clytemnestra, outside the citadel of Mycenae. She was perhaps a royal favourite or princess; at all events the offerings buried with her were of the highest quality. As well as the gold ornaments shown in plate 200 there were these two bronze mirrors whose ivory handles are the finest of their type in Mycenaean art. On both there appear two young women, seated like some ethereal spirits on fan-shaped clusters of palm-leaves. The impression of otherworldliness is heightened by the birds carried by the figures in plate 220. In plate 221 there is poetic feeling in the way the two young girls bow their heads as in deep slumber.

Unfortunately neither handle is particularly well preserved. Both should be later than 1500 B.C. but the stylistic differences in the products of different workshops makes exact dating difficult.

Tsountas and Manatt, The *Mycenaean Age*, p. 187 ff., figs. 82, 83.— Wace, *Mycenae*, p. 36, figs. 55–57.

222 above
IVORY HANDLE OF A BRONZE MIRROR, with rosettes.

222 below
IVORY COMB

Both are from tholos-tomb 2 at Rutsi near Pylos, and are dated by the burials between 1500 and 1440 B.C. The comb is decorated with wild cats chasing ducks and, with the pyxis on plate 223, belongs with the earlier burial of about the beginning of the 15th century. The mirror handle with rosettes was found with some ten swords and knives belonging to the last burial in the tomb, of about 1400 B.C.

Unpublished; pictures and a drawing of the mirror in *Illustrated London News*, 6 April 1957, p. 543.

223 left
IVORY PYXIS. From tholos-tomb 2 at Routsi near Pylos. Rather more than life-size. About 1500 B.C.

The cylindrical pyxis is decorated with alternating rows of spirals and spirals with leaves, divided by astragals. The small handles are in the shape of figure-of-eight shields.

Illustrated London News, 6 April 1957, p. 543, fig. 21.

223 right above
MINIATURE GOLD SHIELD. From the tholos-tomb near the palace at Englianos (plate 157 above). About one-and-a-half times life-size.

The stitches fastening the ox-hide to the frame of the shield are represented by granulation.

223 right below
MINIATURE IVORY SHIELD. From Mycenae. About two-thirds life-size.

There were inlays for the dappled patterns of the ox-hide over the shield. This seems to have been found in the fill of Grave Circle A within the citadel. Both shields may have served as handles or applied decoration to some other object.

Blegen, in *American Journal of Archaeology* 58, 1954, p. 32, pl. 9, 14.

224–225
LEAD STATUETTE OF A YOUTH. From a grave at Kampos in Laconia. Height 12 cm.

The general appearance and dress are purely Minoan. What is unfamiliar is the way the figure is gazing at his hands whose palms are turned down so that he could not have been holding anything very large. This was perhaps an ordinary group of a youth playing with a cicada or a butterfly. The piece is a notable work of art both for its detail and material.

Tsountas, in *Ephemeris* 1891, p. 199.—Tsountas and Manatt, *The Mycenaean Age*, p. 160, pl. 7 opposite p. 158.

226; XL
FRAGMENTARY FRESCO WITH A WOMEN'S PROCESSION. From the palace of the citadel at Tiryns. 226: height of each about 30 cm. XL: Height 39 cm., breadth 33.5 cm.

The Procession Fresco belongs to the second period of the palace at Tiryns and so to the years after 1400 B.C. The composition was of women, or rather girls, converging on one point. The best preserved piece is shown in plate XL and pains have been taken to avoid the parts seriously overworked or restored in recent times. Only parts of the heads are preserved from the fresco shown in plate 226 but they do give clear details of the drawing of the mouth and eyes. There was a similar, though probably artistically finer, Procession Fresco with women in the Palace of Cadmus at Thebes.

Rodenwaldt, *Tiryns*, pp. 80–82, figs. 33–34, pl. 9.—H. Reusch, *Die zeichnerische Rekonstruktion des Frauenfries im böotischen Theben*, p. 31 ff. and *passim*.

XLI–XLII
FEMALE HEAD IN PAINTED PLASTER (Goddess or sphinx). From Mycenae. Height 16.8 cm.

This is particularly important because it is one of the very few extant examples of sculpture in the round in Creto-Mycenaean art. We cannot be sure whether this was a sphinx, for instead of the usual crown the head is wearing only a broad fillet. Notice the dot-rosettes on the cheeks and chin, which might represent tattooing.

Tsountas, in *Ephemeris* 1902, 1, pls. 152.—Evans, *Palace of Minos* III, p. 519, fig. 364.—*American Journal of Archaeology* 1936, p. 205.

XLIII above
FRAGMENTARY FRESCO WITH WOMEN. From Mycenae. Width 13.5 cm., 15th century B.C.

The women are looking from a balcony festively decorated with garlands and double axes. The fragment was found by Schliemann in Grave Circle A and was at first taken for Greek. It is probably from the Ramp House above the graves and not from the palace itself.

Rodenwaldt, in *Athenische Mitteilungen* 36, 1911, pl. 9, who takes it for a Cretan original (p. 228); Evans, *Palace of Minos* I, p. 444, calls it purely Minoan.

XLIII below
FRAGMENTARY FRESCO WITH THREE DEMONS From Mycenae. About life-size.

These three Creto-Mycenaean 'genii' are probably derived from the Egyptian Ta-urt. They had several roles in the religious and superstitious thought of the time: serving goddesses, sprinkling holy water on plants (compare the Tiryns ring, plate 207 and the remarks on it, above), keeping flocks, but also attacking them and wild beasts. Thus there are several scenes with them carrying dead animals on a staff over their shoulders. Such must have been the scene on this fresco. It was in a private house at Mycenae and is of the latest period. Tsountas called the creatures 'donkey-headed'.

Tsountas, in *Ephemeris* 1887, p. 160 ff., pl. 10. The 'genii' are discussed fully, and correctly (*pace* Nilsson) by Evans, *Palace of Minos* IV, p. 431.

227
TALL THREE-HANDLED VASE. From Kakovatos, Triphylia. Height 78 cm. About 1500 B.C.

There were several carefully painted large jars in the tholos-tombs at Kakovatos. This one is decorated with nautili and seaweed. It is of about 1500 B.C. or a little later.

K. Müller, in *Athenische Mitteilungen* 1909, p. 304, fig. 16.

228
THREE-HANDLED VASE. From Deiras in the Argolid. Height about 45 cm.

This bellying vase carries good examples of the stylised palms and ivy motifs of the early Palace style.

Unpublished; given to the National Museum.

229
TALL JUG. Citadel of Mycenae, grave I. Height 33 cm.

Shaft-grave I held several vases of the latest style of any from the Circle. This is one has warts on its spout and ivy decoration. The style and execution are typically Mycenaean.

Karo, *Schachtgräber von Mykenai*, p. 68, no. 199, pl. 169.

It would be superfluous to repeat here the lists of authors and books which are to be found in all the main text-books. A near-complete bibliography of recent literature is given by B. E. Moon, 'Mycenaean Civilization, Publications since 1935' (*Univ. of London Institute of Classical Studies Bulletin: Suppl. no. 3*, 1957); reviewed by E. Townsend Vermeule in *American Journal of Archaeology*, 62, 1958, p. 441. F. Matz, 'Die Ägais', in *Handbuch der Archäologie*, 2, 1, 1950, might also be mentioned here.

For the general reader it should be remarked that the fundamental work on Minoan and, to a great extent, Mycenaean civilisation is Sir Arthur Evans' *Palace of Minos* in four volumes (1921–1935). The scope of the books is far wider than their title suggests and many problems of Minoan-Mycenaean archaeology are discussed, details are closely studied, and all is fully illustrated and enriched by the generation-long studies of the great excavator himself.

The classic study of religion is M. P. Nilsson, *Minoan-Mycenaean Religion*, 2nd edition, 1950.

More for specialists are A. Furumark's, *Mycenaean Pottery* (1941) and *The Chronology of Mycenaean Pottery* (1941). Among other monographs on provincial wares and exports there are F. Stubbings, *Mycenaean Pottery in the Levant* (1951), and Lord William Taylour, *Mycenaean Pottery in Italy and adjacent areas* (1958). The latest work on Minoan seals is V. E. G. Kenna, *Cretan Seals* (1960).

For some problems, particularly about the earlier periods, Schachermeyr's book, *Die ältesten Kulturen Griechenlands* (1955), and article, 'Prähistorische Kulturen Griechenlands' in Pauly-Wissowa, *Realenzyklopädie* (1954), are important.

More general works are F. Matz, *Kreta-Mykene-Troja* (1956); G. Karo, *Greifen am Thron* (1959), and the picture book, C. Zervos, *L'art de la Crète*, 1955, which has a full bibliography. J. D. S. Pendlebury, *The Archaeology of Crete* (1939), gives an important and clear survey of Minoan archaeology.

For Mycenae the books by Wace, Mylonas and Karo have been often cited in these pages, and I have also referred in the Notes to many special discussions of particular topics, especially controversial ones.

INDEX